LOOKING A
LOOKING

VICTORIA AMELINA

When Russia invaded Ukraine on 24 February 2022, Victoria Amelina was busy writing a novel, taking part in the country's literary scene and parenting her son. Then she became someone new: a war crimes researcher and the chronicler of extraordinary women like herself who joined the resistance. These heroines include Evgenia, a prominent lawyer turned soldier, Oleksandra, who documented tens of thousands of war crimes and won a Nobel Peace Prize in 2022, and Yulia, a librarian who helped uncover the abduction and murder of a children's book author.

Everyone in Ukraine knew that Amelina was documenting the war. She photographed the ruins of schools and cultural centers; she recorded the testimonies of survivors and eyewitnesses to atrocities. And she slowly turned back into a storyteller, writing what would become this book.

On the evening of 27 June 2023, Amelina and three international writers stopped for dinner in the embattled Donetsk region. When a Russian cruise missile hit the restaurant, Amelina suffered grievous head injuries and lost consciousness. She died on 1 July. She was thirty-seven. She left behind an incredible account of the ravages of war and the cost of resistance. Honest, intimate and wry, this book will be celebrated as a classic.

Victoria Amelina was killed by a Russian missile in July 2023. She was an award-winning Ukrainian novelist, essayist, poet and human rights activist whose prose and poems have been translated into many languages. In 2019/2020 she lived and travelled extensively in the US. She wrote both in Ukrainian and English, and her essays have appeared in *Irish Times*, *Dublin Review of Books* and *Eurozine*.

LOOKING at WOMEN LOOKING at WAR:

A War and Justice Diary

Victoria Amelina

With a Foreword by Margaret Atwood

William Collins
An imprint of HarperCollinsPublishers
1 London Bridge Street
London SE1 9GF

WilliamCollinsBooks.com

HarperCollinsPublishers
Macken House, 39/40 Mayor Street Upper,
Dublin 1, D01 C9W8, Ireland

First published in Great Britain in 2025 by William Collins
First published in the United States by St. Martin's Press, an imprint of
St. Martin's Publishing Group
1

A catalogue record for this book is available from the British Library

ISBN 978-0-00-872750-5

Printed and bound in the UK using 100% Renewable
Electricity at CPI Group (UK) Ltd

Contents

Foreword

In the middle of a war, there is little past or future, little perspective, little accurate prediction: there is only the white heat of the moment, the immediacy of perception, the intensity of emotions, including anger, dismay, and fear. In her tragically unfinished book—written from the centre of Russia's appalling and brutal campaign to annihilate Ukraine—Victoria Amelina also records the surrealism—the sense that reality has been skewed as in a nightmare, that this cannot be happening. Bombed kindergartens, with Soviet cartoon characters smiling down from the walls. But there are also moments of courage, of companionship, the shared dedication to a cause. In this war, Russia is fighting for greed—more territory, more material resources—but Ukraine is fighting for its life; not only its life as a country, but the lives of the citizens of that country, for there is little doubt about what the outcome of a Russian win would be for Ukrainians.

The massacres, the wholesale pillaging, the rapes, the summary executions, the starvation, the child stealing, and the purges do not need to be imagined, for they have happened before. Russians claim to be the "brothers" of Ukrainians, but Ukrainians reject the kinship. Who needs a "brother" who is a homicidal psychopath and is trying to kill you?

This is the context in which so many Ukrainian artists gave up their primary art to dedicate themselves to the defense of their country and their fellow citizens. Victoria Amelina was among them. Before the war, Victoria Amelina was a talented and well-known literary writer. She was, as we say, award-winning. She published novels and children's books, traveled internationally, and started a literary festival. But all that changed when Ukraine was invaded. She turned to war reporting, researching war crimes for the Ukrainian organization Truth Hounds, interviewing witnesses and survivors.

Many religions have a figure that we may call the Recording Angel—the spirit whose job it is to write down the good and bad deeds of humans. These records are then used by a deity to achieve redress—to balance the scales that the goddess Justice is so often shown as carrying. War crimes are by definition bad deeds. Truth Hounds is a Recording Angel of the atrocities committed against Ukrainians. Amelina is looking not primarily at the war crimes as such, but at the stories of those women who, like her, are attempting to document those crimes, and also at the stories of women under siege: their ruined apartments, their attempts to evacuate, their killed partners, the shattered Lego constructions of their once-happy children. Her writing is hasty, urgent, up close and personal, detailed, and sensual.

She follows in the honorable footsteps of earlier women war reporters such as Martha Gellhorn, who wrote, "It is necessary that I report on this war. . . . I do not feel there is any need to beg as a favour for the right to serve as the eyes for millions of people in America who are desperately in need of seeing, but cannot see for themselves." Artists like Amelina help us to see, but also to feel. They serve as our eyes. Amelina's talent as a novelist was of great service to her, and now it is of great service to us.

Amelina had put together about 60 percent of the book at the time of her death. Much of that material was in raw form—fragmentary, unpolished, unedited. The editorial group putting the book together has said, "While the author managed to finalize the overall structure and write up some of the chapters . . . other sections remain unfinished. They may be composed of unedited notes, contain reports from field trips with no context, or be limited to just a title. The editorial group's strategy is to minimize their intrusions into the original manuscript and, where such intrusions are impossible to avoid, make them explicit to the reader." The resulting text is intensely modern. It reminds us of—for instance—the Pessoa of *The Book of Disquiet* and the Beckett of *Krapp's Last Tape*. Incompleteness draws us in: we long to supply what is missing.

I have found it difficult to write this introduction: How can you draw any conclusions, make any resounding statements, with the subject of the book still in flux?

This war was supposed to be a slam dunk—according to many pundits, it would only take a few days after the invasion in February 2022 to polish off Ukraine—but as I write this, it's been over two years, and small Ukraine has retaken over half the territory seized by huge Russia at the beginning of the onslaught.

War is not static but fluid. It moves, it destroys, it sweeps away everything in its path, it drowns many. Its outcomes and ripple effects are unpredictable.

But as of right now—June 2024—the Russian attempt to take Kharkiv has ground to a standstill; Ukraine has just been told that French military personnel will now operate openly on the Ukrainian side; and the United States has given Ukraine the green light to strike military targets inside Russia, which should impede the cascade of Russian missiles of the kind that just destroyed a deliberately targeted civilian shopping center; and that hit a Kramatorsk restaurant in the summer of 2023, killing Victoria Amelina at the age of thirty-seven.

This is her voice: fresh, alive, vivid, speaking to us now.

MARGARET ATWOOD

Editors' Note

At the time of Victoria Amelina's death, the manuscript of the would-be book was left unfinished. While the author managed to finalize the overall structure and write up some of the chapters (mostly in part I and the conclusion), other sections remain unfinished. They are composed of unedited notes, reports from field trips with no context, or limited to just a title. The editorial group's strategy is to minimize their intrusions into the original manuscript and, where such intrusions are impossible to avoid, make them explicit to the reader. Such intrusions are explained below.

<< . . . >> indicates excerpts found by the editors in the older versions of the manuscript and pasted into the final draft.

Gray font indicates rough unfinished notes left by the author in the draft of the manuscript.

Italic passages are fieldwork reports and other documents pasted by the author into the manuscript.

[. . .] indicates clarifications added by the editors.

[Editors' note] in the body of the manuscript signals to the reader a switch from the polished text by the author to a rough draft or contextualizes the section of the manuscript that follows.

All footnotes are inserted by the editors to add context or to comment on the state of the manuscript (for example, sentences left unfinished and connections undeveloped).

All the prose translations from Ukrainian into English have been made by Daisy Gibbons.

[illegible] Note

[illegible] death, the manuscript of the [illegible] was left [illegible] While the author [illegible] the overall structure and wrote [illegible] of the [illegible] other sections remain [illegible] limited to [illegible] [illegible] reader. Such [illegible] below.

- [illegible] found by the editor [illegible] and pasted into the [illegible]
- [illegible] handwritten notes left by the author [illegible]
- [illegible] other documents pasted [illegible]
- [illegible] by the editor.
- [illegible] the events [illegible] by the [illegible] to add [illegible] connections [illegible]

All [illegible] have been made in [illegible].

LOOKING at WOMEN LOOKING at WAR

What Is This Book?

BY VICTORIA AMELINA

WHILE THIS BOOK BEGAN AS THE WAR DIARY OF A UKRAINIAN novelist turned war crimes researcher following Russia's full-scale invasion of Ukraine in 2022, it has evolved into a story about a number of extraordinary women. The heroines of my book include Evhenia Podobna, a prominent lawyer turned soldier who helps to liberate towns in the Kharkiv region and participates in a historical trial online from the front line; Oleksandra Matviichuk, who leads an initiative documenting tens of thousands of war crimes and wins a Nobel Peace Prize in 2022; and Yulia Kakulya-Danylyuk, the brave librarian in my fellow writer Volodymyr Vakulenko's native village, who manages to find a video that shines a light on the story of his abduction and murder.

My choice of heroines for this book is deeply personal because everything about the Russian-Ukrainian war is personal. Like many Ukrainians, after February 24, 2022, I usually had to make choices that would impact my life more than my writing.

I see this book as a kind of detective story. Since the war began in 2014, and with the full-scale invasion now, I, along with millions of my fellow citizens in Ukraine, have been in search of one thing: justice.

The quest for justice has turned me from a novelist and mother into a war crimes researcher. Over the last year, I have photographed shell holes in library walls and the ruins of schools and cultural centers; I have recorded the testimonies of survivors and eyewitnesses of atrocities. I've done this to uncover the truth, to ensure the survival of memory, and to give justice and lasting peace a chance.

This same urge also slowly turned me back into a storyteller, so that I might tell you the story of Ukraine's quest for justice.

The work of a war crimes researcher requires an understanding of the principles of international humanitarian law. You must learn how to work with deeply traumatized people without traumatizing them even more. It demands that you follow specific protocols that help to uncover all the essential aspects of an alleged war crime. However, one of my mentors in war crimes research, the executive director of an NGO called Truth Hounds, Roman Avramenko, who has been doing this work for nearly a decade, taught me that if I keep two simple goals in mind, I can forget the rest and still get the job done.

First, it's necessary to determine if a case constitutes a war crime according to international humanitarian law. Second, the perpetrators must be identified along with the degree of their involvement in the alleged war crime. I always remember his advice while working on the ground in Ukraine. However, although I try to concentrate on the perpetrators while recording the survivors' testimonies or filming the shell holes, in this book, it's not the perpetrators I search for primarily but the answers to crucial questions about justice we humans have all around the world. What is justice? Who are we ready to forgive eventually? How, meanwhile, can we live with the fact that perpetrators of the most horrible crimes often end up unpunished? How can we change that? And what weapon do we choose to pursue justice in the hardest times? A laptop, a camera, international law, storytelling power, or an M777 howitzer? No choice made by those who want true justice is easy, and for most of us, the outcome of our battle is still unknown.

In June 2022, I wrote to the human rights defender Oleksandra Matviichuk: "I see the tremendous efforts you and your colleagues make to give justice a chance. Yet despite all our efforts, we still might lose. And if we lose, I want to at least tell the story of our pursuit of justice. Please let me work with you to tell your story." Oleksandra replied immediately, suggesting we meet in the Center for Civil Liberties office. Her readiness to let me inside her justice pursuit story turned my war diary into the book you're about to read. I'm grateful to Oleksandra and all the women who became part of this book and my life.

This diary encompasses events from February 17, 2022 until the day we come together near Izyum to celebrate the memory of Volodymyr Vakulenko, the children's writer murdered by Russian soldiers during the occupation, whose war diary I had found and passed to the Kharkiv Literary Museum, dedicated to the Ukrainian writers repressed or executed by the Soviet and Russian regimes. My diary entries are neither regular nor always properly dated. In that regard, Volodymyr Vakulenko's diary and mine are similar.

PART I

The Time of Choices

The Shell Hole in the Fairy Tale

I HAVE JUST BOUGHT MY FIRST GUN IN DOWNTOWN LVIV. I'VE heard that everyone is capable of killing, and those who say they aren't just haven't met the right person yet. An armed stranger entering my country might just be the "right person."

My new gun lies, black and hazardous, on the bed, among all my swimming suits and bright summer dresses. I might need it later when I come back. But not yet. Now I am going on a week-long vacation to Egypt.

"We'll come back to Ukraine on February twenty-fourth, and I'll start going to shooting practice," I explain to my son, who has been watching too much news for his age in the past few months but isn't afraid of the invasion at all.

I put the gun into a safe and our swimming suits into a suitcase.

The invasion didn't happen yesterday, February 16, 2022. So I head out the door, full of hope that it will not happen at all. After all, a full-scale Russian invasion has been rescheduled for the past eight years since 2014.

"Mom, when's the next time we get invaded?" my ten-year-old jokes, like many adults in Ukraine.

At the last moment, I turn around and run to the bedroom. I step on a chair to reach the jewelry box on the higher shelf. What if Kharkiv, Kyiv, and even Lviv will soon look like ruined Aleppo or Grozny? What do I take now if I am not coming home? Ever.

"Mom, we're going to miss the flight!"

I take one pendant, plated with gold and silver, with little rubies embedded in it. I inherited it from my grandma, the only jewelry her mother left her, and thus my oldest family relic. The great-grandmother who left it to us was born in Russia, somewhere on the Volga River. My Ukrainian grandmother and two Ukrainian grandfathers didn't have such old things; for them, everything was gone with the wind in the turmoil of the last century in Ukraine, the heart of the bloodlands.

I put the pendant with rubies on as if it were my soldier's badge.

In line for a security check at the airport, I cannot stop staring at the news on my smartphone. Around 9:00 a.m., an artillery shell hit a kindergarten in Stanytsia Luhanska called Fairy Tale, making a hole in the wall of the children's gym. The photo of the kindergarten is difficult to comprehend: a shell hole in one of the walls, a painted magical island with palm trees and animals on another; yellow ornamented wallpaper, which still makes the kindergarten room look cozy; and numerous soccer balls in the pile of broken bricks.

A couple of years ago, I visited Stanytsia Luhanska, a town near the contact line,[1] along with a dozen other towns in the war-torn Luhansk region, to meet with the community in the local history museum. I was welcomed by its kind deputy director and its bizarre exhibition: the damaged bust of Lenin hit by a Russian shell, the older shells from the Second World War, and the new ones, including those that conveniently got to the museum right through its roof. Through the small window, I looked to "the other side," the territory occupied by Russia or, according to the occupiers, "Luhansk People's Republic," a place from where all the shells, except those from the Second World War, have come. Back then, the deputy director took my books to add to the museum funds, as if contemporary Ukrainian literature were a wonder under the circumstances.

Staring at the picture of the ruined kindergarten gym long enough, I realize what the magic island with palm trees represents: a scene from a Soviet cartoon. Alas, the beloved characters from my post-Soviet childhood, the elephant, the monkey,

[1] The contact line is the 420km strip of land that divided Ukrainian and Russian armies and did not change much between 2015 and 2022.

and the boa, stare from behind the palm trees at the pile of broken bricks, just like I do. This pile is between the Russified little girl I used to be and me.

"No children were killed or injured in Stanytsia Luhanska as no one was in the gym at the time of the shelling," I read in the news. So, we're all lucky.

I often tell myself how lucky we all are, as if arguing with the last line of the famous Serhiy Zhadan's poem, which tells the story of refugees from a city that "was built of stone and steel" but doesn't exist anymore. Serhiy wrote it in 2015 after Russia occupied the cities of Donetsk and Luhansk and the Crimean Peninsula. I only paid attention to the poem in 2018 when I saw it written on a wall on Peace Avenue in Mariupol.

The memories of the places, people, and poems swirl in my head as if the news about the shelling of the Fairy Tale kindergarten in Stanytsia Luhanska changes everything and brings us all to the point of no return.

However, my ten-year-old is trying to see the screen of my phone, and he shouldn't see destroyed kindergartens. Not yet. I close the page with the news and open the work chat. Although technically I am on vacation, my team and I have to complete the funding application for a literary festival we organize in the Donetsk region, not so far from Stanytsia Luhanska, in a small village on the front line oddly called New York. The application is due before the end of the week, by February 25 at the latest, or else we will not be able to launch the project on time. So I have to work even in line for the security check at the airport.

The war crimes researchers and analysts at Truth Hounds are also working. Just a couple of weeks ago, they were in the Luhansk region, providing training and coordinating with the local prosecutors. Now the team is researching the kindergarten shelling in Stanytsia Luhanska and compiling a report. They will call it "Where Did the Shells Come From?" and publish it on February 23, 2022.

It is crucial for them to properly document every major attack; this is what the Truth Hounds team has been doing since 2014. The difference is that maybe the world finally acknowledges the truth: Russia is waging war against Ukraine. Perhaps these days it's us not heeding the warnings as another phase of the war is upon us.

So far, I know only one of the many involved in Truth Hounds, a field researcher under the call sign Casanova, who will later become one of my main teachers in the craft of researching war crimes. I have also met the human rights defender and civil leader Oleksandra Matviichuk. Yet I cannot imagine that in several months I will accompany her to the British Parliament in London, the European Parliament in Brussels, and many other not less important meetings, where we will advocate for justice for the many international crimes that are not yet committed but are, in fact, imminent. Already at our borders are the future war criminals whom I might have met while traveling to Russia as a child, with whom I share my first language and the culture that will forever be part of me, just like Voldemort's magic was part of Harry Potter. Their future victims, survivors, and eyewitnesses, whose trauma will often be comparable to those directly affected, are in their homes: in Irpin, Mariupol, Izyum, Kapytolivka, Bucha, Chernihiv, Kherson, and many other towns and villages, whose names will not become famous. These future survivors and victims include my friends, my fellow Ukrainian writer Volodymyr Vakulenko, and people who are yet to become my friends. Although Casanova will advise me not to befriend the victims, I will break this rule.

But now I am just a woman on vacation flying from a new and shiny Ukrainian airport. I should stop staring at my phone, reading the news, working, and even thinking about my new gun and why I, a nearsighted bookworm, decided to buy it.

The Angel's Advocate—*Evhenia Zakrevska I*

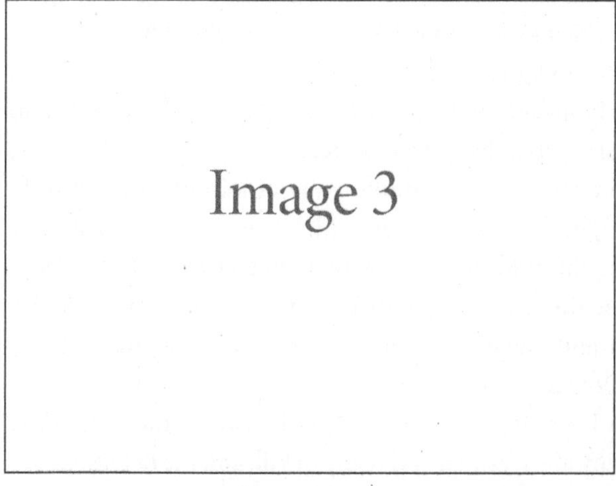

Evhenia Zakrevska

UNLIKE ME, SHE IS ALREADY GOOD AT SHOOTING.

Evhenia Zakrevska, who is a lawyer, first considered joining the army in March 2014.

"We might end up joining the army as this will be the only way," she told her friend Lesya Ganzha, a journalist and human rights activist, eight years ago.

The two women were driving back to Kyiv from just-occupied Crimea in March 2014 and had time to discuss what they had just seen there. Both were active participants in the Revolution of Dignity[2] and went to Crimea as soon as the revolution had

[2] What is known today as the Revolution of Dignity (2013–14) started as the Euromaidan protests in Kyiv's central Maidan square in late November 2013, as the reaction to the president Viktor Yanukovych's refusal to sign a political association and free trade agreement with the European Union. The flag of the EU and the slogan "Ukraine is Europe" became the symbols of the revolution, which saw the president ousted from the country.

been won and the Russian invasion of the peninsula began. They hoped to help prevent the occupation, but it was indeed a job for the army. Ukrainian soldiers didn't do anything, waiting for the orders that never came. Ukraine was all about peace and had yet to learn to fight back.

"The army? But will they even let us join?" Lesya asked doubtfully, surprised by Evhenia's idea.

But she has been thinking about joining ever since, for all the eight years of the war, which was taking its sacrifices like the mythical Minotaur took them in its labyrinth. The labyrinth for the Russian war against Ukraine was the territory of the Donetsk and Luhansk regions, which we all quite inaccurately call the Donbas.

In February 2014, in Crimea, the two women first saw Russian invaders, armed and ready to kill, and the defenseless crowd with blue-and-yellow Ukrainian and Crimean Tatar flags. Indeed, a lawyer and a journalist could not stop the occupation. Evhenia managed to save one of the arrested Ukrainian protesters, and what she saw helped her to contribute to the reports Ukrainians would later submit to the International Criminal Court. Lesya wasn't useless either: she wrote a piece about the situation and the first Ukrainian activists' arrests. Yet that was all the two women could do against the armed strangers at the time. International law or Ukrainian public opinion meant nothing to Putin and his accomplices.

So joining the army remained an option. And Evhenia has been exercising a lot in the past few years. She and her fellow lawyers and human rights defenders often chose shooting practice as a team-building activity; for the lawyers who worked with the cases of the mass shooting of peaceful protesters during the revolution of 2014 in Kyiv, such team-building activities could also work as therapy. They weren't going to be prey. They knew anything was possible.

However, Evhenia Zakrevska is now standing unarmed on Instytutska Street in the heart of Kyiv.[3]

It's February 18, 2022. She is ready for the full-scale war but hasn't joined the army yet. Although the US president, Joe Biden, has already said that Vladimir Putin has decided to invade in full force, there is still a choice, a slight possibility that history will turn out to be kind to the bloodlands this time.

Evhenia still has a choice too. She is one of the country's most prominent lawyers, so she has every reason to let others fight for her. The case of her lifetime, in which she represents the families of the protesters massacred here in downtown Kyiv in 2014, is still being heard in court. Evhenia knows she can win the case; she will ensure that justice prevails and the perpetrators from the Ukrainian unit of Berkut are held responsible. Her expertise is unique enough to excuse her from risking her life in the trenches.

Angels made of colored paper are swinging in the wind on Instytutska Street. The relatives, friends, and survivors of the massacre slowly gather and take a candle one by one. Evhenia takes one too. Approaching the small monument, she recognizes the faces in the photo. These dead are her ultimate clients.

The sky has some unique surreal light today, radiating through the clouds as if the sky, too, remembers the fallen and bends down to the people on Instytutska Street to let them know. Suddenly a rainbow appears over the October Palace. This building once hosted NKVD[4] torture chambers where Ukrainian writers, artists, and activists suffered and died, but since the sixties, it has become an important cultural center. The rainbow seems a

---

[3] Instytutska Street leads up from Maidan Nezalehznosti to the governmental district in Kyiv. It is associated with the mass shooting of protesters on February 18 and 20, 2014, during the Revolution of Dignity.

[4] The People's Commissariat for Internal Affairs, the Soviet secret police agency responsible for internal security and the Gulag prison labor camps between 1934 and 1946; was transformed later into the KGB.

hopeful sign: Maybe this time, Ukrainians will not let their elite be arrested, tortured, and executed?

I am not sure if Evhenia believes in signs. She is the kind of person who does not delegate her job to invisible superpowers. But maybe at this moment, looking at the sky, the rainbow, and the origami angels swinging in the wind, she also believes in some higher justice. She takes pictures with her smartphone: the luminous sky, the rainbow appearing unexpectedly over the winter city, and the angels made by the children of Kyiv in memory of the men and women slaughtered here eight years ago just for defending freedom, dignity, and democracy. Evhenia's best friend, the activist Roman Ratushny, could have been one of those killed. Evhenia risked her life too. It's a matter of chance that they are alive and the others, whose faces are now carved into the monument, are dead.

Evhenia knows who killed them. She knows every painful detail uncovered by all the investigators, prosecutors, and journalists: the chronology of the events, the bullets' trajectories, the shape of the bullet traces in the tree trunks, the biographies of the perpetrators, and the chain of command in the Berkut unit. Its commander, Dmytro Sadovnyk, suspected in thirty-nine murders of peaceful Ukrainian protesters, has run away to Russia.

Even better than perpetrators, Evhenia knows those killed. Ukrainians sentimentally call them the Heavenly Hundred.[5] So to everyone in Ukraine, Evhenia is a Heavenly Hundred lawyer. She knows their names, their faces, and their parents' names and faces.

She decided to be a lawyer after seeing Keanu Reeves in *The Devil's Advocate*. As a child, she resolved to be just like him, or

[5] The participants of the Revolution of Dignity killed by the security forces were named the Heavenly Hundred, an allusion to the central structural units of the Maidan's self-defense—the hundreds.

rather, the opposite of him. Perhaps Evhenia Zakrevska fulfilled her ideal: she's the advocate of the angels now—those angels made of paper by children's hands, swinging in the wind.

She would be a perfect fit for a leading role in a good Hollywood or Netflix court drama—delicate, with deep blue eyes and long red hair.

However, she will cut her red hair soon, following the full-scale Russian invasion. Both she and Lesya Ganzha will finally join the army.

Running Around History

I'M HOLDING MY SON'S HAND TOO TIGHT, LIKE A REFUGEE fleeing her city, pushing through a crowded railway station. However, no one has attacked my city yet. It's February 22, 2022. I'm still like any other tourist here, in Luxor, Egypt. I'm trying not to lose my curious ten-year-old in the crowd chattering in all languages in the ancient temple. Like everyone else, I take plenty of photos, as though it were part of my maternal duty; taking pictures in front of thousand-year-old stones makes human children less fragile too, doesn't it?

Our tour guide, a smiley local woman, tells her stories perfectly. I'm barely able to pay attention, yet I feel myself caught in the waves of time: the pharaohs rule, kingdoms rise and fall, and a nameless someone skillfully carves sacred symbols onto the giant columns of the Karnak Temple. I feel time swirling around me, like the crowd, trying to catch us in history's undertow. Time carries me and holds me just like I hold my son's hand, too tight. Only I feel kidnapped, not protected. What if they attack now, right now? Unable to check on the latest news due to a poor mobile connection, I want the excursion to end.

Unlike me, my kid seems to be all ears. When the guide leads us to the massive stone statue of a scarab beetle and advises us to walk around it seven times to make a wish, my boy gladly goes for it. In fact, he races seven laps around the stone scarab, outpacing the other sightseers even though we've been touring all day in the Egyptian heat. What is the wish worth running so fast in the sun?

"What did you wish for?" the guide asks, assuming he wants a new gadget like any other boy his age. My son doesn't hear the question, or pretends that he doesn't.

However, I don't feel like hiding my ten-year-old's wish. Instead, I'd perhaps like the whole world to know.

"He wished for Vladimir Putin to die," I say.

For just a split second, the tour guide stops smiling. She mumbles something polite and meaningless; I don't blame her. It's not exactly what you'd expect from a ten-year-old.

My son has been wishing for the war to end ever since blowing out the candles on his fifth birthday. Until today, though, he'd simply wished for peace. Never before had he insisted on punishment for perpetrators, on victory for Ukraine, on justice—just on the war ending. But Ukrainian children, or the times, were changing rapidly and inevitably.

Just yesterday, the man to whom my son wished death, Vladimir Putin, proclaimed that the Russian Federation recognized the so-called Luhansk and Donetsk People's Republics as independent states. The recognition of the puppet governments could mean Russia is indeed ready to turn its hybrid war against Ukraine into open aggression. All the panic in the news wasn't bluffing, after all. Our lives were about to change, as the lives of kids in the parts of the Donetsk and Luhansk regions had eight years ago. I squeezed my son's hand tighter.

On the way from Luxor to the hotel, I told him a story from his grandmother's childhood. As a schoolgirl, my mom once stopped preparing for her math exam due to another crisis in the Cold War; she figured exam results wouldn't matter in case of a nuclear apocalypse and decided to enjoy what time she had left.

The apocalypse never arrived, but the math exam was over. As a result, my mother switched her major to history. A fear of war led her to attend the same university where two of the world's most celebrated lawyers, Hersch Lauterpacht and Raphael Lemkin, had studied in the 1930s. In 1944, Lemkin coined the term "genocide," while Lauterpacht outlined what he called "crimes against humanity." Both notions were used in prosecuting Nazis at Nuremberg and, years later, Slobodan Milošević in the Hague. Fortunately, a change in major was the only fallout from my mother's hypothesized apocalypse.

Telling this story to my son in the taxi in the desert, little did I know that in several months even his grandmother would be studying the basics of international law to help document war crimes that would become an inherent part of reality in Ukraine.

"I hope it all ends well for your country," the smiley guide told us after learning about Andriy's wish.

I hope so too. Firstly, I believe the number of Russian troops, which gathered near Ukrainian borders, is not enough to take and keep Kyiv, which we would fiercely defend. Secondly, the ancient scarab magic should also have an effect, shouldn't it?

Upon returning to the hotel, I read that Putin submitted a resolution to use the Russian Armed Forces outside the territory of Russia. Apparently, he has survived so far; my son's naive attempt to save thousands of lives with the Egyptian scarab magic has not been successful yet.

Instead of Putin's timely end, I learn about another death, which makes my heart sink: a Ukrainian dissident and human rights activist, one of the crucial figures in the underground art movement of the sixties in Ukraine, died overnight. I want to tell my son about him, but Andriy is already asleep. But I can tell you: Ivan Dzyuba was the author of the 1965 book *Internationalism or Russification?*, which gathered facts about the oppression of Ukrainian culture and language and violent Russification in the Soviet Union.

A writer at heart, Dzyuba researched human rights violations and genocidal practices. This was not his vocation; history just did not leave him much choice. History is about to limit my choices too. I don't know this yet, but for the rest of the year I will see so many stars above Ukrainian cities. There will be blackouts and[6]

Dzyuba also used to say, "Where there's more pressure, there's more resistance," explaining why some of the most prominent Ukrainian dissidents come from the east of Ukraine. Dzyuba himself grew up in the Donetsk region, near Volnovakha.

Soon there will be no Volnovakha, and there is hardly any consolation in the fact that the Ukrainian dissident will not see the Russian army demolish his hometown. There may be some consolation in that, but it's not justice.

New Home—Casanova I

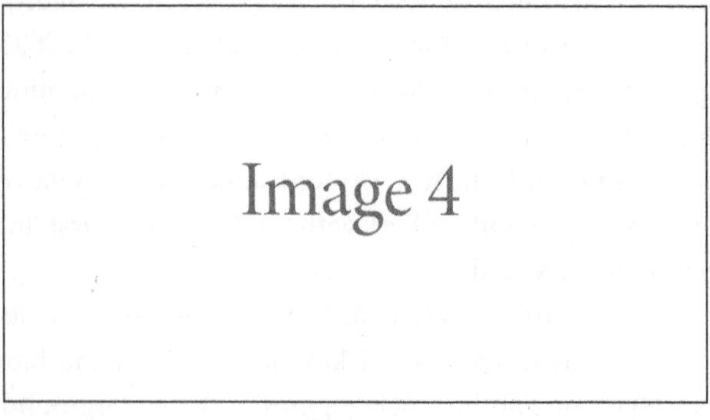

Image 4

Casanova

[6] This sentence was left unfinished.

Her call sign as a war crimes researcher at Truth Hounds is Casanova. She seems about my age, and I'm thirty-seven. She, too, has a son, long hair, and an ambition to write a book. Yet while I quit my day job and did write my novels, Casanova has committed herself to defending human rights and then, since 2014, to researching war crimes. Over the years, many quit the field, switching to less stressful ways of pursuing justice, but not Casanova.

She asked me not to use her real name in the book for safety reasons. Casanova joined missions in the war-torn Donetsk region in 2014 and the occupied Crimea peninsula in 2018. Who knows where she steers next to pursue the ideals of justice and human rights? If she ever gets caught by one of the war criminals she is helping to find and convict, it's certainly better if they don't know she is a key researcher at Truth Hounds.

Casanova is my reason for writing this book: I wanted to write about her. At first, it disappointed me when she asked if she could remain anonymous. I wondered if her mannish call sign, Casanova, would work well for portraying her, a pretty young woman driving minivans, to which she gives cute nicknames, into the war zone. Her old white Mercedes Vito is Birdy, and she is Casanova. However, she told me a story that made me see her call sign differently.

It was the end of 2021, the seventh year of the Russian war against Ukraine, when Casanova decided to quit her job as a war crimes researcher. Dozens of missions to the front line and temporarily occupied territories didn't lead to a single court hearing at the Hague. She resolved not to think about the lack of final results—criminals on the court bench. She kept doing her job well, documenting new war crimes, writing reports, taking pictures of the shell holes, and recording videos of the atrocities in the east of Ukraine. She didn't lose her faith in justice or human rights, no. She felt it was time for a change. Still, the choice wasn't easy; the Truth Hounds team had become her family, and pursuing justice in the Russian-Ukrainian war had kept Casanova going for the past seven years. Yet she planned a brave new life for herself by the beginning of 2022: Casanova and her husband would buy a house and plot of land in Central Ukraine, grow a beautiful garden around it, and live there in the house with the beautiful garden happily ever after.

Casanova already knows what kind of trees she'd have there: apple, apricot, and cherry trees. Those grow best on Ukrainian soil, and the climate is most appropriate. She would even enroll in a master's program at the Kharkiv National Agrarian University to be as good a farmer as she is a war crimes researcher. Her small family would make a living by selling the fruit and inviting people from busy cities like Kyiv and Kharkiv to live their village dream as green tourists—a simple happy life.

She tells me the story, and the name Casanova suddenly has a different meaning: *casa* means "house" and *nova* is "new" in Portuguese.

The garden around the future house, around the *casa nova*, was all well planned, or at least well dreamed. In March 2022, Casanova was going to travel to the Poltava region of Ukraine and find a house with a plot to buy near Myrhorod, in the heart of Ukraine, a canonical Ukrainian town mythologized by Mykola Hohol.

So Casanova quits her job in war crimes research, celebrates New Year in Kharkiv, and drives Birdy to the war zone in the east of Ukraine on the first day of 2022. Her friends volunteer each winter season to bring Christmas presents and entertain kids in schools along the front line. The Kharkiv-based team calls themselves St. Nicholas's Deer, and Casanova is usually their driver. Although playing with kids isn't easy for her, she, like the rest of the team, dons funny deer's horns and watches the fun from the side, so she witnesses not only tragedy in the war zone but joy too. She started 2022 by driving the team to Stanytsia Luhanska, the town where Russian forces shelled one of the schools in 2014 and began the escalation in 2022, which would hit Fairy Tale kindergarten soon, on February 17.

Because of the shelling, several teens from the nearby village in the Luhansk region, Vrubivka, asked St. Nicholas's Deer to evacuate them; their parents didn't want to leave but granted their permission for the kids to go. The team booked accommodation in the Carpathian Mountains. Casanova brings them to Kharkiv but won't drive them farther west; she feels that she cannot go far from Kharkiv now. Unlike me, she has a real plan if Russian forces invade. Throughout February 2022, while I packed my swimming suits and summer dresses for a vacation in Egypt, Casanova bought extra gasoline and studied evacuation routes from Kharkiv to Svitlovodsk. In Svitlovodsk, her Kharkiv friends and their Polish partners set up a shelter in case the full-scale invasion begins. They stocked plastic canisters with fuel, a lot of it. Casanova had sixty liters waiting on the balcony in her Kharkiv apartment so that she would be ready to start immediately.

The Truth Hounds have prepared themselves for the war too. Casanova's ex-boss, the executive director of Truth Hounds, Roman Avramenko, was in the Luhansk region to train the prosecutors there in war crimes research when he received a call from Brussels: leave the Luhansk region immediately. He did, without much hurry. But such warnings came from everywhere, and all eventually appeared to be wrong. So it was only the evening of February 23, 2022, that Roman finally wrote on the Truth Hounds work chat the two words meaning almost the highest level of danger: "Code orange." At that moment, everyone on the team knew what to do, how and where to move. Casanova left the chat at the end of 2021, so she didn't receive that message. She was at her home in Kharkiv.

Despite the dream of settling near Myrhorod, Casanova is

all about the road. She loves to drive minivans that can carry a team of war crimes researchers or volunteers. The work in human rights defense isn't exactly a gold mine, so the minivans she drives are pretty old. Each of them gets a name—or maybe a call sign. If they stall, she talks them into keeping going and not letting the team get stuck in danger. Their names are no secret: the green Volkswagen is Cucumber, the yellow one's Fishy; these are corporate vehicles shared by the Truth Hounds team. Casanova's own minivan is a white Mercedes Vito, and she has named it Birdy. When the attack on Kharkiv started on February 24, 2022, Casanova executed her tasks according to the evacuation plan, carrying passengers with her Birdy.

She'd evacuate as many as possible and get back to researching war crimes. Everyone in war crimes research in the region is all too familiar with Russian tactics; they see the flood of horrible war crimes coming their way.

Her plan for a new home with a garden will have to wait. Near Poltava, where she was going to buy a new house, Casanova stops at a gas station and messages Roman Avramenko, the organization she left at the end of 2021 to start a new life.

"Any vacancies?" she inquires with bitter irony.

"Well, of course. What would you like to do?" Roman replies.

On February 27, she posts on her Facebook page: "Dear all, I am alive and well, my family is safe. Obviously, I'm back to volunteering and 'work.' Well, you got it. Please send me information about the shelling of civilians in the Kharkiv region (in personal messages only)."

Casanova doesn't speak Portuguese. And the dream about the house and the garden appeared, of course, much later than Casanova got her call sign. Still, it seems to me that it's this idyllic Ukrainian vision of a house surrounded by the cherry trees, *casa nova,* that she is protecting by remaining incognito. And even when Casanova begins to speak again to the eyewitnesses and war crimes survivors, I will keep seeing her "new home" as if shining through the reality of destruction, injustice, and human pain.

She Was the Evidence—Iryna Dovhan I

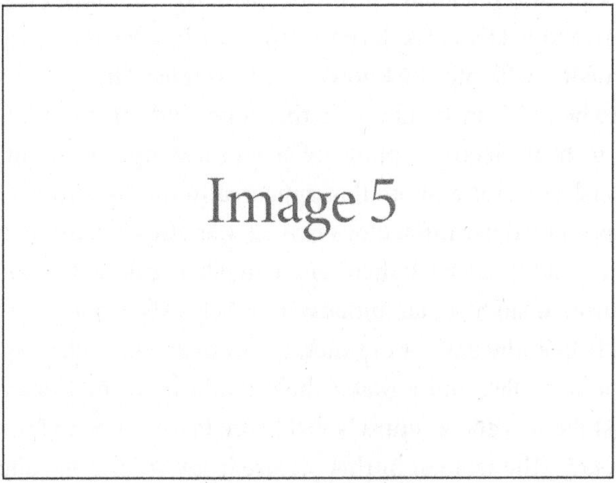

Image 5

Photo of Iryna Dovhan

Iryna Dovhan already has her new home and new garden. The old ones she had to leave behind in the Donetsk region in 2014. Fleeing to join her family in Mariupol, she could only evacuate her shepherd dog, Matilda; two cats;, and her daughter's prom dress, which the girl never got to wear due to the occupation. Most of the valuables had already been stolen from the house, while Iryna was held captive by Russians. And, of course, she couldn't evacuate the trees or the flowers she had been growing for about twenty years.

Iryna's new home near Kyiv is serene on February 23, 2022,

when, at about 11:00 p.m., she receives a message from a friend in the army: "They will attack in full force in several hours."

She jumps to her feet and goes to tell her husband. But he is already asleep. She watches him sleeping, phone with the message in her hand, and decides not to wake him up.

They have tried to spare each other whenever possible during these eight war years. In 2014, when the lawyer Evhenia Zakrevska interviewed Iryna about the horrendous days in Russian captivity in occupied Donetsk, Iryna didn't describe what the Russians, from what will later be known as the Wagner Group, actually did to her. Her husband was in the room, and she did not want him to hear. Seeing a photo of her beaten up on one of the Donetsk squares, a photo that appeared in the *New York Times* and prompted her miraculous release, was already hard on him. What could he do back then? He remembers calling the hotline of Euromaidan SOS, an initiative that helps Ukrainians get free legal help in the darkest of times; the woman who picked up the phone was Oleksandra Matviichuk, the head of the Center for Civil Liberties and a future Nobel Peace Prize winner. He could only say, "The woman in this picture is my wife. What should I do?"

Fortunately, he didn't have to do anything to release Iryna; the photo by Mauricio Lima did it all. He only needed to take good care of her afterward. So after they fled the Donetsk region in 2014, he sold everything he had left, including his childhood apartment in Mariupol and his car, so that Iryna could have a house with a garden again, in safety, near Kyiv.

Now Iryna is waiting for the attack on her new home, new garden, and new life. She ran away, but Russia is catching up. She hopes the friend who sent her the message is wrong, but she is ready anyway. She first encountered Russian soldiers in Donetsk in 2014, so, after all, the worst has already happened to her. She wasn't ready back then. Her survival came as a miracle, or as a famous photographer who could make the case known to the world overnight, making it impossible for the Russians to slaughter her quietly. But now Iryna doesn't count on miracles.

She has been stocking food in the basement of her new house for her children and grandchildren to survive on. She has been training as part of a medical unit to help the Ukrainian army win. So she waits until 2:00 p.m. on February 24 for them to attack and falls asleep, snuggling beside her husband, knowing they are ready for something no one can actually be ready for.

She will know that Russia has caught up with her when she opens her eyes. In Russian captivity, she was beaten up and got a concussion, so her hearing is not perfect now. But it will be impossible not to hear numerous explosions in Vasylkiv, where her son and two grandchildren now live. She will wait until they escape and the entire family gathers in her well-prepared basement. She will hug them all, one by one, take her backpack, and leave. Her husband will drive her to the agreed-upon meeting point for her medical evacuation team, in Hostomel.

Their small car will be one of the few going into the town while everyone else is fleeing it, running for their lives. She will see the Russian helicopters in the sky over the Hostomel airport. But that will not stop her. Since 2014, Iryna has been the live evidence of the Russian aggression in the east of Ukraine. She has met with the International Criminal Court prosecutors in the Hague and given dozens of interviews, emphasizing that Russian soldiers, not only their Ukrainian collaborators, tortured and raped women in 2014 in Donetsk. But now, the evidence of the Russian aggression—black Ka-52 alligator helicopters—is above her head. So in this moment, it seems she no longer needs to prove anything to the world; she needs to help Ukraine win, and its soldiers live.

In fact, Iryna will return to the Hague soon to talk about gender-based violence, war crimes, and accountability again. But she does not know it yet, jumping into a minivan with other paramedics and going to save the lives of the Kyiv defenders. On February 24, the Hague seems too far from Hostomel. Black Russian helicopters seem much closer.

My February 24

Our flight to Ukraine is scheduled for 7:00 a.m., February 24, 2022. When we take a taxi to the airport, it's still dark in Egypt. Everyone else in the half-empty seaside hotel seems to be sleeping peacefully, and I decide not to wheel but to carry my suitcase past dark bungalows so that no one is woken up because of me. Or maybe I just want to hear the quietness of the world as if I already know it is about to change forever.

It's 4:00 a.m. in Egypt and in Ukraine. I look up: the sky's clear, and the constellation of Ursa Major is shining brightly above our heads. Other constellations do too, but I don't recognize them. I first saw such a starry sky in Luhansk when I was five. We lived in Lviv back then and there was always too much light pollution to see the stars well enough to learn how to recognize constellations. In Luhansk, the relatives we visited lived in a house, on a street that was dark enough during the night to see all the stars above. Someone showed me, a five-year-old, Ursa Major back then in Luhansk. Perhaps it was my mom. So the sky full of stars became one of my memories about the city. Stars meant my childhood and Luhansk for me. I grew up, Luhansk was occupied by Russians in 2014, the world changed, but I haven't learned to recognize any other constellations. And February 24 is not a day to learn about constellations.

I ask my son to hurry up; if we miss our flight, we'll be stuck in Egypt, beautiful but not easy to navigate for a family that does not speak Arabic.

On the ride through the desert, I'm trying to read the news. The connection is poor again, almost nonexistent. Despite all my efforts, I manage to receive just one message, short, like a World War Two telegram from the front line. It reads: "Explosions in Kyiv."

I am gasping. This must be a mistake. Many sounds may seem like distant explosions when you are scared. And what if these are just fireworks, someone's joke? We've read too much scary news lately, we looked at the toys in the piles of the broken bricks, not the stars, we thought about all the wrong things and made the wrong wishes. Besides, the explosions could have all kinds of explanations. What if this is a gas explosion? Gas explosions are a possible thing. The bombardment of a European capital is not. Not anymore, I mean. Never again, right?

"Can you see the stars through the window?" I ask my son.

"I cannot," he replies, too sleepy.

"I can see Ursa Major, the Great Bear," I lie, so he keeps trying to see the constellations despite the glare from my phone's screen on the window while I try to contact our family and friends in Ukraine. I don't quite remember who in particular I write and call; I mostly fail anyway. The desert is endless.

"Oh, I see it!" shouts my boy about the Great Bear.

We thank the driver and rush into the airport building. When we get home, everything will be clear.

"Do you know what happened?" the Egyptian official asks me as soon as we enter the building. I don't reply for a moment, so he keeps repeating as if helping me to realize:

"You cannot go to your country."

"You cannot go to your country."

I can and I will, I think. I rush to the blue screen with the departures. This will be the last time for a long while that I see Ukrainian cities on such a screen: Lviv, Kyiv, Kharkiv. I will search the blue screens in every airport, hoping the nightmare will end.

In an hour, we are the only ones left in the tiny airport of Marsa Alam, Egypt. The desperate crowd of Ukrainians left the building heading to the buses brought by their tourist agency. The Ukrainians are to be taken to some random hotel, so they won't prevent passengers from happier countries from boarding their flights. I booked the hotel and the flight myself and had no agreement with a tourist agency. So when everyone else boarded the buses, we stayed. The airport official asked us to leave.

"You cannot stay here," the guy in the airport uniform repeats. He likes repetition, apparently.

I explain that we have nowhere to go, but he doesn't seem to understand.

"We had a revolution like yours in 2011; we, too, protested against injustice. We succeeded, and Russia is punishing us for that," I said suddenly. I could also mention I wrote a book about three revolutions,[7] including the one in Egypt. But war isn't a time for small talk.

The guy interrupts me: "Shhh. We cannot talk about the revolution openly now. Okay, you can sit here near the entrance."

I thank him, sit on the floor, and start looking for flights.

How does it feel to be stuck in an empty airport in a foreign country, knowing that the ruthless enemy is attacking the cities you love? I feel a mixture of fury, grief, and . . . relief. Yes, I also feel relieved. It seems shameful yet inescapable to feel this way, and I justify myself by thinking I'm not the only writer who has met the beginning of an apocalyptic war with something other than despair or anger.

[7] Victoria Amelina's debut novel, *Fall Syndrome* (2014), focuses on three revolutions: the Tunisian Revolution of Dignity (2011), the Egyptian Revolution (2011), and the Revolution of Dignity in Kyiv (2013–14).

Czesław Miłosz, Polish-Lithuanian poet and Nobel laureate, described how he felt in 1939 when Nazi Germany and the USSR attacked Poland. "The nonsense was over at last," he wrote; "The long-dreaded fulfillment had freed us from self-reassuring lies, illusions, subterfuges; the opaque had become transparent."

I once accidentally bought Miłosz's book in Kraków, the city to which I am desperately trying to find tickets now, sitting on the floor in the empty terminal. The reasons for Milosz's relief were not the same as mine, but I agree with the main point: the nonsense is finally over.

My son's last birthday wish was never going to come true: the war he was growing up with never ended but evolved, grew and morphed into a full-scale war we have not yet seen. We are entering an open battle with Russia. It is time for everyone to call the war a war.

The season of phantasmal peace is over; everything is illuminated like this empty sunlit terminal in the middle of the desert. There are no tickets to Kraków from here. I don't know where to go. And I recite a poem by Derek Walcott in a whisper:

. . . and this season lasted one moment, like the pause
between dusk and darkness, between fury and peace,
but, for such as our earth is now, it lasted long.

I guess when the world ends, some people cry, some scream, some go silent, some swear, and others recite poems. To be honest, I swear a lot too. Over time, I will also learn to laugh a lot again. The end of the world isn't as quick as everyone imagines; there's time to learn. Yet there are no instructions.

War Instructions No One Wanted—
Zhenia Podobna I

Zhenia Podobna

On the night before the invasion, Zhenia Podobna stays up late in her new apartment in Irpin. She is editing emergency instructions for the public television company where she works making documentaries. Their office is downtown, on Khreshchatyk Street, and the emergency instructions are to be executed if the war reaches the Kyiv region.[8] Almost no one believes in such a scenario. Zhenia does. Her colleagues assume her worry stems from a trauma suffered during the years she worked as a war correspondent. But unlike her neighbors in Irpin, at least Zhenia's colleagues do not blame her for "panicking," and she is allowed to edit the instructions adding whatever she thinks is crucial.

[8] The office of the television company was relocated to downtown Kyiv after the Russian attack on the television tower on March 22, 2022.

Around 2:00 a.m. on February 24, Zhenia decides the instructions are good enough, pushes the Send button, and falls asleep. It is the last moment she remembers before the first explosions prove her right. Although being right is definitely not what she wanted.

Zhenia runs up and down the stairs of her apartment block, all eight floors, knocking on every door:

"Wake up! We have to get ready!"

"Wake up! We're under attack!"

"Wake up! We're at war!"

Zhenia is sure that now her neighbors will finally do what they should have done long ago when warned about the possible invasion: prepare the basements, stock food and water, and plan where they would get electricity in case of a power outage. However, the neighbors still laugh, swear, and ask Zhenia to leave them alone. It's too early for war; everyone wants to sleep.

She rushes to the local supermarket, which seems an ideal shelter, with a basement, a stock of food, and possibly an electric generator. Zhenia wants to explain all this to the supermarket employees; now they will finally listen to her.

It's about 5:30 a.m. on February 24, 2022. People worldwide switch their TVs on. They don't know the names of the towns yet: Hostomel, Irpin, Bucha. Yet they are perhaps more aware of how grave the situation might be in the Kyiv region than the people around Zhenia.

At this moment, perhaps, the airport employees in Egypt are already telling me that I cannot fly to my country; they also know. Everybody knows.

However, supermarket employees in Irpin prepare for an ordinary work day; they tell the war correspondent Zhenia Podobna to calm down and let them do their job, as the customers will soon be coming in. So Zhenia and her parents find an open basement in one of the apartment blocks nearby and organize a bomb shelter there themselves. The supermarket will soon cease to exist—shelled, destroyed, and looted.

Around noon Zhenia heads up to her apartment on the eighth floor near the beautiful lake. She hears the sound of helicopters and looks out the window. What she sees will haunt her for months: black "alligators" flying like crows over the Hostomel airport. Looking at them, Zhenia knows Kyiv might fall. Terrified by this sudden realization, she cannot move away from the glass, as if destined to watch the war from a jar. Her home, her city, and her parents seem defenseless against the black alligators, the occupiers they're carrying, and their weapons. Time stops for Zhenia.

Iryna Dovhan is watching these same helicopters from her car, heading to Hostomel: about thirty Ka-52 alligator attack helicopters, flying low, firing cannons and guided missiles at the Ukrainian defenders below. But while Iryna is concentrating on joining her medical evacuation team, Zhenia observes the scene in the sky as a war correspondent. She ponders what these helicopters mean. Once the Hostomel airport is under Russian control, the transport airplanes will bring thousands of occupiers directly to the gates of Kyiv. She knows that she is potentially watching the end of her world. For a moment, it seems that the Russian plan is working and Kyiv will be occupied in a matter of hours, not even days or weeks. Zhenia's world is gone.

Then the unexpected happens: one of the helicopters goes down, disappearing in the black smoke. Zhenia looks at the dirty cloud over Hostomel airport and sees not just one alligator destroyed, but the entire myth of Russian invincibility destroyed. This first helicopter hit, not a victory but the slightest chance for it, is widely visible and becomes a sign for many. The burning Russian alligator means we should fight not only because it is better to die fighting, but because we can win. Quite a difference. Now Zhenia can even plan for the future, and it includes finding the person who downed that first helicopter, talking to him or her, and telling the world their story.

So Zhenia gets back to work, cleaning the basement nearby for her neighbors, who become less and less sarcastic as the explosions get closer, the helicopters fly lower, and Russian jets appear in the sky.

The Russian jets and the alligators eventually suppress the Ukrainian defense. Yet the continuing resistance means that all the big Russian transport Il-76 planes, with troops, armor, and fuel on board, have to turn back midway and return to Russia.

Meanwhile, on the ground, Zhenia hides her awards for her work in the war zone in the sand she has for her pet, an old chinchilla named Busya. Zhenia is regretting not having time to safeguard her husband's war medals; they are all on his uniform, and she has no time to unpin and hide them in the sand as well. She cannot take her awards or her husband's uniform with her, knowing the Russian army as an enemy all too well since 2014. If anyone or anything gives away that she is related to the Ukrainian Armed Forces, she and her parents can only hope for their death to be quick. She says goodbye to her apartment and heads to the street, where her father's car is already waiting. In her head, she now has two dreams. The first one is, of course, to come back home soon. But this will not happen, as the apartment will be destroyed. The second one is to find the soldier who shot the first alligator over the Hostomel airport and thank him or her. Just like perpetrators and victims, the heroes should also have names and faces. But this is no time for research: Zhenia knows the Russians are heading to Kyiv, and Irpin is right on their way.

Jammed roads force Zhenia to choose a more daring route via Hostomel and Borodyanka. Near Korosten, in the dark, she sees a military convoy. Zhenia hopes it's the Fourteenth Brigade of the Ukrainian Armed Forces moving to intercept the Russians.

One of the tanks trying to run over their car makes her doubt that. She calls her friends in the army to ask them what is going on. The answer is short and scary:

"Those are not our guys."

Zhenia sees that the vehicles are all marked with v.

In several months, Zhenia will open the door of her apartment in Irpin and say quietly, "Welcome, this is my home." Her voice will suddenly change, as if she lacks air, and I will follow her through the half-burned rooms.

By then, I'll be a war crimes researcher, still a beginner but hopefully an apt one. I will have experience wandering the ruins of strangers' homes. I will be trained by Casanova to talk to survivors of heinous war crimes. I will talk to them. But nothing will help me to find words for Zhenia, my fellow writer, a war correspondent, whom I admire, and my dear friend. I will be silent while she walks me through her half-burned life:

"Here are my books. See, I told you it is a miracle. I am lucky. All my neighbors lost everything, yet I still have my books."

She will climb on a chair to take something from the upper shelf and accidentally find a red necklace:

"I made it myself. I do things like this when I'm nervous; it helps. This one I made, waiting for the news from my friend on the front line in 2014."

"And this is the bedroom. The floor here could collapse at any moment, as the shell hit the apartment precisely under this place. And I was here, in this room, when it all began on the twenty-fourth."

It will be risky to stand in that bedroom above the shell hole. But I will know why Zhenia shows it to me. She will be letting me in so I can do for her what she has been doing for many other women—so I can tell her story. And I will be more scared of failing Zhenia than of falling through the floor of her cozy bedroom with its still-lovely curtains and pillows miraculously intact.

Zhenia will turn away, wiping tears from her face, and apologize for no reason. I will tell her that crying is good and normal. Yet quite cynically, at the same moment, I will contemplate if I can take a picture of her like this. Would an emotionally intense photograph be good for the story? I'm not a journalist; I'm not used to taking pictures or filming when instead I can help, hug at least. But a picture did free Iryna Dovhan from Russian captivity. And though I am certainly not as good or famous a photographer as Mauricio Lima, who took the picture of Iryna Dovhan being beaten in Donetsk, I will decide that sometimes recording and intervening *is* indeed the same. So I will pick up my phone and take a picture of my crying friend.

The American writer Susan Sontag thought that photographing was an act of nonintervention. "The person who intervenes cannot record; the person who is recording cannot intervene," she wrote in her book on photography. I remember it well: the characters of my unfinished novel about the war argue about that all the time, and as an author, I was perhaps on the side of those who'd choose to intervene, not record. However, I'll know that Zhenia lets me, of all people, in, so I can record; thus, somehow, this recording, this storytelling, is an intervention in itself.

There are cases when photographs save lives, like when Mauricio Lima saved Iryna Dovhan from Russian captivity, but that's not the case here.

The world will be used to seeing Zhenia's apartment building as a horrifying background for the photographs of world leaders and stars visiting Irpin after liberation. I won't take pictures of myself there.

This Is Europe

FINDING TICKETS FROM EGYPT IS CHALLENGING EVEN THOUGH I don't care much about the destination; it is enough for it to be Europe. Eventually, I find tickets to Prague. The airfare is crazy expensive, but I don't want to stay even a day longer: the palm trees, the swimming pools, and the whole relaxed atmosphere contrast too much with what is happening in Ukraine. I need to get home.

At the airport, citizens from the countries of the European Union check in to the Prague flight and head to the security control area; all Ukrainian citizens are asked to wait. I can recognize the Ukrainians among the Czechs without looking at their passports or hearing them talk. We no longer look like tourists; we are all something else already: refugees, soldiers, or someone else in the middle. We don't know who we are yet.

We try to explain at the check-in counter that Ukrainians have been able to travel to the European Union without a visa for several years. So we can enter the Czech Republic routinely, like tourists. But everyone sees it too: we are not tourists anymore.

The night airport is not a place to explain that "Ukraine is Europe" and that this slogan of the Ukrainian Revolution of Dignity is perhaps the very reason for the invasion;[9] this argument won't work. No one has to let us in.

At the same time, the first refugees from Ukraine cross the land borders to Poland, Slovakia, Hungary, Romania, and Moldova. But I don't know anything about that. We await Prague's

---

[9] What is known today as the Revolution of Dignity (2013–14) started as the Euromaidan protests in Kyiv's central Maidan square in late November 2013, as the reaction to the president Viktor Yanukovych's refusal to sign a political association and free trade agreement with the European Union. The flag of the EU and the slogan "Ukraine is Europe" became the symbols of the revolution, which saw the president ousted from the country.

decision for about an hour, discussing the rumors about a Ukrainian who was not allowed to board his flight to Germany earlier in the day.

"And what if they don't let us in?" my ten-year-old asks me.

I don't know the answer. I remember all the news and documentaries about the unwanted refugees I have seen and *The Terminal*, a 2004 American comedy-drama film starring Tom Hanks. Hanks's character is stuck in New York's John F. Kennedy airport terminal, unable to return to his native country or enter the United States, stuck in between, like us.

An hour later, the verdict arrives for us: "You can board."

I still worry about passing through border control upon landing. But being stuck in the airport in Prague might be a bit easier; the languages are similar, and they have many coffee shops in the terminal, as far as I can remember.

In the Prague airport, the border control officer, a young woman, glances at my passport and then stares at me. She seems to be more interested in the expression on my face than in my passport details. Perhaps she is new to the job and has not seen anyone whose country is being bombed. Maybe she is looking not at me but at war. She stamps our passports without asking any questions. I nod and take the documents without a word as well. I cannot mumble, "Thank you." I am sobbing.

"Why are you crying, Mom?" my son asks.

"Because we are home," I say.

"But this is not Ukraine," he says, confused.

"This is Europe," I answer, as if this word, "Europe," is a password that should explain everything to my child. It isn't, of course. The term "Europe" will be redefined in the next few days. The world is transforming, and the meanings of words are changing; I feel that in my inability to pronounce "war," the quietness of my son, and the gaze of the Czech border control officer. I weep not only because we are let in, but because it seems that in looking at me, people have started seeing not me but war. I am war. We Ukrainians all became a war. Nothing else about us matters now, only it—the catastrophe that has just begun.

I buy train tickets to Poland; through worried Europe, I'm heading home to Ukraine. There I will be just myself at war, not war.

Of course, my son is not coming with me; we are about to part. But he doesn't know this yet.

A Writer from K.—Iryna Novitska I

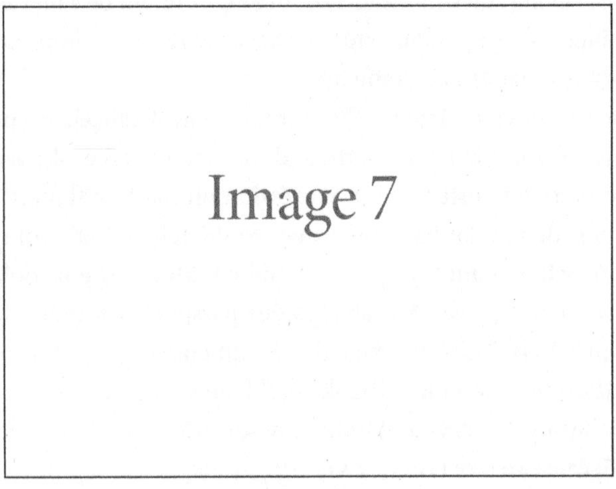

Image 7

Photo of Iryna Novitska

AT 7:00 A.M. EXPLOSIONS SHAKE THE WALLS OF IRYNA NOVITSKA's house shake: *it* has begun. At this moment her neighbors jump to their feet, perhaps. Iryna has not been able to jump to her feet for almost a decade. Even when the full-scale war begins, she has to move slowly into her wheelchair.

Like every Ukrainian, she then feverishly reads the news and messages. Russian troops are advancing toward Kherson and are already less than 200 kilometers from where Iryna is, in the Dnipro region, and moving quickly. But she's not concerned about her safety. At the other end of the country, in the Kharkiv region, the Russian army is advancing toward a small village near Izyum. There lives Iryna's son, Vital'ka, a fourteen-year-old child with autism spectrum disorder, and her former husband and good friend, the Ukrainian writer Volodymyr Vakulenko.

Iryna cannot move fast, but her thinking is quick:

"Please take Vital'ka and leave," she writes to Volodymyr.

She will keep asking him to evacuate every day while there is still a connection. On March 7, she will receive the very last messages about her son and the situation. Volodymyr will describe to Iryna what he sees from the window as the Russian army enters his village: "At the end of the convoy was a black Niva car. Someone from counterintelligence. I deleted all my contacts." That will be his last message ever.

Their story started in 2006. An alumnus of a culinary school, Volodymyr Vakulenko worked as a janitor at the Izyum compound feed plant and volunteered in a provincial center for creative local youth; his own creative writing aspirations were yet to be fulfilled. Iryna, a postgraduate student in Ukrainian literature and an editor at one of Lviv's publishing houses, got increasingly involved in her new part-time job at a website for aspiring authors like Volodymyr. The website, Poetry Workshops, was founded in Lviv, and did not usually attract poets from as far east as Izyum. That fact and the fierceness of Volodymyr's poetry attracted Iryna's attention. His pen name was Volodymyr Vakulenko-K. Soon she learned the letter "K" stood for his native village near Izyum—Kapytolivka. Volodymyr loved Kapytolivka deeply, although he was perhaps hardly loved back. This small village is central to his life and will be central to his death.

"Two souls, alas, dwell in my breast": Iryna likes to quote

Goethe's *Faust*, remembering how she saw Volodymyr at the time they met: he was still searching for his identity and his place in history. Iryna had an experience making history already. In the winter of 2004, she took part in the civil resistance that would later be known as the Orange Revolution, a series of events in Kyiv and throughout the country that deterred fraud in Ukraine's 2004 presidential election and secured Ukraine's democratic vector. Volodymyr observed the Orange Revolution from the other side of the barricades: while Iryna was in Kyiv protesting for the pro-Western and ultimately just pro-Ukrainian candidate Viktor Yushchenko, Volodymyr went to Kostyantynivka, in the Donetsk region, and observed the camp of supporters of the pro-Russian candidate Viktor Yanukovych; Volodymyr tried to understand their pro-Russian views but couldn't support them. This choice of Volodymyr's, which he was making back then, at the time of Orange Revolution in 2004, would make him an obvious target for the Russian regime in 2022.

In 2006, when Volodymyr and Iryna met, he was already on the way to becoming someone Russian occupiers would definitely want to eliminate in 2022—a Ukrainian who wouldn't agree to flip his identity to Russian, neither for privileges of belonging to imperial culture nor even for survival. Iryna helped Vakulenko complete the transformation.

Back then, she'd pay for the whole night in the internet cafe in Lviv, located on the street named after Dzhokhar Dudayev, the first president of the Chechen Republic. Volodymyr connected from Kapytolivka, where the streets were still named after Soviet leaders and Russian writers, like everywhere in the former USSR. Could they imagine that in seventeen years there would be a street named after him in Kapytolivka, he would be dead, and she would try to get to his funeral through the war-torn country in a wheelchair? Of course not. They spent nights chatting about life, poetry, and politics. She guided him through the poetry of Arthur Rimbaud, the love philosophy of Roland Barthes and Ivan Franko, the Ukrainian Executed Renaissance writers, and the generation of the Sixtiers. Iryna and Volodymyr read each other's poems and told each other news from the opposite ends of Ukraine. Until, later the same year, they moved in together. Or, rather, he moved to Iryna.

As much as he loved Kapytolivka, in Lviv, there were more opportunities for an aspiring writer. Vakulenko took part in poetry readings and joined an artistic community that spent time on Virmenska Street—Ukraine's Montmartre, where writers, musicians, and painters met. The magnet for the creative crowd, a gallery named Dzyga, hosted exhibitions, concerts, and readings. Vakulenko did his best to be noticed. Yuriy Izdryk, the founder of the best-known Ukrainian literary magazine, *Chetver* ("Thursday" in English), invited Vakulenko to help him curate one of the magazine's issues. Iryna keeps the copy of issue #30 to this day. Vakulenko didn't become all that popular as a poet. But in 2011, his first children's book came out.

In 2008, Iryna gave birth to their son. The doctors had to do a C-section due to the child's improper position in the womb. For three days they wouldn't show the child to the mother. When Iryna first saw her son, she noticed scratches on his tiny body and a mark on his forehead.

"Did anything go wrong during the operation?" she asked. But no one would answer her. In independent Ukraine, the medical system was still unreformed, and women were especially vulnerable, in both gynecologists' offices and birth beds. Iryna didn't insist; more than anything, she wanted to get out of the hospital and be home with her son and husband. They named the child Vital'ka.

When he was two, Iryna noticed that his vocabulary was too

scarce compared to other children's. He would also avoid eye contact. He is fine, Volodymyr would insist. However, in about a year, they got a diagnosis—autism spectrum disorder.

Iryna tried to teach the boy as much as possible; he even learned some numbers and letters. The child just needed more love and understanding, Volodymyr believed. He seemed to understand his son without words, as if speaking his unique nonverbal language. The couple argued more and more often. Busy and stressed about her child, her marriage, and writer's aspirations she had to abandon, Iryna felt pain in her legs but didn't know what was going on until it was too late. In 2011, she lost the ability to walk. Their marriage was falling apart just like Ukrainian democracy; Viktor Yanukovych, a pro-Russian oligarchic candidate against whom Iryna protested in 2004, won the presidential election in 2010 and was consolidating power to try to turn Ukraine into a state like almost any other in the post-USSR space—an authoritarian one. But Iryna didn't have the strength to think about politics anymore. Her life was drastically changing; she had to adapt to using a wheelchair.

However, there was yet hope she would be able to walk again. At the end of 2013, she went to Crimea, where in the Saki sanatorium, a doctor named Lyudmyla helped her stand again. Not walk yet, but stand. It was a lot for Iryna.

"Come again, you might even be able to walk with support," the doctor promised before Iryna left Crimea in the beginning of February 2014.

Full of hope that she would walk again and restore her marriage, Iryna returned to Lviv and learned that Volodymyr left for Kyiv to participate in the protests,[10] which by that point had turned into real struggle between the prodemocratic protesters and the police and government-paid militias, called *titushky*.

[10] The protests in question are those of the Revolution of Dignity (2013–14).

Volodymyr was beaten by titushky in Mariinsky Park, his head severely injured. Yet unlike many others, he came back home alive and with victory. Weren't they lucky?

The Yanukovych regime fell; the now former president himself ran to Russia. This victory was too bitter, with more than a hundred dead or missing and Russian troops entering Crimea.

With the Russian annexation, Iryna never got a chance to see Dr. Lyudmyla again, and so never got her chance to walk. Her marriage with Volodymyr had also had a chance, but it, too, vanished. With the beginning of the Russian aggression in the east, Volodymyr decided to move back to Kapytolivka. Izyum was right on the way from Kharkiv to the Donbas, and it was convenient to help both the army and the affected civilian population from there.

A couple of years later, Iryna met someone else; he was incredibly handsome and smart and also used a wheelchair. Volodymyr continued to live with his father and Vital'ka. Iryna moved to the Dnipro region to be with her new husband.

So by February 2022, Iryna and Volodymyr could only communicate via the internet and phone, just like at the beginning of their story, when she'd connect from Dudaev Street in Lviv and he'd connect from Kapytolivka.

The question of whether Izyum and Kapytolivka were too close to Russia to be safe was at the heart of their talks for the first two months of 2022. Volodymyr and Iryna talked every day, but they did not make a decision.

On February 24 at 7:00 a.m., when the walls of Iryna's house in the Dnipro region shake from an explosion, Volodymyr Vakulenko is the first person she talks to.

"Please leave with Vital'ka," she begs him again.

But he will never leave.

As If You Were Going to War

On February 24, 2022, thousands of Ukrainians begin moving westward to evacuate, and thousands start moving eastward to join the defending forces. It is as if a flock of forty-million birds is disturbed by a loud sound and rises into the air, covering the sky to the horizon. The roads are jammed immediately. The lines at the Polish-Ukrainian border, which have never been short, break all records. By the time I reach the border on the afternoon of February 26, tens of thousands are escaping Ukraine on foot, in their cars, and on buses at the checkpoint. Yet only two vehicles are crossing the border into Ukraine. I am in one of them, a gray Dacia Duster that belongs to the Polish writer Ziemowit Szczerek.

Ziemowit is going to Lviv to evacuate his friend's family and kindly agrees to take me and my cargo on board. Our car's trunk is full of medicine, hygiene stuff, and canned food we bought hastily in a Polish supermarket. I also got a canister full of gasoline and a small souvenir bottle of Polish vodka at the last Polish gas station. When my friend Sofia called from Ukraine and I described to her what we were bringing, she laughed:

"Guys, you're packed as if . . . as if you were going to war!"

I am not sure whether her laugh was hysterical or ironic. Perhaps it was both. I laughed too. What was happening couldn't be anything but a Kafkaesque dream anyway. Now, at the border, the dream is turning into reality.

Only a few are crossing in the east direction, and at some point, we happen to be in a line for those fleeing Ukraine. There are simply no control booths for people traveling east. No one expects us; all resources are stretched to let people escape the war. So we melt into the line of evacuees who have spent the last two days at the border, and I secretly look at them, just like the Czech border officer looked at me yesterday.

Not that I have never seen my people escaping war. I did. Part of my family had to evacuate from the Donetsk region in 2014. My sister-in-law, or just sister, as this is what I call her, moved from the Donetsk region to Kherson. Grandma Hanna moved to Lviv and died there, daydreaming of returning to her little old house on what had become a contact line in 2014. I have numerous friends from Donetsk, Luhansk, and various towns in Crimea who carry the keys from their houses in their pockets, ask remaining neighbors to water plants in their abandoned apartments, and teach everyone to say "See you in Donetsk," like Jews say "Next year in Jerusalem." I am used to all that, and I myself dream of the starry sky over Luhansk, the vast squares full of sunlight in Donetsk, and the smell of the cypress trees near the little Crimean town of Simeiz.

But I have never seen Ukrainians fleeing the country en masse, frightened, desperate, ready to spend days at the border, ready to leave everything behind, maybe even the keys from home.

They don't have much with them.

"Hey, you have a cute bag," I tell a little blonde girl dragging a pink suitcase behind her; I hope it is full of her favorite toys, so she won't end up missing them, like my son is already missing his Lego. The girl's mother looks scared, though she is hiding it from the child; the girl seems to be treating the whole thing like a sudden vacation, obviously proud of having her own suitcase.

"Where are you from?" I ask.

"Zhytomyr," the girl replies.

That is right, I think; people from Kharkiv or Sumy must still be crossing the country to reach the border.

"Do you plan to go into Ukraine?" the Polish border officer asks, frowning.

"I do," I reply, as if I'm marrying someone, perhaps my country.

Unlike the Polish officer, the Ukrainian one on the other side of the border does not ask anything; he gets it: I'm just going home.

Then we drive past the people at the pedestrian crossing point. Their crowd looks like a giant moaning creature with hundreds of hands, mouths, and eyes. The giant must be in pain. I want to turn away but make myself look: I have to stop seeing the suffering creature and start seeing individual human beings. They are primarily women and children, like my son and me. Men have not been allowed to leave the country since yesterday. The young men I notice are perhaps foreigners, scared and arguing uselessly in their languages. The border guard can hardly understand them. He is yelling something in Ukrainian to the entire public; the creature doesn't hear him. The guard seems more desperate than polite, trying to ensure no one dies in a fatal crowd crush today. I don't usually empathize with border guards, but I wish this one luck.

We continue our hour-long trip past the line of cars. I am watching families arguing in their vehicles, strolling around them to warm up, carrying their babies, walking their dogs, heading to the bushes because there are no restrooms along the road, or leaving their vehicles to walk on the roadside in the hope of crossing quicker on foot. It seems like I'm going past my entire country that suddenly had to run for its life, past all Ukraine's fear, despair, and anger. I take out the tiny souvenir bottle of Polish vodka I bought at the gas station. I didn't know why I bought it; now I do. The line is about forty kilometers long; the souvenir bottle seems too small for the experience.

Ziemowit is going to travel back to Poland tomorrow. As a Polish citizen, he may have the right to pass the line and go directly to the crossing point for the European Union citizens. For me, it's different; it was easy to cross into Ukraine, but I would have to spend about four days at the border to get out again. Fortunately, I don't plan to return to Poland soon, although that is what I promised my son. I lied to my child, and I will keep lying; war is a source of bad habits.

I reach my apartment in Lviv on the evening of February 26, 2022. It feels cold and empty without my son and dog running to meet me as usual. A siren starts wailing. I lie on the corridor floor and wail much like a wounded siren. I'm afraid to go inside to see my son's books, toys, and bizarre Lego creations: houses, castles, space shuttles, and replicas of famous buildings. During the following months, he will worry for them: Could I tell the displaced children to please not touch his Lego? They can take anything they need, play with his toys, read his books, and sleep on his bed, but they can't touch his constructions; they took so much time to build.

I will lie to my child, saying his Lego stuff is unharmed. But our home will turn into a small shelter. I won't even see who will destroy all my son's Lego houses and when. At that exact moment, the real cities of Mariupol, Popasna, Volnovakha, and Borodyanka will be razed to the ground.

As High as Her Mountains, as High as Her Drone—Evhenia Zakrevska II

On the morning of February 24, the lawyer Evhenia Zakrevska and her husband are not the first in line to the territorial defense headquarters. It's all because of her stubbornness: even after the first explosions are heard in Kyiv, Evhenia wants to head to the court and participate in the scheduled hearing, as if nothing can stop justice—at least not Putin.

Evhenia's fellow lawyers doubt that going to court in a rain of Russian bombs is a sensible idea. Still, she insists: "The purpose of this war is to destroy the Ukrainian state and all its institutions. Therefore, the institutions, including the courts, should work." Evhenia's arguments are always powerful—in court as well as in life.

Besides, the hearing she wants to attend on the first day of the full-scale war is of historical importance, one of the Maidan cases, as everyone in Ukraine calls the cases of peaceful protesters killed during the Revolution of Dignity. It's hard to accept that Putin will again interrupt the trial: Russia has already demanded that some of the accused be exchanged for Ukrainian POWs, and the exchange happened in December 2019. But even that did not stop Evhenia Zakrevska. So she refuses to believe that the full-scale war can stop her.

Yet by 9:00 a.m., it is clear that the courts will not open.

Like all of us, Evhenia has to decide who she is in wartime, and the role of a lawyer seems unattainable. Evhenia looks at her husband and picks up her backpack, stuffed for the occasion, packed for war as carefully as when they used to go hiking in the mountains together. He picks up his war backpack as well. They leave their apartment near the Protasiv Yar, a park in the Solomyansky district of Kyiv, which, together with Roman Ratushny, Evhenia managed to protect from influential construction companies. Together they merge into the long line of volunteers outside the territorial defense office eager to defend the capital.

Is Evhenia scared? Well, yes. She is too far back in the line, and the office may run out of guns before they get to her; she fears ending up unarmed, already not a lawyer, but not yet a soldier.

But when Evhenia's turn finally comes, she gets her Kalashnikov. The situation is fatal, but she is game: she has managed to officially join the territorial defense of Kyiv, and what more can you wish on February 24, 2022?

Soon Evhenia's unit will be on the outskirts of Kyiv, behind the villages of Stoyanka and Belogorodka. By February 27, the Russian forces will reach Stoyanka and entrench there. Evhenia's unit, consisting mainly of novices, will train to meet them. But Evhenia's main task will be waiting for her first, most crucial, and potentially only battle. If any Russian tanks break through, her unit is to stop them and delay the Russian convoy for as long as possible. And her only weapon will still be the AK-74 she was so glad to receive on the first day of the war. She will try to procure anti-tank weapons for her unit, and she will succeed, but not enough. So she will learn how to stop tanks with a Kalashnikov:

"Aim at everything that shines. Aim at the optics," the instructors say.

She is good at shooting; she can do that.

"Tanks! Tanks!" someone yells on the radio. She jumps to her feet, puts her body armor on, and grabs her AK-74, repeating to herself, "Aim at everything that shines. Aim at the optics."

But no, it's a false alarm.

Then comes another alarm. And another. But it's false again. All of them will be false. Russian tanks will never reach the outskirts of Kyiv. Evhenia will have more time to learn and will soon be fighting in the Kharkiv region, where I will meet her.

Chernihiv Airstrike [—Vira Kuryko I]

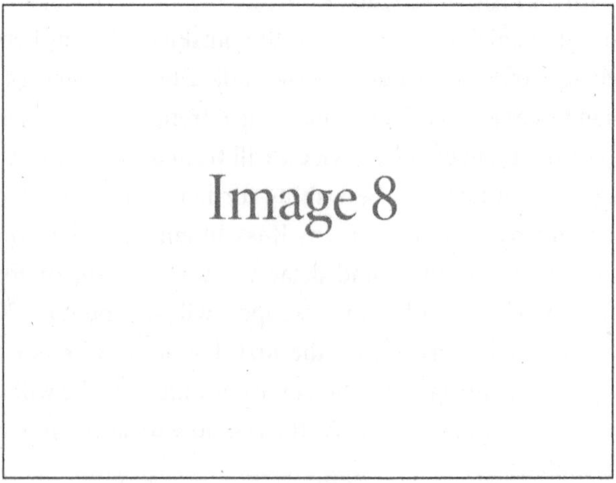

Image 8

Vira Kuryko

On March 3, 2022, unguided aerial bombs are raining down on the city of Chernihiv, killing at least forty-seven people and leaving many more homeless.

I don't know who to call. It feels like someone close to me is there, but I cannot remember who that is. I have visited the city several times, of course. I was last in Chernihiv in summer 2021 and stayed in a hotel, Ukraina, in the city center.

On March 12, this hotel will be destroyed too, hit by a FAB-500 missile. In the summer of 2021, I couldn't even imagine that. Back then, sitting in one of Chernihiv's cozy cafés, I first heard about the young, talented local writer Vira Kuryko. Chernihiv's festival manager Inna couldn't stop talking about her and her brilliant nonfiction debut.

The book, *The Street of the Involved*, told the story of ordinary Soviet people who lived next to the famous Ukrainian dissident, one of the so-called Sixtiers generation, Levko Lukyanenko in

Chernihiv. After his death, these ordinary people opposed renaming their street after him; they all were involved with the regime, to different extents. Some spied on Lukyanenko. Some just didn't care. The idea seemed brilliant to me, though I've never met the author. I knew only her name: Vira Kuryko.

Later I will learn what happened to her that day, March 3, 2022, when the unguided aerial bombs landed on the Chernihiv apartment buildings. Vira Kuryko came back to Chernihiv. Without knowing, she and her husband passed already occupied villages, luckily avoiding mortal danger.

Heart Under Occupation—Iryna Novitska II

From Volodymyr's last message, Iryna knew that Kapytolivka was occupied on March 7, 2022. She didn't know that the occupiers didn't allow civilians to leave the village and searched men at numerous checkpoints, one of which was right in front of the house where Volodymyr and their son live. However, she was already aware that there had been no gas since March 1 and no electricity since March 3. Now there was also no internet or cell connection.

March 2022 was freezing; the temperatures near Izyum reached negative 18 degrees Celsius. People spent time near the fires in their yards, cooking, quietly sharing news from the neighbors who managed to reach someone by phone, and warming themselves together like in ancient times, waiting for the spring and the Ukrainian army to come.

At first, Iryna tried not to worry too much. Volodymyr was the only caregiver for their disabled son and his elderly father. The three generations of men lived together in a small house with a garden, the kind of house Casanova might have considered for starting her new life without war crimes research. Volodymyr had a disability himself: his health was first impacted by the trauma he received while serving in the Soviet army in Russia when he was young and then by the injury on Maidan in 2014.

Iryna knew about the cruelty of the Russian army and how the empire treated people like Volodymyr, Ukrainian writers, and activists. Her degree in Ukrainian literature made her all too familiar with numerous examples in the history of Ukrainian literature in the nineteenth and twentieth centuries. Yet she didn't expect history to repeat itself in her lifetime. It seemed impossible that the Russian occupiers would hurt two vulnerable civilian men and a helpless boy in the tiny house in Kapytolivka.

However, on March 13, 2022, everything changed for Iryna. Perhaps for every Ukrainian lucky not to experience the occupation, there was a piece of news that made them realize how desperate the situation in the occupied territory was. For Iryna, this was the news about the execution of Volodymyr Kononov, a Ukrainian who offered a hopeful example for her as someone active and successful in Ukraine despite being in a wheelchair. Volodymyr had lost his right arm and left leg due to an injury at a metalworking plant almost twenty years earlier. Since 2014, he had been helping Ukrainian soldiers in the east, bringing them food and sometimes even taking fighters to positions in his car. With his wife, he fell into the hands of the "militias" and spent ninety-eight days in captivity, but even that didn't stop or break him. Kononov founded his business and kept helping the soldiers. Now the media was reporting: the famous volunteer Kononov had been shot dead by the Russian invaders in his wheelchair in the Luhansk region, near Severodonetsk.

Iryna gasps, realizing: If the invaders didn't spare this man, why would they spare Volodymyr or even her son?

So Iryna starts spreading the information on social media: She cannot reach Vakulenko. He might be in danger.

I see these messages about Volodymyr missing in the beginning of April and immediately write to Tetyana Teren and my other PEN colleagues; we have a small chat on Signal dedicated to evacuating and helping writers in danger. Notifying PEN is a sensible and practical thing to do; we can quickly spread the worrying news among our fellow writers worldwide. However, the next thing I do is completely impractical: I open my chat with Volodymyr Vakulenko.

He only wrote to me once, in the summer of 2021. He asked me if he could be invited to the literary festival I was managing. But the program of the festival was complete; Ukrainian writers were eager to come to the war zone. So I had to decline Volodymyr's request. Busy with the festival, I forgot about this chat immediately. Now I reread it and gasp. In 2021, Volodymyr wrote to me jokingly: "It's not the last festival, and I'm not going to die . . ." He did not want me to feel bad that I had to say no. Volodymyr's last words were: "And if you need any help, just knock."

I will knock on the door of Vakulenko's house in Kapytolivka in six months when the Izyum region is finally liberated by the Ukrainian army. I will come to Volodymyr's house not as a fellow writer, and not as a festival founder, but as a war crimes researcher.

Evacuating Deborah Vogel

I GREW UP IN A SMALL APARTMENT IN A NINE-STORY GRAY Soviet building on the outskirts of Lviv. My grandfather used to be a Soviet colonel, a fighter pilot, actually. For his long and perhaps controversial service, the Soviet regime granted him and his family, consisting of his wife (my grandmother) and their two daughters, a tiny two-bedroom apartment near a tank repair plant.

We, the children and grandchildren of the Soviet military, grew up there to the sounds of tanks firing and all the windows shaking several times a day. The tanks were regularly tested after being repaired at the plant. These explosions meant no danger to me; they were the sounds of my childhood. To this day, I can stay calm when I hear explosions in a war zone. I remember not even noticing shelling in Avdiivka sometimes when visiting the town as a writer after 2014. The Soviet regime arranged my life so I was better prepared for war than a normal person.

When I was sixteen, my mother and I managed to buy another tiny apartment in a building nearby, even closer to the tank plant than my grandfather's. It was so close to the plant that during working hours, I could hear the plant workers talking to each other right outside my windows. It didn't occur to my mother and me that the tank repair facility outside our windows would become a legitimate target for missile attacks in a war.

We expected that since the Soviet Union collapsed, along with its militaristic culture, the tank plant would eventually be closed and the land sold to developers. But that wasn't what happened.

So when I called my mom on February 24, 2022, the first thing I said—or yelled, rather—was:

"Mom, take your documents and leave now! They could strike the plant at any moment!"

Actually, I shouted "Now!" several times, I'm sorry to say.

My mom listened to me, but she did not move too far from her father's home, i.e., only about two hundred meters further from the military facility.

There, in the apartment of an old Soviet colonel, our beloved grandfather and father, deceased before he could see the madness of the Russian aggression in 2014, we all came together on March 6, 2022.

Five women of different ages—my mother, my aunt, my sister, my eight-year-old niece, and I—are gathered in the living room full of memories. I look at the numerous photos on the shelves as though they could give me advice. After all, hadn't all my ancestors had to survive war, occupation, and genocide?

We have important things to discuss. Firstly, what do we do with the frightened Maria, my niece? Her father, my sister's husband, isn't there to discuss this with us; he lives in the barracks now as he, like many, volunteered for the army on February 24. Secondly, who will care for my ten-year-old son, who is already safe in Poland but quite lonely? His father, a senior vice president at a technology company, will have to keep doing the job that requires him to travel all around the United States, trying to convince the customers that thousands of Ukrainian engineers can still be trusted with developing cutting-edge solutions, even as the bombs are falling (they will prove that they definitely can, by the way). His important job means that at least money isn't an immediate problem for all of us, but it also means that he cannot care for the children.

There is one more problem, the fussiest one: our white shepherd dog, Lyra. I left her with my mom the day before I went on vacation to Egypt. Since the first day of the invasion, Lyra has been on a critical mission of psychological support for Maria, who has to hide in the corridor to the sound of wailing sirens and misses her father, who decided to join the fight. Yet the dog is one of the vulnerable too. What if she gets scared of explosions at the tank plant and runs away, for example?

While my dog and lovely niece happily snuggle on the corridor floor, the safest place in the apartment, the rest of us argue fiercely about what is best for everyone. Or at least not unbearable. But I am the only one with a car and a driver's license, so the choice is largely mine.

The news keeps coming, one story more horrible than the

next, and my work chats are full of messages about the humanitarian needs in the Donetsk region, Kyiv, Chernihiv, and Kharkiv, and the writers who need help evacuating or a place to stay in Lviv on their way to safety.

So I feel like I cannot leave Ukraine even for a couple of days to evacuate my family. I stay for the night in my childhood home, feeling illogically safe in the apartment so close to a legitimate military target for Russians.

In the morning, my sister's husband, Petro, comes to visit; his short visit might mean he is here to say goodbye before being deployed to the front line, but there is no time to ask. I hear the door opening at about 6:00 a.m., and little Maria rushes to it, yelling "Daddy!" and jumping, like a monkey, to reach for his hugs. I watch Maria hanging on Petro, looking like an unfamiliar hero in camouflage, and I make up my mind:

"I'm evacuating you all tomorrow," I say to my mother in a low voice, not to interrupt the moment Maria and her father are having. "He is defending us, so I will at least ensure his daughter is safe. That is how I can help. Please start packing."

I go back to my apartment, now known as Noah's Ark, and try to pack too: I take my son's warm clothes, the book I read him at bedtime, and our dog's toys. I don't take any of my clothes; I will return soon.

I turn to the bookshelves, approach, and stare at them, on the verge of crying. I take books, one by one, look at them, and put them back on the shelves. Should I evacuate some books too? Which ones? I have too many.

I end up taking three books: *The Executed Renaissance*, an anthology of writers killed by the Soviet regime in the 1930s; a poetry collection by Hrytsko Chubay, a genius Ukrainian poet of the Sixtiers generation, who was broken by the KGB and perhaps even forced to testify against his friends; and a book by Deborah Vogel, a young Jewish poet who chose to write in Yiddish and was killed in the Lviv ghetto, like thousands of other Jews, in 1942. I grab these three books not only because I love the writing. It is my irrational, even silly, attempt to save them: the writers who have already been executed, a genius who has already been broken, and a woman who has already been slaughtered with her little son. I'm evacuating their books today, wishing I could have evacuated them too.

On March 8, International Women's Day, I'm driving my mother, my sister, my niece, and my dog, who is also a she, to the Polish border. We spend more than twenty hours there. March is cold, and I cannot keep the car's engine running: I don't know how long we will have to wait, so we risk running out of gasoline before we finally make it to the border. I'm cold, and I want to sleep. No one else in the car can drive. My sister just wakes me at night: "Wake up, go! They are moving," she exclaims. I start the engine and drive another ten meters. Then the cars stop again. The line of the vehicles, full of refugees, is barely shorter than eleven days ago when I was going in the opposite direction, into Ukraine.

We get to know our neighbors. We argue with those trying to pass the long line and go directly to the border. We defend each other. In front of my car is a woman from Kharkiv in a black Mercedes-Benz with a fussy black cat in the front passenger seat. I don't know her name, but a woman in a black Mercedes with a black cat helps me stop those who want to cut the line, and she treats Maria to cold dumplings she has brought along for the trip. She lets me down at five in the morning, suddenly starting the engine, driving forward, and passing the line ahead of us while everyone else sleeps. She knows many kids are in line, and she's rushing past them with a cat. I try not to judge her. She is from Kharkiv, and she was driving from Poltava nonstop. And she shared her dumplings with Maria. These dumplings and our dog kept Maria warm and not too hungry on that difficult day and night.

Still, I cannot help but exclaim, not expecting an answer: “Hey, why would she do that to us?”

We stay there waiting, feeling betrayed by a stranger with a fussy black cat and guilty for running away or evacuating a dog instead of maybe taking someone else with us.

The tank repair plant won’t be hit until March 26, 2022, but there is no way to know that, of course. Every day my mother, aunt, sister, and eight-year-old niece would have to be prepared for the area to be hit, hiding in the corridor because there are no bomb shelters.

On March 26, when Russians finally hit the plant with missiles fired from the occupied city of Sevastopol, the windows in my mother’s apartment will break. But she won’t be there.

Invisible Refugees—Tetyana Pylypchuk I

Image 9

Tetyana Pylypchuk

WHEN I WAS EVACUATING MY FAMILY AND A FEW BOOKS FROM my library, including *The Executed Renaissance* anthology, another more important evacuation happened on the other side of Ukraine.

On the morning of March 8, 2022, the territorial defense soldiers help the staff of the Kharkiv Literature Museum to load the manuscripts, letters, and first editions of the Ukrainian writers of the twentieth century on a train heading west. Tetyana Pylypchuk, the director of the museum, boards the train too. It is hard for her to leave the city, which itself is crucial for Ukrainian literary history, but she is the one responsible for the unique collection, almost everything tangible that is left from the Executed Renaissance generation. She won't leave the collection unattended even for a second; if a missile were to hit, she preferrs to be near too. On the train west, Tetyana and her two male colleagues take turns standing guard like soldiers in the dark. Even at night the lights on the train are off, and the blinds shut to protect the passengers from the shards of glass in case of an explosion. The train, full of refugees, rolls through Ukraine in darkness and silence, past the war-torn Kyiv region, farther west.

The passengers on the train flee Kharkiv, Balakliya, and the Izyum area, where the writer Volodymyr Vakulenko has decided to stay behind. Only one compartment has no passengers, unless the writers whose papers Tetyana is rescuing are invisible refugees.

Their archive would mean nothing to the rest of the world; they are the weird ones, Ukrainians by choice: They are the Executed Renaissance, slaughtered, buried in mass graves in the 1930s, and prohibited from being remembered in the Soviet Union. They are the Ukrainian Sixtiers, sent to the camps in the 1960s and 1970s for daring to remember. Their works were not translated in time to become part of world literature and European discourse. But for people like Tetyana Pylypchuk, who is guarding them in the dark, they mean the world.

It wasn't always like that for us, though. Like me, Tetyana grew up speaking Russian and reading Dostoevsky, Tolstoy, and Bulgakov. Then she majored in Russian literature at Karazin University in Kharkiv. But once, as a student enchanted by the Russian classics, she visited the Kharkiv Literature Museum. Intrigued by the fact that her hometown had a hidden Ukrainian literary history she had no idea about, she worked at the museum as a volunteer. Together with other young people who gathered in the museum, including the future literature star Serhiy Zhadan, she resolved to help the rest of Ukraine learn the truth about its twentieth-century writers.

The key to the truth was on 9 Kultury Street in Slovo House. Its walls, unlike most Ukrainians, remembered the writers of the Executed Renaissance, as they all lived in this one big house with five entrances and sixty-six flats meant for the best of the best of Ukrainian intelligentsia. Contrary to the typical Soviet blocks, Slovo House had spacious rooms full of light, which turned out to be just holding cells. Almost everyone here was doomed for arrest, suffering, and death. A black car would come at night, and steps were heard on the stairs. The writers and their families froze in their beds: Are they coming for me? Then the sense of relief when a neighbor is taken, not you, made them feel ashamed, perhaps. Many feel the same now when the enemy airplane drops its bombs, but not on you this time. Your survival instincts tell you to be happy. But you don't want to be happy; instead, you want to remain human.

A day before the evacuation of the museum archive, Slovo House was hit. Despite the danger, Tetyana rushed through the cold Kharkiv streets to see the extent of the destruction. She was worried that the building would be gone, worried about the inhabitants whom she got to know over years, and about apartment 40, where her team organized an artistic residency, inviting writers and scholars who wished to explore Kharkiv.

This apartment that once belonged to the executed writer Petro Lisovyy became a place of bohemian parties, poetry readings, and philosophical discussions. But a Russian missile spared it, damaging the facade of the second entrance only and breaking the windows in apartment 21, which once belonged to the writer Ivan Dniprovsky, whose archive Tetyana is evacuating. He wasn't the brightest of the generation, but his archive was the only one left. Dniprovsky died from tuberculosis before the NKVD could come for him; thus, his apartment wasn't searched and his archive was not confiscated, enabling Tetyana and her colleagues to research Slovo House and its executed inhabitants. Now it is on the train, traveling farther and farther away from Kharkiv.

The archive will remain in a safe location (which I have been asked not to disclose for obvious safety reasons) till victory. Tetyana comes back home several days later. Her collection is safe in the west; her family has evacuated too. She is now alone in the city. She tries to open the door of her apartment building, but finds it locked from the inside, bolted by her frightened neighbors. It's almost curfew, it's freezing, and it's starting to get dark. But she can go to Slovo House; she has a key to apartment 40. She arrives at Slovo House and stays there till May. This area of Kharkiv is often hit; perhaps Russians are targeting the nearby hospital. But to Tetyana, apartment 40 on the first floor seems safe. What once was a happy residency and a holding cell becomes a shelter during the war.

Tetyana gets back to work. She cannot invite visitors to her museum, but her team can keep telling the truth online. On March 21, 2022, she organizes poetry readings.

Some seventy miles away, on the same day, Volodymyr Vakulenko is finishing his diary in the occupied village of Kapytolivka near Izyum. He writes about the Poetry Day, the wedge of cranes in the sky, and his faith in victory.

Noah's Ark

My apartment in Kyiv seems as far away as lasting peace. Many of my friends move in the opposite direction, from the east to the west. Many of my fellow writers from Lviv and Kyiv are already volunteering at the Lviv railway station, meeting confused, frightened evacuees and helping them navigate the city or find transport farther west to the Polish-Ukrainian border.

My friend Kateryna Mikhalitsyna is a children's writer, poet, and translator. Now she reads urgent announcements at the railway station: she can write and translate the announcements on the go, and typical announcements aren't helpful anymore. The timetable and the circumstances change daily, if not hourly.

My friend the poet Ostap Slyvynsky volunteers here too. Simultaneously, he starts the project he calls War Dictionary, asking people to send him examples of how the meaning of all the words change. I try to contribute to the War Dictionary, but language fails me to the extent that I cannot even describe it.

My apartment turns into a shelter. A family with three kids and a dog, a family with a grandma and a cat, and a family with a hamster are all my guests. I will not remember most of their names. I will remember, however, how I'm waiting for my friends from Bucha.[11]

I see their posts on social media first, then they disappear. I read about the green corridor in Bucha. Then I read about how the occupiers shoot at the cars in the green corridor. Then, finally, on March 12, my friend writes to me from her husband's phone that she is no longer in Bucha; she got to Kyiv. She will be in Lviv soon.

---

[11] The poet and journalist Olena Stepanenko; her husband, the Belarusian poet Siarhey Prylutski; and their son.

I know a massacre is happening while I meet the newly displaced, drink tea with them, go to the humanitarian aid warehouses, and negotiate with the brave truck drivers. I know what happened to Iryna Dovhan and hundreds or perhaps thousands of others in the Donetsk region.

When she finally comes, I don't ask her anything. She looks at my warm apartment, the running water, the electricity, and the food, and says nothing. Her little son hasn't talked at all for several days.

The next day, she says that she and her friend stopped eating to have enough food for the children. She says: I saw something horrible during the evacuation but cannot remember it.

She might seem okay and even smiles at times. My friend only starts to cry when talking about her cat. On February 24, she left her apartment and went to her friend's house in Bucha, leaving the cat behind, but just for a day or two. They could never return for the cat. It would cost them their lives, and she couldn't risk her son's life for the cat. Even for the cat.

"But the Russians are breaking into every apartment anyway," she says with weird hope. She doesn't care about her flat or belongings. "I hope they broke the door, so the cat could sneak out."

"Of course, they broke in," I try to comfort her, remembering how she showed me the photos of her cozy blue kitchen last summer.

In the morning, when she wakes up, we make coffee in my kitchen and hear a loud pop. Olena winces.

"This is not what you think," I say.

Only it is. Then we hear an explosion. The news says the Yavoriv training center was hit, killing and injuring many who had just volunteered for the army.

Olena is going west with her son in a few days, and Noah's Ark continues to operate. There are more hits around the city, but we get used to them and don't dare to complain; we compare everything not to the average life but to Mariupol now.

"The smoke is going away, and your Noah's Ark is still here for you to come to," I write on social media after another explosion that covered High Castle, the city's highest point, in black clouds of smoke.

The Executed Library and the War Diaries of Librarian and Writer—Yulia Kakulya-Danylyuk I

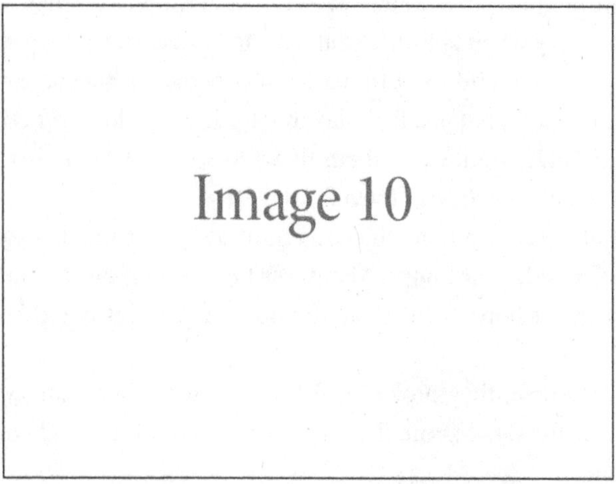

Image 10

Photo of Yulia Kakulya-Danylyuk

The village of Kapytolivka near Izyum is small but has its Writer and Librarian. The Writer is Volodymyr Vakulenko-K. Yulia is the Librarian.

Yulia's library, hidden between the only school and the only kindergarten in Kapytolivka, across the street from the town hall, is small, cozy, and perfect. She calls it home; she is happy here.

At 6:00 a.m. on February 24, she gets a call from a friend: there are explosions in Balakliya and Borova, where her parents live. Her twelve-year-old son is still asleep. Her husband, Dima, a carpenter, has recently joined the army as a driver and is already in Kostyantynivka, in the Donetsk region. Via phone, he assures his wife that they will not let Russians through. Her bosses in the regional culture department tell her the same. No one says the word "war" at all, as if that's not what explosions mean, nor Putin's night address, nor martial law. So she decides to go to the library.

Her library is the only library in Kapytolivka, and she is the sole librarian. People come to her not only for books. For example, on February 24, 2022, a woman came to ask Yulia to help her install an application on her smartphone. The library is not just a library here but a help center for the elderly, a safe space for women, and a club for children. It has to be open for everyone in hard times. So Yulia keeps it open.

The day seems ordinary; there are no more explosions. Readers even come to borrow books.

She is one of the few friends of Volodymyr Vakulenko in his native village. Others consider him a weirdo, and remember his troubles with alcohol, although he overcame those many years ago and was proud of his little victory over himself. He even quit smoking after Yulia told him he was a slave of cigarettes; Vakulenko was all about freedom, so he replied, I'm not a slave, and never smoked again. Yulia has always kept his books and even the photocopies of the newspapers that mentioned him in the library. She was proud of being the librarian in a village with its own resident writer.

The day the invasion begins, she sees the writer Volodymyr Vakulenko from afar. He waves to her, but she does not have time to walk in his direction. She will regret this as this is, in fact, their last chance to talk.

The Writer and the Librarian of Kapytolivka will never see each other again.

They will both stay in Kapytolivka. They will both start keeping their war diaries. Yulia's is more consistent. She writes it in a neat notebook with blue ink, in nice handwriting that reveals that she used to be a schoolteacher. Volodymyr will write in red and black ink, crossing out many lines and adding new ones. And his handwriting is not so easy to read.

The librarian starts her diary on February 24, 2022, and when no one can pronounce the word "war," even herself, she notes in her journal:

The war began in Ukraine. Russia invaded us . . .

Volodymyr might disagree with her first line, perhaps; this war started in 2014, he would remind her. He will retrospectively describe the first days of the invasion in a poetic way:

The sun was not in a hurry to warm up the land. Slowly, timid tulip sprouts emerged from the ground. No one covered them to protect against the frost. After the bombed-out buildings in the city, there was no time for flowers.

Both Librarian and Writer will note how quickly they have adapted to the horror. Volodymyr will write:

You get used to everything; the main thing is who you remain amidst all this. The "Grad" explosions stopped bothering me at all.[12] *I'm not afraid of dying suddenly, but I have no privilege to die. I'm not alone, so I have to survive.*

[12] The BM-21 "Grad" is a self-propelled 122mm multiple-rocket launcher designed in the Soviet Union.

On March 12, 2022, [Yulia writes]:

It's incredible how quickly one can learn to live in new conditions! Just a few days ago (a week), I was terribly frightened by the sounds of explosions, airplanes, etc. But today, I hear how grad rockets are fired near the village council toward Izyum, and I chop wood. Yes, I had to learn how to chop wood because I have to heat my neighbor's house to preserve at least one heating system. So, while the grad rockets are firing, I chop wood. The jets fly, and I stoke the boiler. I already know by ear how far it all is, and whether there is a threat to life. Thank God, there were few "arrivals" in the last few days, mainly from us. So, sleeping at night is possible, which is essential for the nervous system functioning. Still, my hands yet tremble sometimes for no reason at all. And as for my tired head, I won't even mention it :))

Today, I finally managed to find a connection and talk to Dima. And I also wrote to my parents and some girlfriends. Even [my close friend] Lapulya called me. Well, how could it be otherwise? :))

I'm so glad that my parents will finally hear that I'm alive and well. I know how worried they are. And I heard Dima, thank God! I think he was happy to hear me too.

The grad rockets are firing again. You don't even pay attention anymore.

Today, I went to the library. I picked up some of my things; it's a pity that I couldn't take everything. It is painful to look at the books, everything is scattered, dirty, and smoky.

The young boys almost begged me, saying that they are not guilty and already want to go home. The strangest thing is that I wasn't scared of them at all. I just wanted to tell them a lot! I told them that they are not an army, but a disgrace because they are robbing stores, people, behaving like cowards, and burying their equipment behind people's homes. I said that they and their children are cursed and will never wash human blood from their hands. The boys silently listened to everything, heads down.

Yulia is sure she is keeping her diary just for herself. If she is lucky, no one will ever read it. Who would be interested in the journal of a village librarian? Perhaps only the occupiers who would like to conceal their crimes? She tries not to describe too much, so they cannot accuse her of spying on them.

Volodymyr is afraid of the occupiers finding his diary too. Yet he also has hope that the world will hear him one day.

On March 17, 2022, Vakulenko writes:

Today is the tenth day of the occupation. I understand that these manuscripts will end up in the hands of the FSB, which is supposed to arrive after the "Z" division of the Russian army. However, I still hope to hand them over to international organizations in case of a prolonged occupation, as they will be governed by the rules of the international community.

There is no internet connection in Kapytolivka. It is divided by the Russian checkpoints. It is shelled, so walking far is quite dangerous. The librarian and the writer live on the different ends of the village. Thus, Yulia does not know that Volodymyr is being taken away for questioning. She also does not know that he buried his diary in his garden, so his war diary is already over, and so will be his life soon. Yulia will still keep her diary, occasionally documenting the fact that the abductions of the civilian men suddenly intensified on March 24, 2022. She will not know that Volodymyr Vakulenko is one of those taken on this day.[13] Here is what she writes while he is being taken away in a white

[13] Volodymyr Vakulenko was taken away for questioning the first time with his underage disabled son Vital'ka on March 22, 2022. On that occasion, they were released. However, on March 24, he was captured and taken away, never to be seen alive again.

minivan marked with the letter "Z" they have both learned to despise:

[Editors' note: The fragments below are taken from the diary of Yulia Kakulya-Danylyuk]

03.24.2022

People are killing people. They are doing so not only for territory or food but for no reason at all. Maybe they're scared. Afraid that if they don't kill, they will be killed tomorrow. Fools . . .

Sometimes, when I'm very scared, I imagine that I am water. I seep into the ground, hide in cracks, flow deep down to underground springs. But then a shell comes flying, everything trembles, the earth shakes, and even water cannot find peace. There's no peace to be found anywhere right now . . .

03.25.2022

Every day is chaotic. And every day there's hope that this day will be the last of the war. But they keep shooting and shooting, day and night. The sounds are splitting my head, because they're shooting somewhere close to us. Endless echoing shots, helicopters, machines. You watch this and sometimes you think it's not happening to you, but some horrible movie. Yesterday I wrote a note during the day, and now real "action" has begun. The "DPR" militants are doing wonders with us. They catch soldiers, put guns to their heads, look for the slightest sign that they might be involved with the Armed Forces of Ukraine or the Defense Forces. When I heard all this, I was really scared. I realized that the real "Germans" had come, the real "Gestapo." Now every corner of Kapytolivka has its own owner, and we have to ask for his permission for everything. I cannot even imagine what I would do if they came to me!

By March 28, Kapytolivka's Writer will be in captivity, tortured, or already dead. His war notes will be in the black Ukrainian soil, waiting to be found one day.

Kapytolivka's Librarian will keep writing, not knowing that now she is the only one left to document the events in the village:

> *03.28.2022*
> *The most disgusting thing is that I'm scared all the time. There's no phone because we're not allowed to use it. I can't describe everything that's happening here, all the events, because I just want to forget all the horrors.*

She knows one of the men on her street was taken; she knows he might not ever come back. She is right; the man's body will soon be found in Kapytolivka.

Yulia is the one left to write, but she is in danger too. The wives of the Ukrainian soldiers cannot feel safe here. And she is afraid to leave the village: at the checkpoint they might already have her name noted. So she stays. So she keeps writing her diary.

Last Sparkling Wine from Bakhmut, Last Vase from Popasna, Rome Statute in My Bomb Shelter

I KEEP GOING BACK TO THE MEMORY OF WHEN I WAS [THIRteen years] old. It's New Year's Eve, so according to the Soviet tradition, the women of the family are chopping boiled vegetables in a small kitchen to make lots of salads with mayonnaise for the dinner table. They don't need my help, so while everyone but my grandpa is in the kitchen, I wander around the sixty-square-meter apartment where the six of us live. There is no one in the living room, but the TV is on for some reason. It was almost always on in my childhood and always broadcasting the Russian public channels. Suddenly the New Year's program changes to an urgent address by President Yeltsin.

"I am tired. I am leaving," he says. Then he talks about Putin. I wish I could say I feel alarmed, yet I don't remember worrying. Instead, I feel excited: I have just witnessed history in the making. I run to the kitchen to let my mom, my grandmother, and my aunt know the news.

There is a rule one learns at the beginning of a war, the rule of two walls: during the bombing, you'd better be two walls from the nearest window. Of course, it is better to be in a real bomb shelter, but there are not a lot of those. In fact, if you live in a small apartment or an apartment with many windows, you will not even be able to follow the rule of two walls.

When my apartment in Lviv was full of displaced people, I left it and went to the apartment on the top floor downtown, which I had recently bought. There was no furniture, refrigerator, or even electric kettle, but I was alone.

The apartment has too many windows, including skylights, so it is impossible to follow the rule of two walls. The only place without windows is a small wardrobe, in which I had planned to store my numerous dresses. I put a rug on the floor, so it will not be so cold, and find a sleeping bag, which my husband and I used many years ago in the Himalayan mountains in Nepal. This sleeping bag and the wardrobe are my bomb shelter now. I call it my nest. My back aches, I start coughing despite lying on a rug, and I feel like I will never be able to open this wardrobe and search for a dress without remembering March 2022. Yet I sleep pretty well here, not waking up when the air raid siren goes off. Maybe it's because I'm exhausted. Or because I know I'm already as safe as I can be, even though I'm on the top floor of the building dangerously close to the Lviv television tower, which might become a target. I'm in my nest, my bomb shelter, and my fortress. I bring books in here: the poetry of Paul Celan, Hryhorii Chubay, and *Survival as Victory*, Oksana Kis's book about Ukrainian women in the Russian gulags. I cannot read; I mostly keep these books for company. I wanted to be alone, so I could cry, wail, or read Paul Celan aloud. But I only whisper his poem, which I know by heart, *Todesfuge*, Death Fugue, perhaps the most famous poem about the Holocaust.

The air raids sirens go off, but it seems nothing ever happens. Or rather, it does, only not here. Others die; I don't. It seems I don't need to sleep in the wardrobe. I can sleep near the window and look at the night city, dark and weary. Even in Lviv, people believe all the lights should be turned off during the curfew hours for safety. I cannot understand how it would save us from a guided missile; missiles do not target the lights but operate by coordinates. But perhaps the memory of the Second World War kicks in, and so those who do not turn off the light on time get angry messages from their neighbors:

"You're exposing all of us to the enemy!"

"Who on the fifth floor has strange violet lights on? Maybe these are insurgents signaling the Russians?"

"Sorry, it's me. I use violet lights. I am just your neighbor," someone replies.

Lviv has not been bombed for a long time, and I cannot understand why. No one here understands. It is illogical: Lviv was always regarded as a nationalistic center in Russian propaganda. Why, then, do they destroy Mariupol but leave Lviv untouched? They have long-range weapons.

I feel guilty for not being a target. This feeling is as illogical as Russians not bombing Lviv, but I cannot help it.

I feel relieved when I finally hear explosions while lying on the floor in my blue sleeping bag in the evening. I stop replying to the endless messages in the volunteer groups coordinating evacuation, humanitarian aid, and accommodation for the displaced. I let myself just lie, look into the dark, and wait for what will happen. Nothing happens.

But every time I walk home through the beautiful streets of the old town, its market square, Virmenska Street with its fourteenth-century church, I try to remember every detail of every building, each bas-relief, each atlante and column. Will Russians ruin all this? Will these streets only live in my memory? On one of the walls on Valova Street, I see a poem by Serhiy Zhadan and cannot help but think about the poem on the wall in Mariupol, on Peace Avenue: Is it still there? Or is it already gone, together with the building and its people?

Perhaps military experts know that Lviv cannot and will not be bombed like the cities in the east, north, and south. But I don't know that. I know nothing about types of missiles, our air defense, and Russian jets. I have no time to find out. I am busy learning other things: how to put together a military first aid kit, for example, or what documentation is necessary to accept humanitarian aid from the United States, or how to find a truck and a driver ready to go to Kyiv, Kharkiv, Chernihiv, or Sumy.

There are also new cultural projects. For example, Tetyana Teren, the executive director of PEN Ukraine, came up with the idea of putting quotes from Ukrainian poetry into the first aid kits.

"Can you imagine a soldier reading poetry while looking for scissors to cut his clothes and treat the wound?" I ask, though I love the idea.

I cannot remember if we actually started putting poetry into the first aid kits; perhaps not. The days seem one long endless day of February 24. I cannot remember what happened yesterday. I don't call my son. I don't call my mom. I only talk with the people who need help or can provide it. I'm connecting them, connecting, connecting, as if weaving lace or building a beehive.

Tetyana has more viable ideas for cultural projects too. For example, she starts the Dialogues on War, a series of online discussions in which Ukrainian writers talk to their foreign colleagues about what we are going through.

On March 26, I am walking to where Tetyana is staying in Lviv: we have agreed to watch one of the Dialogues on War live together and discuss all the projects PEN Ukraine is planning. I pass Zamarstynivska Street, exhausted from work at the warehouse. I raise my head and see the plaque dedicated to Raphael Lemkin, the lawyer who coined [the term] "genocide." I stop. This plaque seems out of place; it belongs to another story about achieving justice, acknowledging the truth, and saying, "Never again." All of it is gone now, isn't it?

I love *East West Street*, by Philippe Sands, and how it weaves in the changes to international law with people's lives and historical narratives. I realized we might be at the beginning of a new stage of transformation of international law, and I would like to help this transformation happen as a citizen and writer. I don't think law and human rights should be fields reserved for people with law degrees. Law is ultimately about human beings, or at least it should have people at the center; this makes law similar to literature. Maybe I can do something other than sorting medicine, moving boxes, and collecting money?

The Canadian writer Margaret Atwood and the Ukrainian writer Natalka Sniadanko talk online today. But I hardly listen. I want to bring more books to my bomb shelter nest. I want to reread *East West Street* and maybe read something about international law, like the Rome Statute or the Geneva Convention. I don't even know yet that there are multiple Geneva Conventions, not just one, but the idea is already there. I will find the Rome Statute easily on the internet, strange reading for strange hard times.

Berezil and Bucha

"The Maklena Grasa performance in Kharkiv will take place on February 26, 2022, at 18:00." The announcement is still available online. It seems you can press the Buy button on the website and get your tickets to the parallel universe where the invasion did not happen, and so the theaters in Kharkiv are full of light, laughter, and applause, and the year 2022 is known as the year of the hundredth anniversary of the Berezil theater.[14] But the missiles were launched at Kharkiv, the Russian troops crossed the border from the Belgorod region into Ukraine, and the premiere did not happen on February 26, 2022, nor later in March.

Maklena Grasa is the last play by Mykola Kulish and the last production of Les Kurbas as the director of Berezil in 1933.[15] It premiered in Kharkiv, the unfortunate capital of the Ukrainian Soviet Republic from 1922 till 1934. The plot is simple. Maclena, a teenage girl from a poor family, tries to earn money in various ways, including prostituting herself, in order to save her family. The original version of the play is forever lost. Only its Russian translation survived, and it was then translated back into Ukrainian—a painful metaphor for the history of Ukrainian literature.

Kulish set his play in Poland, but setting the play outside of

---

[14] An avant-garde theater founded in 1922 by the Berezil artistic association as an experimental studio under the artistic direction of Les Kurbas. In the early 1930s, Kurbas and Berezil became the targets of Soviet critics' diatribes and were denounced for inaccessibility to the masses. In 1933, the theater was purged.

[15] Kulish (1892–1937) was the pioneering playwright of the Ukrainian avant-garde. He was arrested in 1934 and murdered in 1937 in Sandarmokh, in theKarelia region, as part of the mass execution of political and other prisoners that marked the twentieth anniversary of the 1917 revolution. Several of Kulish's plays were staged by Les Kurbas at the Berezil theater. Les Kurbas (1887–1937) was the leading Ukrainian avant-garde theater director. He was arrested in 1933 and, like Kulish, executed in Sandarmokh in November 1937.

the Soviet Union saved neither him nor Les Kurbas. The Soviet regime accused both artists of trying to distort the perfect reality of the Soviet Union—a weird claim in times of the Great Famine, which killed millions of Ukrainians. Peasants, including children, appeared on the streets of Kharkiv, looking like ghosts, not asking for food anymore, just dying silently. Under these circumstances, how could a performance show the Soviet reality as darker than it already was? A rhetorical question.

According to the memoirs of Yosyp Hirnyak,[16] one of the actors who survived the Great Terror, Les Kurbas put it this way:

> As for the lack of enthusiasm for our reality . . . for the past four days, as I walk to my theater, I pass by the body of a woman who died of hunger . . . Nobody is removing her body. Such scenes do not inspire enthusiasm.

After the play premiered, one newspaper called it "fascist slander against the socialist reality"; the propagandists on the state-sponsored Russian channels, like Russia Today, could have used this same expression now about today's Ukrainian art.

In 1933, just like now, the play was only one more excuse. The entire generation of Ukrainian elite was to be wiped out. On November 3, 1937, both the playwright Mykola Kulish and the theater director Les Kurbas were shot dead together with almost three hundred other Ukrainian creatives, civil leaders, and politicians.

No one was ever prosecuted and punished for the Great Famine, nor for the Executed Renaissance. Some of the perpetrators were later executed too, but not for what they did. The Soviet terror machine erased them because while mass murder may not be so easy to start, it is even harder to stop.

---

[16] Yosyp Hirnyak (1895–1989) was one of the most prominent actors at the Berezil theater.

The huge poster reading MACLENA GRASA 26/02/22 18.00 might still be on the theater building, yet I, of course, cannot see it from the warehouse in Lviv. I also wouldn't dare to ask any of my friends who remain in Kharkiv about the poster. I ask them only one question now: How are you? They lie to me, saying they're okay. I keep helping to procure, pack, and coordinate trucks, minivans, and cars going from Lviv to Kharkiv and other cities with humanitarian aid and ammunition, like blood cells carrying oxygen. I don't know if I'll ever see Kharkiv again, but I have to do my part of the job so I stand a chance to see it. Every time Kharkiv is hit, I think about the theater where the premiere of *Maclena Grasa* should have happened: Is it still there?

Russian forces dropped two 500-kilogram bombs on the Drama Theater in Mariupol, killing the families who had hidden inside. I imagine the sound of the plane approaching and the bombs falling, but I cannot even begin to imagine what happened inside the building, when the roof exploded and the walls collapsed. Can the same happen to the Kharkiv theater? The Kyiv theater? Or even the Lviv theater I can see from my balcony, just like my friend Oksana Stomina could see Mariupol theater from hers? The only difference is that it has already happened there, and it only *might* happen elsewhere. What is the likelihood it would happen in Kharkiv? Serhiy Zhadan stays at night at another theater, the Puppet Theater in Kharkiv. What if this theater is hit? People die in the streets, at playgrounds, like the one near the Slovo House, where both Kulish and Kurbas once lived. People die while queueing for the humanitarian aid that I'm helping to pack.

I do not have time for international news, but I imagine Kharkiv is in the news a lot. Would it be in the news because of the premiere of *Maclena Grasa* at the Kharkiv theater? The hundredth anniversary of the modern Ukrainian theater, one of the most important phenomena in Ukrainian culture? No. The world would still know nothing about the Executed Renaissance, the genius Ukrainian playwright Mykola Kulish, the innovative Ukrainian theater director Les Kurbas, and their brilliant theater, Berezil, founded in 1922 and eliminated by the Soviet regime by 1937. Perhaps it still does not know, despite the fact that Kharkiv is in the news. But I would agree to Ukraine still being just a large blind spot on the map of Europe, "a post-Soviet country near Russia," as everyone called it, if only Kulish's *Maclena Grasa* would premiere again in the Kharkiv State Drama Theater on February 26, 2022 at 18:00.

Today is March 31, 2022, an anniversary of Berezil, one hundred years since Les Kurbas founded it in 1922.

If not for the full-scale invasion, on this day we would remember Les Kurbas, Mykola Kulish, and their theater. But we are at war. So March 31, 2022, does not become the one hundred year anniversary of Berezil. Instead, it becomes the day of the liberation of Bucha.

How will we remember it from now on? What will I think about every year on March 31? About Berezil or the Bucha massacre, uncovered right after the liberation of the town? Perhaps both. Because aren't they connected, the Bucha massacre and Berezil? Bucha was an idyllic town till 2022. Berezil was a unique modern Ukrainian theater founded in 1922. Both were executed.

Among the Guiding Stars—Oleksandra Matviichuk I

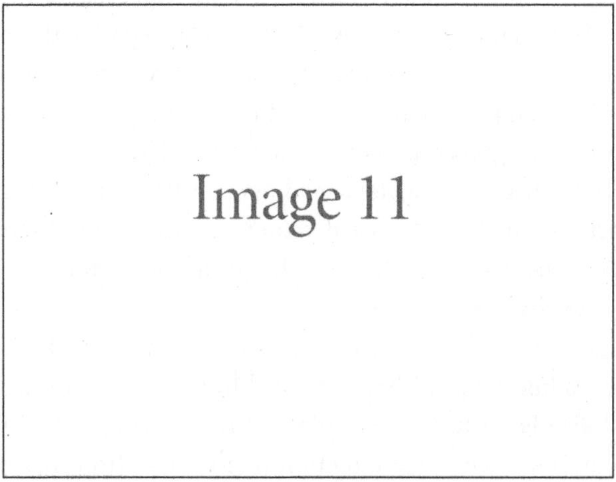

Image 11

Photo of Oleksandra Matviichuk

Another critical event related to Berezil happened long after the theater ceased to exist and its director and leading playwright were executed. In 1962, sixty years ago, young people of the generation we know as the Sixtiers gathered in the October Palace on Instytutska Street in Kyiv. They came together to commemorate Les Kurbas and his unique Ukrainian theater. That gathering was a brave enterprise: the Soviet regime had done everything it could to erase the memory of Kurbas completely, so it would have been wiser not to talk about him publicly in the capital of Soviet Ukraine. But the creatives who gathered on Instytutska Street in 1962 believed that times had changed after Stalin's death and were courageous enough not to care about the possible consequences of their actions. A year before, Les Taniuk, a young theater director obsessed with restoring the memory of his great predecessor, traveled to Russia to find the place where Les Kurbas was murdered. That evening on Instytutska

Street, Taniuk and his friends dared to talk about Les Kurbas and Berezil quite freely, at least for the time.

The response to truth is often even more truth; that is why regimes fear even small bits of it. After the official part of the event ended, a woman from the audience approached Taniuk and told him bitterly that there was no need to travel as far as Russia to uncover mass graves: some are right here, in Kyiv.

The woman was a witness, and her words eventually turned at least three of the Sixtiers generation—the director Les Taniuk, the poet Vasyl Symonenko, and the painter Alla Horska—into researchers of Soviet crimes.

I have yet to become a part of this sad tradition of Ukrainian creatives finding out what happened to their dead colleagues. I will also learn to find witnesses as if following in the footsteps of those who paid attention to a woman from Bykivnia and came to the village to uncover the Soviet regime that created the first Kyiv mass grave of the twentieth century. I do not yet pay attention to the part of Alla Horska's biography about crime research, but over time I will notice how much we have in common.

In March 2022, I can only think about Horska's magnificent monumental artworks and worry about them. Most of her mosaics are located in the Donetsk region, three of them in Mariupol: *Blossoming Ukraine*, *Tree of Life*, and *Kestrel* [*Boryviter*].

The latter is the most precious to me. I have never seen the mosaic, only a prototype, which looks like an exquisite painting. The actual mosaic in Mariupol is even more beautiful: the artists deviated from the prototype a bit, adding more blue and making the figure of the white bird more streamlined.

I first saw the prototype of *Kestrel* at the Sixtiers Museum in Kyiv before the full-scale invasion in the summer of 2021. Interestingly, then and there, in the museum that contains Horska's works and Taniuk's manuscripts, I also met Oleksandra Matviichuk, the prominent human rights defender leading a substantial war crimes documentation and monitoring effort.

It was no accidental encounter: Tetyana Teren, our mutual friend, celebrated her birthday at the museum. The Sixtiers have always been guiding stars for us, our link to the Executed Renaissance generation and thus to the entire history of forever endangered Ukrainian culture, so Tetyana fulfilled her dream of celebrating her thirty-fifth birthday among them.

At the time, I was a novelist and the director of a literary festival in the Donetsk region. My participation in human rights action was limited to campaigning for the freedom of my fellow writers, like Oleh Sentsov, Stanislav Aseyev, or a mathematician turned journalist from Crimea named Osman Arifmemetov.[17] Standing on the sunlit terrace of the Sixtiers Museum in Kyiv with a glass of wine, I could not imagine that, just like the artist Alla Horska, I might soon spend less and less time writing and more researching the untold stories about mass graves in Ukraine.

Oleksandra Matviichuk, on the contrary, had always dreamed of being a theater director, like Kurbas or Taniuk, but chose to pursue justice rather than an artistic career. Early on, she discovered the world around her was full of injustice: Oleksandra remembers how she discovered that Vasyl Stus, an outstanding Ukrainian poet and perhaps the most legendary dissident among the Sixtiers, was killed in a Russian camp when she was three.[18]

---

[17] Osman Arifmemetov is a journalist from Simferopol and a streamer of the Crimean Solidarity NGO. He was arrested by Russian security agents on falsified charges of terrorism in 2019 and sentenced to fourteen years in jail by the Southern District Military "Court" in the Russian city of Rostov-on Don. Victoria Amelina was the ambassador of his case within the #SolidarityWords human rights campaign, which supports Ukrainian prisoners of the Kremlin. When Arifmemetov heard about Amelina's injury in the Russian strike on Kramatorsk, he wrote her a letter of support. PEN Ukraine received the letter when Amelina had already died of her wounds.

[18] Vasyl Stus (1938–1985) died in the Soviet concentration camp Perm-36 only six years before the fall of the Soviet Union.

Oleksandra had realized a simple thing many in Europe began to understand in 2022: evil is not somewhere in the past; it is here. Heartbroken because of Stus's story, Oleksandra, who came from a Russified family, resolved to switch to Ukrainian. Little did she know that she would soon meet one of the Stus's close friends, who, like him, in 1972 was sentenced to seven (years in jail) plus three (years in exile) for "anti-Soviet propaganda." Stus did not survive, and he inspired Oleksandra to pursue justice; Sverstiuk survived and became her mentor.[19] They met through poetry: [Yevhen] Sverstiuk led a contest of artistic poetry recitation, and Oleksandra's choice of poems made an impression on him: "You're so tiny, but you chose such powerful poems," he said, seeing perhaps yet hidden strength in Oleksandra herself. Sverstiuk expected her to follow her dream of becoming a theater director, although he himself had to spend less time writing and more covering political issues his entire life. Yet Oleksandra chose law, becoming a Shevchenko University law school student in [2001].

Then she quit her well-paying job at a bank because she witnessed too many human rights violations and couldn't look the other way. She decided her long-term passion for human rights should be her full-time job.

As a teen, Oleksandra was often the one typing Sverstiuk's essays. He had lost his health in the Russian labor camps and could not see well enough to type himself. Oleksandra loved to help him.

Yevhen died at the end of 2014, after the Revolution of Dignity and the initial Russian invasion. At the time, Oleksandra's

---

[19] Yevhen Sverstiuk (1928–2014) was a distinguished literary critic, publicist, and political prisoner. In 1972, he was arrested and sentenced, for his involvement in the dissident movement and his defense of political prisoners, to seven years in strict-regime labor camps in Perm Oblast and five years' exile in Siberia.

organization and Oleksandra herself, like many others, were already busy documenting war crimes and crimes against humanity in Ukraine.

The Center for Civil Liberties first started doing the job just because it was the rational thing to do. During the worst days of the revolution, it seemed that the bodies of protesters killed on Instytutska Street could just vanish. The team started taking pictures and publishing them; even if human rights defenders were killed or arrested too, the word would be out already.

Now it seems that our entire lives were already defined by the encounters with the Sixtiers.

Influenced by the Western humanistic culture and the Ukrainian Executed Renaissance, the Sixtiers created remarkable artworks and had equally impressive but hard lives. They could be compared to the hippie movement or the Beatniks in the West, yet Ukrainian Sixtiers had to operate in a totalitarian and anti-Ukrainian Soviet state. The most prominent of them served sentences in the Russian camps. Some, including my favorite poet Vasyl Stus and the artist Alla Horska, were killed by the regime.

The party on the terrace was followed by the excursion. And among the works on display I saw the colorful sketch of the beautiful *Boryviter* by Alla Horska. When Oleksandra and I met, she already had plenty of experience in documenting war crimes and crimes against humanity as well as organizing such research work. Yet I wonder if back then we could think of Alla Horska not only as a painter and dissident but also as an investigator. Now, in 2022, this side of the Sixtiers movement seems much more understandable, close to us, and important.

Standing there looking at the sketch of *Kestrel*, constructed as a huge mosaic in Mariupol on Peace Avenue in 1967, we could not imagine that we would never be able to see the mosaic again. The mosaic that took Alla and her colleagues months to create will be destroyed in a matter of seconds by Russian shelling in 2022.

What still remain are this colorful sketch in Kyiv, the memories of Alla Horska, and the inspiration she is for Ukrainian women determined to uncover the truth about the horrible crimes.

The NKVD murdered her in 1970. It was hard to deal with her like all the other Sixtiers, by sending her to the camp first; she was too high profile in Soviet society due to her father, a well-known member of the communist party.

Alla risked her life to tell the truth and be on the right side of history. Oleksandra Matviichuk, whom I met at the Sixtiers Museum, was always known for doing the same.

PART II

Looking for My Way

Returning to Kyiv

My problem is that I promised my son I would not go to Kyiv, but would stay in Lviv. I decide to buy a ticket to Kyiv at about 8:30 p.m. on April 2. The train leaves at 10:35 p.m. the same day. The curfew starts at 10:00 p.m. That doesn't leave me much time to think. I believe the trip is quite safe, but I still cannot not think about the risk: if something happens to me, the last thing my son will know about his mother is that she lied to him. But it's good to be a writer; you can ask other writers to help. So I write to my friend, the marvelous children's writer Kateryna Mikhalitsyna:

"You are a children's writer, so you must find a way to explain why I lied. Will you?"

"I will," she assures me. "Go."

I start messaging those of my fellow writers who didn't leave Kyiv: Svitlana Povalyaeva, a poet, civil activist, and the mother of two extraordinary sons; Olya Rusina, a journalist and another marvelous Ukrainian children's writer; and Larysa Denysenko, a writer, a lawyer, and women's rights activist. Svitlana tells me she and her husband will meet me at the station.

Image 13

Photo of Svitlana Povalyaeva

Image 14

Photo of Larysa Denysenko

"Why would you wake up so early?" I try to protest.

But my friend insists that taking a taxi in Kyiv might still be unsafe: How would you know who the driver is? I'm not sure it's a valid reason, but I gladly accept the offer; I have missed Kyiv and my friends. I'm eager to see them.

The train is almost empty. It is my first trip by rail since the beginning of the full-scale invasion. Many still fear traveling to the recently besieged capital. A polite elderly attendant asks me to keep the window shut and pull the blinds down for safety. The blinds will supposedly protect me from shards of glass in case of an explosion. But in the middle of the night, I wake up suffocating. It seems too silly to die from lack of air during a war.

I approach the steward; he is not sleeping.

He lets me open the window; perhaps I do look like I am more likely to die from the lack of air than from the shards of glass.

"But please don't turn on the light," he asks.

"I won't," I promise.

For the rest of the night, I sit on the bed, watching Ukraine rushing past me, yet also getting closer, filling me, just like the wind coming from the outside fills my lungs with much-needed air. I am home every minute of the way to Kyiv. So if an explosion did happen nearby and I died hit by glass shards, I would die absolutely happy.

I shoot a video of the dawn somewhere between Zhytomyr and Kyiv and send it to my Kyiv friends, who are still in Lviv.

I am a bit sleepy in the morning, but my sleepiness vanishes as soon as I see Svitlana. She and her husband take me home to my apartment on the nineteenth floor in downtown Kyiv.

Almost all the building's inhabitants have moved out. But the concierge, Iryna, welcomes me back, beaming; it seems she considers me a sign of victory. She knows I was born in Lviv and have apartments there too. I could have chosen not to go to Kyiv, yet I am here.

"Have you seen how they damaged our building?" she asks.

The damage is minor: just bullet traces on the facade. Also, one of the windows got broken by a shot; we are so lucky that the owners had already evacuated by that time. But we just laugh at all that: Isn't this a happy outcome compared to what could have happened?

Svitlana is amazed by the views from my nineteenth-floor windows.

"It's possible to see so much from here!" she exclaims, while I'm remembering where my teapot is and looking for cookies. The Russian Kyiv offensive was so short that the cookies I bought before the full-scale invasion haven't even gotten hard.

Svitlana tells me what I have missed while being in Egypt and then in Lviv: both her sons, Vasyl and Roman Ratushny, are in the army now; her neighbor and friend Evhenia Zakrevska and her husband, Mykhailo, are in the army now; and basically, all our friends are either in or helping the military. Her younger son, Roman Ratushny, took part in liberating Trostyanets, in the Sumy region, several days ago. He's so proud to be a part of the 93rd Mechanized Brigade, named after Kholodnyi Yar, a Ukrainian partisan state that existed on part of the lands of the former Ukrainian People's Republic from 1919 to 1922. He beamed when he joined; she wailed louder than the air raid siren after he left. Her elder, Vasyl, has defended Ukraine in the east since January 2015, but the younger one, Roman, had seemed to be made not for war but other fights. He and Evhenia Zakrevska defended Protasiv Yar together, a park I can see from my balcony. He was meant to be an activist, and I used to joke how she [Svitlana] is the mother of Ukraine's future president, so she should start writing her memoirs right away—but that was in 2021.

Through March, she helped the military, the neighbors, and the dogs around her. She celebrated her birthday on empty Andriyivsky Uzviz, the street people used to remember as the place where the Russian writer Mikhail Bulgakov had rented an apartment in Kyiv. In March 2022, only a few places were open, including Chasing Two Hares, a café named after a famous Ukrainian play by Mykhailo Starytsky; a Crimean Tatar restaurant, Musafir; and a small bar that somehow kept selling prohibited alcohol to anyone, including foreign war correspondents. Of course, nothing related to Bulgakov was.

She also got married in March. The latter she considers the least important, of course.

"We did it in case one of us dies or gets into emergency care, you know. It's better to be married during the war," she explains.

She and her husband have lived together for over twenty years and raised two sons.

"Congratulations anyway," I say.

We laugh. We keep laughing when we go to my balcony and pose for a picture under the clear Kyiv sky. We cannot stop laughing.

Then Svitlana suddenly doesn't feel well. She is unsure what is wrong with her, but I have an idea.

"Listen, please try taking this. You're probably having a panic attack," I explain. Svitlana takes the pill I give her, a tranquilizer, and soon starts to feel better.

We no longer laugh. We no longer pretend. Bucha, where the exhumation is happening now, is some dozen kilometers away. If not for our friends and Svitlana's sons, what occurred in Bucha might also have happened here, in Kyiv. They are both on the front line—even the future president of Ukraine, Roman Ratushny. But after all, how could he not be there? That is why I said I would vote for him one day: if, at twenty-two, you do not compromise with evil even for a bit, at about forty, you might be a decent presidential candidate.

We do not talk about all that anymore. I thank Svitlana and Khmara, her husband, again, and he takes Svitlana home to the tenth floor in the building up the hill of Protasiv Yar, the park Roman and Evhenia keep defending—now not from Ukrainian construction companies, but from the Russian invaders.

Two Women, One Dog, and Countless Victims of Gender-Based Violence

"It's so quiet," she repeats from time to time.

I've already heard this from my friends who evacuated from Bucha, Kyiv, Kramatorsk, and Kharkiv. Everyone who lived through the constant artillery bombardment says the same: it's impossibly quiet. Silence scares them.

"It's okay. It will pass. You all say that," I tell her.

"Oh really? Everyone?"

"Everyone."

Larysa and I meet on an empty square in Obolon, a northern district of Kyiv, where people stopped a Russian tank in the last days of February. Later, it seemed the tank was a military vehicle, not a tank, and there is also no certainty that it was indeed Russian. But the heroism of the Obolon citizens is unquestionable anyway: they were ready to stop Russian tanks. It's just that the Ukrainian military managed to stop them farther away.

Still, Obolon wasn't a good place to be either at the end of February or in March. The sound of shelling was particularly loud in this district of Kyiv. You could not forget about the constant threat nearby. Larysa also could not forget what might happen to her if the Russian troops managed to enter the city. She is a lawyer and a women's rights activist, an active member of the Ukrainian women lawyers nonprofit Yur-Fem. The first case of the Russian invaders raping a Ukrainian woman came to her in March. A friend wrote that there was a woman in Mariupol who needed help. Larysa, scared, devastated, and enraged by what was happening in the Kyiv region, replied that she was ready to help. What else could she reply?

She also had no doubts about what was happening just a dozen kilometers to the east of the Obolon district of Kyiv, in occupied Bucha, Motyzhyn, Andriivka, and other villages. She was ready to help and the cases kept coming.

"Can you help this woman?"

"Yes, I can."

It's the first time I see Larysa without makeup, in gray, nondescript clothes, and with a lost look on her face. She was always the brightest, a brunette with beautiful eyes, flowery suits, colorful jewelry, and an incomparable expertise in law and women's rights. Now, a month after the full-scale Russian invasion, it seems that only the expertise remains. Larysa looks like her own shadow. I brought her colorful candies as a present; she is looking at them in disbelief as if colors all went away, broke into shades, and disappeared as if washed away by tears.

She talks. I listen. She has been listening to women throughout her law career; I have to listen to her now. Suddenly she stops, looks at me, and asks:

"Can you see the future? I mean, I can see today, but I try to imagine our life in several years and I cannot. Even half a year or a month is hard. I just don't see it."

"I see it," I say.

She waits for me to elaborate.

"I see the future. I mean, we might get hit by the Iskanders at this very moment. But at the same time, I somehow see Ukraine after the war. I don't know if we are in the future, but there is Ukraine after the war," I say, and turn away.[1]

Larysa nods and tells me how there are no bomb shelters, and her elderly parents won't go there anyway. So she has been hiding in the corridor, "behind two walls." Suddenly her mother calls:

"Are you all right? When will you be home?" she asks, afraid to be alone and to lose her daughter.

Larysa calms her down and we keep walking: two women talking about the unspeakable and a cute bulldog boldly called Lucifer. In half a year, in September, I will see a bulldog in liberated Izyum, sitting next to a woman cooking food on a fire in front of her damaged apartment building. I will send Larysa the picture. By that time, Larysa will have returned to her colorful suits and bright earrings. But right now that seems impossible.

"That magazine interviewed me and they wanted to take new pictures of me. Take the old ones, I told them. Yet they insist. But how will I look at them? I go to my wardrobe, open it, and cannot understand what I'm seeing. The same with cosmetics. I don't know how I can use them *now*."

An Artist Who Starved to Death: Lyubov Panchenko from Bucha

"On April second, they brought Lyubov Mykhailivna [Panchenko] to a hospital in Kyiv, but we didn't know and were searching for her everywhere. We were given completely different addresses, and there were various rumors," Olena Lodzynska began her narrative. "Only when she was being transferred from

[1] As a result of this conversation, Victoria Amelina wrote the poem "Word in the dictionary [future]." It can be found in appendix I.

one department to another in this fifth hospital did someone finally notice the search request." (At first, she was admitted to the therapy department, but when they saw that bedsores had formed due to immobility, she was transferred to the surgery department.)

Throughout the month of the Russian occupation, eighty-four-year-old Lyubov Panchenko was in her own house, dying of hunger. It was only when her house was shelled that someone remembered her—a neighbor rushed in and helped her come to her senses. Later, Lyubov Mykhailivna was evacuated. Lyubov Panchenko is a professional artist-designer of Ukraine, an honorary citizen of Bucha, a laureate of the Vasyl Stus Prize, and a member of the Union of Ukrainian Women, and belongs to the group of renowned artists of the sixties who revived Ukrainian culture during the Khrushchev Thaw.

The artist cannot return home to her house in Lisova Bucha because during the hostilities, the doors and windows in her dwelling were shattered by the explosive blast of a projectile that hit the barn. Even if the house were in perfect condition, she still could not be alone because she is bedridden. She requires full-time care, including spoon-feeding and changing diapers.

The only positive aspect is that the artist has entrusted her artistic heritage, which was preserved in her house before the war, to the Museum of the Sixties (otherwise, during the occupation, everything would have been looted).

On the eve of the war (February 2, 2022), Lyubov Panchenko crossed the border at the age of eighty-four. Museum workers and other supporters of the artist's unique creativity greeted her. At that time, she was well-dressed, walked independently, joked, and was genuinely happy to have guests.

Now the woman is completely exhausted from prolonged starvation due to the Russian occupation. She is bedridden and looks extremely emaciated, making it hard to look at her.

Olena Lodzynska, the head of the Museum of the Sixtiers in

Kyiv, where Lyubov Panchenko's works are preserved, shared these details.[2]

Those Who Write "For the Children" on the Missiles

<< How to prove Peter Pomerantsev[3]>>

Even if all Russian propagandists stop, their words will continue to kill Ukrainians.

On Friday, April 8, 2022, Russians killed fifty-two more Ukrainian civilians, including five children, in a missile attack on a railway station in Kramatorsk. One of the deadly missiles that hit the station had the words FOR THE CHILDREN painted on its side. People unfamiliar with Russian propaganda might wonder what these words mean. Why would somebody write FOR THE CHILDREN on a deadly missile?

I have been following the dehumanizing fake content produced by Russian media during the past eight years. The propaganda about "Ukrainians killing children" first appeared in 2014, after Russia occupied parts of the Donetsk and Luhansk regions, with the scary tale of a crucified boy. The terrible crucifixion fake and many others have circulated in the Russian media ever since. The myth about Ukrainians killing children in the territories occupied by Russians never made any sense—well, as much as the myth about Jews killing Christian children never made sense. Terrible lies and hate speech about neighboring nations never make sense, but they always work: justifying further crimes against those falsely accused.

---

[2] On April 30, 2022, Lyubov Panchenko died from exhaustion in the hospital.

[3] This sentence was left unfinished. Peter Pomerantsev is the author of *This Is Not Propaganda* (2019), a book about disinformation and propaganda.

On April 8, the Russian missile struck an area where Ukrainian families waited for trains so that they could be evacuated. I have been at that railway station in Kramatorsk many times. As a writer, I went to speak and read to children in the Donetsk region affected by war since 2014. At a literary festival last autumn, we even built "a light machine that would stop the war"; the idea came from a book by my fellow Ukrainian authors Andriy Lesiv and Romana Romanyshyn. We brought a string of lights and let the kids color the bulbs; everyone applauded as it lit up the room. Now Russian bombs are falling on the place where we experienced this joyful moment. And I cannot help but wonder whether the children who colored the bulbs were among those killed by the Russian attack on the railway station.

"A light machine" from a Ukrainian book couldn't save anyone. The missile with the words FOR THE CHILDREN, inspired by Russian media and books, completed its horrendous task successfully. And I cannot help but think that all the Russian TV staff, the "journalists," the producers, the news writers, the managers, and even their assistants always knew the truth. Still, they continued to work for the propaganda machine for years, earning their money and probably vacationing next to you and me, somewhere in Italy or Florida.

Now some propagandists leave Russia and proclaim they are anti-war. However, what does it matter if a missile labeled "FOR THE CHILDREN" can still hit the families trying to escape? Didn't all those working for the propaganda machine know that their dehumanizing lies about Ukrainians would have irreversible consequences? Did they think their words could lead to war crimes?

It was not only the media. Russians have also been publishing books and shooting films mocking and demonizing the Ukrainian people, our Ukrainian language and traditions. Russian fantasy books portrayed Ukrainians as mere monsters, just like the Russian news did. Russian nonfiction "history" books on Ukraine have little to do with facts. Some of the titles include: *Ukrainian Catastrophe: From American Aggression to World War?*, by Sergey Glazyev (Moscow: Book World, 2015); *The Collapse of Ukraine: Dismantling of the Substate*, by Rostislav Ishchenko (Moscow: Yauza, 2015); *Bloody Crimes of the Bandera Junta*, from the Antimaidan Library series, by Alexander Kochetkov (Moscow: Book World, 2015); and *Ukraine: Was There Ukraine?*, by Anatoliy Tereshchenko (Moscow: Arguments of the Week, 2017). I wonder how the authors of these books feel now. Are they anti-war?

In March 2022, one of the propagandists, Maryna Ovsyannikova, appeared on Russian TV with a NO WAR poster. Had she even been trying to address the Russian audience? Why was the text half English? Russians now have such contempt for the West that using English to convince them doesn't seem like a sensible idea. Besides, the anti-war slogan doesn't eliminate the root cause of the war—the hatred and contempt toward everything Ukrainian. The poster said nothing in support of Ukraine. No wonder, unlike real Russian dissidents such as Yuri Dmitriev, Anna Politkovskaya, and others incarcerated or killed by the regime, Maryna Ovsyannikova didn't even end up in jail; instead she ended up hired by the German media company Die Welt. Her performance changed nothing for the Ukrainian people. Still, when interviewed on the streets, many ordinary Russians say they support the war, as Ukrainians must have deserved it. Moreover, some say the Polish, Lithuanians, or Estonians might deserve to be next.

The words FOR THE CHILDREN on the deadly missile reveal how Russian media and the creative industry are also responsible for the war crimes. It is not just Putin's war, but a war of all those who made the hatred machine work and gave in to hatred for Ukrainians.

"A light machine that will stop the war" is a lovely idea for children; the adults should know better: stopping the war is not about chanting anti-war slogans. It is not possible without holding numerous Russian propagandists accountable for their lies.

People inspiring their army to write FOR THE CHILDREN on the deadly missiles are as guilty as those pressing the buttons to launch the attack. The difference is that the latter can stop killing. But the hatred initiated by the propagandists' words leads to more and more deaths and cruelty toward Ukrainian civilians.

Hate speech in the media and books is more like radiation; it continues to kill. And we are yet to understand how to make Europe a safe place again.

Till They Have Voices—Iryna Dovhan II

BEFORE 2014, IRYNA DOVHAN HAD A BEAUTY SALON IN THE Donetsk region. So as a beauty professional she knows what to do with her face to become unrecognizable. She could, for example, intentionally burn her skin with too harsh peeling. She could change her hair too, of course. Perhaps she could cut it off in an ugly way and then put a headscarf on. Becoming unrecognizable is the only way for her to survive the occupation, and Iryna Dovhan is preparing for one in her new home in the Kyiv region.

She spent several days in the forest as a combat paramedic, but then she fell. Running with body armor is not an easy task for a sixty-year-old. She had a torn ligament that severely limited knee movement but didn't want to admit it to the team's commander for a week. But as soon as it became obvious that the combat paramedic Iryna required care herself, she was sent back home. There she could only sort medicine and wait to see how the battle for Kyiv would turn out.

Following Maria Lvova-Belova—Kateryna Rashevska I

Image 15

Kateryna Rashevska

[Editors' note: The unedited draft version of the section "Following Maria Lvova-Belova—Kateryna Rashevska" from the manuscript is contained in fragment A of appendix I. Below, the section is organized by the editorial group in accordance with the logic of narration and presented without repetitions.]

Kateryna Rashevska is a young lawyer from a small village in Poltava Oblast; somewhere here, in 1399, Western civilization, represented by the Lithuanian prince Vytautas, lost a battle with Eastern civilization, represented by the Tatar horde.

Kateryna has blonde hair, wears suits, and defends people from grave human rights violations. Transferring Ukrainian children to Russia is just one of them. Yet Kateryna is especially passionate about it. Firstly, because she loves children. Secondly, because as a lawyer she is very interested in the history of the

Holocaust and Article 6 of the Rome Statute. And Article 6 is, of course, Genocide.

In the final days before the full-scale invasion, Kateryna watches another documentary about the Nazi policies toward Jews.

Maria Lvova-Belova was born in the Russian city of Penza. She has blonde hair, wears lovely long dresses, and helps Putin transfer Ukrainian children to Russia. Four months before the invasion, Putin appointed her as Russia's so-called Presidential Commissioner for Children's Rights to become a partner in one of his crimes. The crime is defined in Article 6 in the Rome Statute under point (e): "forcibly transferring children of the group to another group."

As a child, she sang in a church choir and dreamed of marrying a priest and having many children. Her dreams have largely come true. She is married to a Russian Orthodox priest. She has five biological, eighteen adopted, and one stolen child, a teenager named Philippe from Mariupol, whose bravery I admire. According to Lvova-Belova, Philippe hasn't been a very obedient "son," to put it mildly.

Kateryna Rashevska also dreams of having children, yet she has been too busy in the past eight years of the Russian-Ukrainian war, so she has none. She works for the Regional Center for Human Rights (RCHR), an NGO founded by the internally displaced Ukrainians from the temporarily occupied Crimea. Before 2022, she was the only one in the office whose life was not affected by the Russian aggression. The RCHR first encountered cases of Ukrainian children being transferred to Russia in 2014: the children from occupied Crimea were adopted by Russian families. Gathering information about these cases was the first task given to Kateryna at RCHR.

Kateryna and Maria are very different women. Article 6 of the Rome Statute connects them.

Maria does not know the connection. Kateryna has been thinking about Maria since March 2022. In April 2022, she learned that the first group of children taken from Ukraine were transferred into Russian families. Among those, she saw two boys who had a grandmother. Kateryna wrote about children transferring and adoptions on social media, but her messages did not attract much attention. In March and April there was a lot going on.

What Kateryna finds and saves starting in March 2022, following Maria Lvova-Belova everywhere from social media to the Russian state-sponsored television channels, will feed into the submission RCHR will make to the International Criminal Court on October 25, 2022.

Evacuating New York

My apartment in Kyiv doesn't have many old things: a large wall clock from the Brezhnev era; a porcelain rooster; childhood photos of my son's father, taken in the eighties in the Donetsk region; and finally my family photos, the faces of my son's great-grandmothers and great-grandfathers. I took them all off the walls of a house in a small town on the contact line in the fall of 2021, less than six months before the full-scale invasion. I don't know what came over me, but suddenly I was scared for all these things: they needed to be saved, taken away, evacuated. Of course, people would have to be saved. But things do not have to consent to the evacuation; many people still have not agreed to leave their homes.

I keep calling people in New York, a small town in the Donetsk region, from where the clock, the rooster, and the photos come. In October 2021, I organized an essay contest for the high school students there. I know the winners well because their prize was a trip to Kyiv and Lviv. Now I want to make sure these girls leave the area, which is being shelled heavily and might be occupied at any moment. But I cannot even convince my good friend Anna or her daughter, Yasya, who has cystic fibrosis and needs urgent treatment after spending more than a month in her basement. Yasya wanted to stay, as her father and fiancé fought near her home, i.e., on the very front line.

After visiting Hostomel, Irpin, and Bucha as a volunteer, I message and call again. I am not capable of describing what I just saw. But I say to one of the mothers:

"I will help you to find accommodation in Lviv or abroad. Please just take the evacuation bus or train. But you have two daughters, so you must evacuate."

It seems to me that it is pretty clear to any woman on earth what I mean by saying that young girls must evacuate the town which is about to be occupied.

"But maybe it will all go away somehow . . ." the mother replies to me in Russian.

I hang up and cry for the girl named Myra, whom I showed Kyiv and Lviv in January 2022, and her elder sister.

Yet my calls are not in vain. In a couple of days, I will receive a message: "We are in Kryvyi Rih."

Anna's daughter, Yasya, agrees to leave her town in the Donetsk region when I say there is a chance she will get cystic fibrosis treatment in Europe. In Ukraine, the life expectancy of people with cystic fibrosis is brief. They often do not even reach adulthood. Anna's son, Yasya's elder brother, has already died from the disease. Anna and her husband, Vitaly, always knew they would have to watch both their children die. But now there is a chance: European clinics started giving Ukrainian refugees with cystic fibrosis the medicine that could change and prolong their lives.

"Okay, if there is a chance to get the medicine, I am evacuating," Yasya writes to me.

Her father has joined the army and is now fighting "near home," in the Donetsk region. So now everything has changed. Yasya might live longer, and he might die.

"Maybe he doesn't want to see his daughter die," I think, wondering if this is good news. It's hard to understand what is good news right now. Yasya's blood saturation is below 90 percent, and she is very weak, but she boards the evacuation bus in Toretsk alone. I contact the doctors in Lviv:

"If she doesn't feel well, will you please provide urgent care in Lviv until I can take her further?"

"She might not survive the trip!" the doctor yells at me. "She should not go as far as Lviv. She should stop somewhere in Zaporizhzhya!"

"No, she is going where she can be helped," I say. "She wants to live; that is why she left her basement in New York."

Yasya will survive the trip.

On April 22, I will bring Yasya, a girl with cystic fibrosis from the Donetsk region who doesn't speak English at all, to Dublin. I've been told that in Ireland, she can get a medicine called Kaftrio and get a chance to live till her forties.

Yasya's father will die near Bakhmut in August 2022, and his body will not be recovered. He will not get to see his daughter die. Yasya still hasn't gotten Kaftrio. New York stands. Many houses, three schools, a kindergarten, and a library are damaged or ruined. But New York stands; the front line in this area didn't move an inch.

Skovoroda Museum Destruction—
Tetyana Pylypchuk II

The morning of May 7, 2022, is like any other morning for Tetyana Pylypchuk. Listening to the comforting noise of coffee slowly boiling on the stove in the Slovo House, and distant explosions somewhere in the northeast, she scrolls through the news. The words "missile" and "museum" appear on the screen abruptly and make her heart rate increase. She sits at the table to read the news one more time. Then she starts calling her fellow volunteers who could drive her to Skovorodynivka village, some kilometers from Kharkiv. There, at about 11:00 p.m., the eighteenth-century building, which until recently housed the Literary Memorial Museum of the philosopher Hryhorii Skovoroda, was hit with a fire and burned out.[4] The memorial room, called the "quiet cell," where Hryhorii Skovoroda lived and died, was gone. The exhibition, Tetyana knew, had been evacuated before.[5] But the building itself was perhaps even more important. For the first time she cries, feeling that weird relief I felt on February 24, 2022: what you feared for so long is already happening. Everything is clear: The Russians will ruin our museums, libraries, universities, and what can we do?

Someone tells Tetyana that she can document the destruction, secure the evidence and follow through so the perpetrators will not go unpunished this time.

On the same day she has a call with

---

[4] Hryhorii Skovoroda (1722–1794) is an iconic Ukrainian philosopher, theologian, and poet. He suggested that the meaning of human existence is that heart, morality, and creative (congenial) work are the foundations of an ideal society. His writings have influenced generations of Ukrainian thinkers u*f*p to this day.

[5] According to Tetyana Pylypchuk, only the most valuable objects from the collection were evacuated. The exhibition burned down.

[Editors' note: Victoria Amelina did not finish this chapter. What follows is her unedited notes with Ukrainian excerpts translated into English.]

Anastasia Cherednychenko

Vasyl Rozhko—Poshyvailo—Lviv branch

Poshyvailo also filled out the ICCROM forms and started this cooperation

these forms are not effective

Skovorodynivka

we give

We had a Ukrainian Security Service representative with us and he documented this for criminal proceedings

It was good that the architect was there, as it wasn't possible to fill them out without the architect

and they started the communication process with the local authorities

Need to get an understanding on building aspects, what exactly was damaged, how much, and what can be done with it

Also about cultural preservation, rebuilding

iccrom is the architect

The Ukrainian Security Service requested these materials

What has been damag—

Anastasia called

I phoned her

I knew what it was about

I had been in contact with UNESCO—they'd seen the news and got in contact themselves

It was during a weekend and they wrote to me about what was happening

She was with Mariia Zadorozhna in the evacuation headquarters

They had carried out similar expeditions together before

A female photographer
plus a drone operator from Poltava who was sent by the evacuation headquarters

In fact, this expedition was organized by Vasyl Rozhko and Mariia Zadorozhna
The three of us, me Poshyvailo and Mariia talked on Zoom

The Zoom happened when we already understood the dates

12–13 May
He was standing opposite the museum

The director and employees
She was confused

broken leg
The park was lovely, beautiful

A new project was supposed to be starting on February 24, 2022 in the Skovoroda museum
A well-thought-out exhibition—in order not to have a Soviet anniversary
celebration
a rethinking of the exhibition
content and form
Tania Pylypchuk was at the head of it
They spoke with the founder of Khartia, since he had to be there
The local authorities thought about an anniversary celebration
She was with Skovorodynivka as is what should have happened

We went inside
We didn't go straight to the forms because we didn't cross over there straightaway

Wonderful weather

Next to the building there was even a neat flowerbed—daffodils and tulips were in bloom

documentation

we had

We drank tea with the museum employees and Tania had with

right opposite the museum

Skovoroda was on our left

We drank tea outside, had sandwiches and cakes

The explosions exploded, whereas the birds sang

When we returned, there was black smoke on these fields on the side where the russians had been located

My first trip away from Kyiv since the 24th

Vahanova: was she helpful necessary? She had gone to work and was a little late

and when we passed through

That was what will happen with Kha

There was a story that created Kharkiv

In 2007 when she lived in Kyiv she started visiting Ukrainian dissident Yevhen Sverstiuk. Yevhen Sverstiuk had a habit of inviting

Easter and Easter dinner at his home on the left bank of Dnipro. It was Raskova Street; after his death it became Yevhen Sverstiuk Street.

Yevhen Sverstiuk left his last diary to the Kharkiv Literature Museum.

Lukyanenko came to Sverstiuk funeral.[6]

[6] Levko Lukyanenko (1928–2018) was a Ukrainian politician and dissident and the author of the Declaration of Independence of Ukraine.

[Editors' note: The notes below contain pasted fragments from the article "The First Exhibition Was Dedicated to the Tortured Poet: The Kharkiv Literary Museum Came Back Home," by Hanna Shchokan, published in *Ukrainska pravda: Zhyttia* on March 23, 2023.]

The archives of the writer and translator Ivan Dniprovskyi, who lived in Kharkiv after 1923, became the core of the collection.

"Ivan Dniprovskyi died in 1934 from natural illness, so he was not subjected to repressions, and because of this nobody conducted any investigations of him or deleted any of the documentation. There are still letters from other writers, Dniprovskyi's own manuscripts, and photos—all the things that were deleted for other artists. This archive is very valuable—it is the foundation for our collection on the 1920s. And this is the foundational theme we find ourselves talking about today." Tetiana Ihoshyna [the keeper of the Kharkiv Literary Museum collection] recounted.

Currently the museum cannot exhibit the originals and present exhibits using objects held in the museum's stores and which belong to the National Museum Fund.

"We closed our exhibition on February 24 last year. Before the full-scale invasion started—we were ready, we felt that it could happen. On February 16 the most valuable part of the collection had already been packed away. After the beginning of the full-scale invasion, we evacuated it as first priority. Then the evacuation of second priority items. The most valuable and irreplaceable museum items—manuscripts, first of all—were evacuated to safer cities in Ukraine," said the deputy director.

During 2014, authorities kept telling the museum team "Don't get into politics," but they didn't get into politics; they just presented exhibitions about Ukrainian poets.

In January 2014 they held an event after which the audience asked "So it all didn't start just now?"

"Book on trial"
Before February 16 the basement was ready

This year, Berezil Theater turns 100.
And Les Kurbas would be 135..

We cannot go without celebrating these dates—which is why we are inviting you to Les Kurbas birthday celebration on February 27.

On the program:

-a presentation on the 2022 residency concept, held in a laboratory format
-a lecture by theater expert Yana Partola about Les Kurbas and the Berezil Theater
-20s-and 30s-style canapes—find out what people ate in Ukraine 100 years ago
-we will dine on 1910s to 1940s era crockery manufactured by the Budy faience pottery factory outside of Kharkiv which was donated to the residence by the well-known Ukrainian lawyer and Kharkivite Andrii Vyshnevskyi

We should have been gathering here with you today in the museum gardens for our traditional Ladder Readings. It would have been cold, we would have treated you to tea, and you would have stayed until the last verse. There would have been one performer reading you poetry from the top rungs of the ladder, and another from the bottom.

This might now seem like a parallel reality—but we really don't appreciate it when someone ruins our plans.

Our ladder readings were not stopped by the pandemic, and they won't be stopped by the war.

Throughout the entire day today, we will be uploading poems by Kharkiv poets who have been forced to leave for other cities.

As we dream about a great event in our garden, for now we can overcome the distance with poetry.

Khvylyovyi
Youth falls frame

On the maps of 1654—the year of the Pereiaslav Agreement. And the russians were very eager to incite the myth that Kharkiv is a russian city. Kharkiv 300 years on—1954—the division of Ukraine from russia—

We are not going to evacuate

we evacuated as a second priority

We filmed the dissidents of the sixties—and once more back underground

Ivan, go home there's no vodka here—Prague, 1968

in order for Europe to remember—in order to show how history repeats itself

and I thought

maybe we would wake up and it's no longer our flag flying above us

On the 3rd floor—the flag is visible, I checked

The Ministry for Culture gives the contact of an individual in Ukrainian Railways and the individual is called Mykola Hryhorovych

When it was all dismantled she had already decided that the first exhibition would be about how they dismantled the collection using the example of one institute to show how Kharkiv created recollections of its past.

but it won't look like that

I'll bring the first and only exposition piece for the first exhibition for Tania

But the big exhibition is about how we

very actively fueled the myth that Kharkiv is a russian city. Kharkiv 300 years 1954 reunification of Ukraine with russia

When they were filming the sixties, they went underground again.

Ivan, go home, there is no vodka, Prague 1968
so that Europe remembers—to show the repetition of history
and I thought
maybe we wake up and our flag is no longer flying
on the 4th floor—you can see the flag and checked

The Ministry of Culture gives the contact of a person in the national railway

when they were dismantling, she had already decided that the first exhibition would be about how the collection was dismantled—using the example of one institution to show how Kharkiv remembered its past.

the first and only exhibit for the first exhibition will be brought by Tanya.

But the big exhibition about what us

blankets, water, canned goods, dry alcohol, candles, matches, flashlights, batteries

the book on the dock—filmed on February 24

the first explosions called from the Department of Culture and said you can go to work

we run to work
in storage boxes and in the basement
March 8 evacuation

The Enemy's Face, or Oleksandr Shelipov's Killer

In May, the first Russian soldier charged with a war crime in Ukraine is testifying in court in Kyiv. There are more than a hundred journalists in the courtroom. They are primarily interested in the perpetrator; it's his story that the audience wants to hear. All the headlines are about the killer; not Oleksandr

Shelipov, who lost his life; not Oleksandr's wife, Kateryna, who lost her husband.[7]

I read about the perpetrator, too: he is twenty-one and says he was only following orders. His weirdest words make headlines: "I fired so they'd leave me alone."

Kateryna expresses something so much more human, saying she doesn't mind if the murderer of her beloved husband is exchanged for one of the Azovstal[8] defenders. Her words do not make headlines: kindness gets fewer clicks. Yet it's deep and interesting, and Kateryna is so much more than the killer everyone wants to see, hear, and understand, as if understanding will help bring evil to an end. But there's nothing to understand in him. We can look for the trauma that made him destructive and find a trauma. Yet it's not his traumas that made him fire at a senior citizen on a bike but a simple desire to be left alone, nothing else.

Another Russian military officer, Private Ivan Maltisov, who testified in court as a witness, said he didn't try to stop Shelipov's murder because he "didn't think about it then."

He is as dull as Shishimarin. While reading Hannah Arendt's *Eichmann in Jerusalem*, I thought her subtitle, *A Report on the Banality of Evil*, was not precise enough: it should have been the emptiness of evil, not the banality. There's nothing to look at without Hannah in the room at Eichmann's trial.

Everyone knows the name of the perpetrator. Similarly, for every book about a Ukrainian, Zaluznny or Zelensky, there seem to be five books about Putin.

---

[7] On May 18, 2022, Vadim Shishimarin pleaded guilty to fatally shooting the unarmed civilian Oleksandr Shelipov.

[8] The Azovstal plant became one of the most symbolic sites during the siege of Mariupol in 2022.

War Crimes Research 101—Casanova II

On April 9, 2022, I wrote to Casanova:

"Listen, do you still document war crimes?"

"Sure," she said.

"Do you need volunteers?"

"Well, yeah."

"I have to finish some things, but I could join from April twenty-ninth."

"Thank you! But let's see how you feel, okay?" she replied, meaning, of course, that I am too vulnerable to do the job, a creative with a history of depression—or at least this was how I read it, so I decided to play it cool.

"Yes, sure. But since I repeat the names of those who have to be punished for what they did here, I think war crimes research is exactly what would help me feel better."

I'm here by Casanova's invitation.

The office of the Truth Hounds NGO is in the Podil district of Kyiv, a lovely historic neighborhood, also known as the Lower City. The office looks ordinary with desks, computers, a coffee machine, comfortable sofas, and even an office cat (later the cat appears to belong to Roman Avramenko). The view from the windows is lovely, and the employees can smoke on the balcony facing one of Kyiv's green hills. At first it seems the only thing that gives away that this is the office of a team that has been researching heinous war crimes for the past eight years are the drawings on the blackboard in the meeting room. They depict artillery craters and their traces on asphalt. I already know, of course, that the size and shape of the craters left by the explosion can provide clues about the type of projectile; I did some research on the internet, trying to understand what else I should study apart from the Rome Statute and Geneva Conventions to become a war crimes researcher. Then I notice a piece of artillery shell on a bookshelf.

The drawings and the piece of deadly shell do not attract anyone's attention but mine, as if they were just common diagrams and a nice souvenir brought back from an ordinary boring business trip; they are routine in this office. People make coffee, eat cookies, and chat about anything but war.

The training does not begin with studying missile types or their traces on the asphalt and on the walls. Instead, like any training, it starts with introductions. People, who, like me, volunteered to become war crimes researchers, sit in a semicircle and introduce themselves. We say our names and why we are here. There is not much pathos in what people say. Someone says she is from the occupied city, but doesn't make it clear if anger has something to do with her decision to try war crimes research. No one says the words "injustice" and "justice" aloud. I don't either.

Most of us, young men and women, make joining the war crimes research effort seem like a casual thing to do. They say they are already somehow involved in the human rights movement, but now need to learn more about war crimes and international humanitarian law. They don't vow to bring anyone to justice.

The training seems too ordinary, too normal, too routine to be about the unspeakable, life and death, crime and punishment.

Only one of the women speaks differently, not hiding her good intentions behind weak explanations. She speaks Belorussian.

"My name is Anisia. I am Belarusian. Ukraine gave me shelter when I really needed it, persecuted in my country. I want to do something for Ukraine now, when Ukraine is in need of help."

I like her and her reasons yet wonder if she will be able to work without speaking any Ukrainian. Sure, she knows Russian, but I'm pretty sure it will not be enough. (By the time Anisia and I go on a field mission together in the Kharkiv region, she will speak fluent Ukrainian).

When it's my turn, I decide not to say I write books for a living; this sounds a bit pretentious.

What I do say is:

"My name is Victoria. I work in the cultural sector. I'm here because I want to be useful in wartime. I moved boxes and sorted tactical medicine at a warehouse till now, but maybe I can do something else too."

Casanova smiles; I guess she likes that now she is not the only one undercover here.

Casanova is one of two lecturers today. And after the introductions, her fellow lecturer, Roman Avramenko, opens the theoretical part of the training with an introduction to the basics of international humanitarian law. We are not expected to become lawyers, but there are key principles, Roman and Casanova believe, that will let us identify potential violations and ask more questions.

War crimes researchers should aim to obtain the most complete information about the alleged violation of international humanitarian law: who, what, where, when, why, how, and what was the result (the so-called five W + H questions and the "so what" question). To obtain the above-mentioned information, the following data should be collected from the person being interviewed:

A brief description of the interviewee, including their occupation, education, place(s) of residence, date of birth, and other personal and contact information

The date and time of the incident(s) being discussed in the interview

How the witness can confirm the date and time of the incident(s), such as events they recall happening around the same time (a national holiday, a sporting event, a family celebration, the start of military operations, public statements by officials or leaders, international events, prior known incidents, etc.)

How the interviewee knows the time the incident(s) occurred (such as the time displayed on their watch at the moment of the incident, a part of their regular daily routine from which they can conclude the time of the incident, a television or media broadcast that happens at the same time regularly, text messages sent during the incident, etc.).

The contextual elements to be considered in the incident report include the weather conditions at the time of the incident(s) (rain, wind, snow, sun), whether it was light or dark outside, and whether it was night (full moon, new moon). The location should be described, including the address and any particular objects in the area. A hand-drawn map of the location where the incident occurred should also be included. Photographic or video evidence taken by the interviewee or their close relatives should be submitted.

The interviewee's location at the time of the incident should be identified to ensure that they can provide accurate information (whether they were at the scene and witnessed everything firsthand or were hiding and only heard about the incident from neighbors). A list of the affected areas resulting from the shelling should also be included, including the addresses of damaged buildings and the location of shell explosions. The interviewee should describe what they saw (flashes, bright colors in the sky, projectile trajectory), heard (shots, explosions, whistling, rustling), and felt (vibrations, oscillations, effects of shock waves). The direction of the shelling from the interviewee's location should also be determined (from a certain direction, from the side of a specific settlement or object, "to the right or left," etc.).

The type of weapon used in the shelling or attack should be identified (firearms, mortars, artillery, what caliber, etc.) and how the interviewee obtained this information. The interviewee may be considered a professional witness if they have previous or current military experience or have significant experience living in conditions of hostilities and have started to distinguish between types of weapons. After the incident, experts should contact the interviewee and confirm the type of weapon used. The interviewee may also have information about the forces involved in the conflict and their location, from having seen it themselves, hearing from friends, or seeing it on the news.

Whether the attackers were visible, how many of them there were, what they looked like, and what elements suggest their affiliation with one side or the other (military uniform, insignia, etc.) should be noted.

Were there or are there objects nearby that could be a legitimate target of shelling (military bases, deployment locations, firing points of the conflict party, ammunition depots)? Are there objects nearby that are considered protected from direct attacks (educational institutions, hospitals, churches, humanitarian aid institutions)?

Was there a warning about possible shelling, and how was it done (sound signal, warning from military personnel from one of the parties, warning in the media, rumors and where they came from)?

Did the respondent suffer personally and how? Information about civilian casualties as a result of the attack (injured, killed)?

What are the consequences of the attack (damage to objects, physical and psychological trauma, financial losses)? What official documents can the respondent provide to confirm their words (excerpts from doctors regarding injuries, acts from state authorities regarding destruction and damage to objects)? Does the respondent have any physical evidence collected after the incident, and how did they obtain and preserve it?

At the end of each witness/victim interview, they are given the opportunity to review documented testimony and correct any possible errors or inaccuracies in the record. If possible, the final text of the interview is printed on-site and provided for the respondent's signature. A representative from Truth Hounds and the respondent also sign a two-copy agreement on the possibility of using the collected data for the purposes specified in the agreement and the obligation of Truth Hounds to ensure the confidentiality of the collected data. All testimonies are collected from each witness separately and independently. The presence and influence of other eyewitnesses or anyone else on the witness's testimony is not allowed.

Building a case should be like writing a novel. In order to do it right, you have to know everything, every detail. If you don't see how it all happened, the reader won't either. Convincing international judges must not be easier.

War crimes research involves collecting and analyzing a wide range of evidence, but the key element is always witness testimonies.

In addition to collecting evidence, war crimes researchers also provide support to victims and their families, helping them access medical care, legal assistance, and other forms of aid. They may work with local communities to raise awareness about human rights violations and advocate for justice.

One of the key challenges in war crimes research is ensuring the safety and security of researchers and witnesses, particularly in war zones.

The Truth Hounds director Roman Avramenko went briefly to Yahidne in April and heard right away about the infamous school basement and Ukrainian men executed for no reason.[9]

The fun part of the training is over, yet we also have several documents to read before we can join a mission. In one of those I find this phrase "All field materials regarding the events after 24.02.2022 on the workspace should be uploaded to the '24-02' folder." In the folder I find subfolders named for the regions of Ukraine. There are already hundreds of testimonies, yet there will be thousands. The testimonies will then become entries in the database. I will not have access to it; for security reasons, only database operators have access. There the testimonies we collect become something an AI algorithm could parse into investigation results, perhaps. Each perpetrator is an entity; every episode.

Casanova's first witnesses in 2022 were those whom she evacuated from Balakliya and other towns of the Kharkiv region.

The training is ongoing. I attend the theoretical course for two days, but the entire weeklong first field mission is focused on training. I start working with some of the best war crimes researchers in the field, and they guide me. That does not include all the nights I spent reading the Geneva Conventions and the Rome Statute to the sound of wailing sirens. Such reading isn't necessary to document war crimes in the field, but it is essential for a deeper understanding of why and what we research.

---

[9] Editors' note: this sentence was highlighted in green by the author. The idea was not developed.

Coming Together in Kharkiv, or Time to Save a Beetle

The six of us, me and five of my fellow Ukrainian writers, arrived in Kharkiv by train. At night, when we boarded it in Kyiv, I couldn't see how many passengers the train would eventually carry. It was almost dark on the platform, and people sneaked into the carriages one by one, like fireflies, with cell phones glowing in their hands. In the sunshine of Kharkiv morning, I was happy to find there was a crowd of us, fearless passengers, pouring onto the platform, hurrying to the monumental nineteenth-century station building I hadn't seen for six months.

The last time I was here, I was heading to the city of Kramatorsk, in the Donetsk region, through Kharkiv and Izyum. Izyum was occupied by Russians, and we received the dreadful news about our colleague, the children's writer Volodymyr Vakulenko, who the occupiers had abducted. The city of Kramatorsk was under constant shelling. And Kharkiv was too. Traveling here, we were prepared for air raid sirens and explosions to be the first sounds we'd hear upon arrival. Yet besides the passengers' steps and chatter, it was quiet on the sunlit platform. People with backpacks like us, visitors, and those with kids, pets, and suitcases, coming home maybe for the first time since February, didn't look scared. They fascinated me with their as-if-there-were-no-war look. That may be why I was the last to notice a fragile creature on the asphalt. My friends had already surrounded it and discussed what to do with this big lonely beetle stuck amid this unexpectedly crowded platform. I noticed another woman stop to help the beetle as well but then look at us and move on, as if trusting that the creature was in good hands. She was right.

The poet Ostap Slyvynsky took and carried the stag beetle to safety, carefully but confidently, as if carrying a landmine. The beetle was safe.

The crowd dissolved, disappearing in the Kharkiv subway, taxis, and private cars. The city turned out to be empty at this time of day.

We were searching for our hotel on foot when the air raid siren went off, as if the Russians wanted to fulfill our expectations for horror instead of a lovely morning. There was nowhere to hide, so we kept walking, led by Google Maps and vague memories; perhaps neither worked well for us as we realized we had to cross the avenue, yet there was no pedestrian crossing. Someone suggested we go back to the previous one. It was an air raid alert in Kharkiv, so we'd better hurry to our hotel, and there were no vehicles in sight. Yet that was what we did: walked back to the crossing and then waited for a green light.

I bet we had a better chance of being hit by a missile than by a car. I also bet every one of us knew about these probabilities. Yet we followed the rules. And I was already writing this piece in my mind.

There are no clear rules for surviving the war. You can follow all the recommendations, go to bomb shelters in a timely fashion, carry a first aid kit, try to evacuate, and still get killed. There are no rules for surviving, but there are still rules for living. It was in our power to save bugs, cross the empty streets on a green light, be polite, be elegant, and be human.

The reality of war rarely met the expectations created by my favorite books and films. Every instant was full of meaning, conscious, or even crucial: bringing blankets to a family of refugees in March, saving a beetle now, buying a drone so Ukrainian soldiers would see and kill the enemy time after time.

Later, in September, after the Ukrainian counteroffensive in the Kharkiv region, I'll talk to an occupation survivor near Izyum. He will be a rare find: neither he nor his family or close friends had been kidnapped, tortured, or killed; they'll be safe and sound, although they don't know that yet. As a war crimes researcher, I'll almost be wasting my time on this lucky survivor. But the man will need to talk to someone to reflect on the occupation. So I'll justify talking to him by his vague memory of the airstrikes' dates and times and will listen to him for about two hours in his backyard. We'll end up having tea with sweets in his house, damaged by shelling, chatting with his wife, and looking at the last of his rabbits to survive the occupation. And in the end, this man told me that with occupiers in the village, he felt like an insect, meaning anything could happen to him, and no one would care.

There I'll remember this beetle we have just saved in Kharkiv and how others were ready to stop and help the poor insect. And I'll feel again that it all made sense. Although the war wasn't over, war was the time to save the smallest insect and each other.

Practical Lessons with Casanova and Without Her

[Editors' note: One of the previous ideas for the book structure was focused not on the heroines but on unexpected lessons learned by the war crimes investigator working in the field. This chapter contains remnants of the previous structure focused on some of the lessons learned. What follows below is a rough draft with unfinished sentences and unedited notes.]

THE MAP OF MARIUPOL

We sit in his car, and his car must be his only home. He was born in Donetsk and lived in the Kyivskyi district, near the airport, which was destroyed in 2014. His boss refused to stay under occupation and relocated his employees to Enerhodar. But the war would not end, and so they came back and worked in the occupied city till 2017. He was no hero or perfect patriot. He only stopped working in the occupied [territory] because the so-called Donetsk People's Republic (DPR) nationalized the plant in 2017. In 2018, he came to Mariupol. He would still visit his mother occasionally in the occupied city.

Here, a journalist would ask the interviewee how his mother is now, whether their political views are the same, and whether they call each other. Casanova does not ask. I do not dare to ask either. The question about his mother would lead to emotional pain, that's all. And we are interested in the details about the destruction of Mariupol. It is clear that it is ruined, but how, exactly? When particular streets and buildings were destroyed? With what weapons? And by whom? In the end, we will be able to identify pilots, units, commanders, and their role in the war crimes and crimes against humanity committed in Mariupol.

The man continues to talk, looking in front of him and sometimes putting his hand on the wheel, as if driving on an invisible road:[10]

> *On the night of February 23, we said goodbyes late after a corporate event. On the morning of February 24, 2022, the boss called and said not to go to work—war. The first shelling started overnight from February 23 to 24. I didn't hear the shelling because I was in the city center, on 4 Peace Avenue, near the Drama Theater.*
>
> *They told us to stay at home, and we stayed at home. I wanted to go to Metinvest to retrieve equipment, but they no longer allowed entry. Ukrainian military personnel had entered to defend the plants.*
>
> *I think tanks arrived at Azovstal on February 24 to defend the*

[10] As a result of her mission to the Kherson region in August 2022 and recording testimonies there, Victoria Amelina wrote the poem "This Weird and Smoldering Summer." It can be found in appendix II.

plant from the side of the "DPR," from the side of Pishchovyk [a small village near Mariupol].

We heard explosions on February 24 during the day. They were firing from the Pishchovyk side. They started shooting at Azovstal.

The Pentagon [a local nickname] area started to get hit.

On February 25, 2022, the heating was turned off.

On February 28, the power went out, and on March 1, 2022, it was turned back on.

On March 2, 2022, the power was turned off permanently.

Communication was still working. I could make calls within Ukraine but not within Mariupol because the base stations in other areas had likely been disabled.

Communication disappeared in the evening of March 5, 2022.

In other areas, communication was lost earlier.

Close flybys began on March 4, 2022.

On March 5, 2022, airplanes started flying approximately every hour. I think they were dropping bombs (I only saw planes with missiles a few times near the port).

I walked on Italian Street because it was narrower than Peace Avenue, and I thought I could hide there faster. Every other house was already damaged. Wires were lying on the ground everywhere. In some places, there were holes through the buildings. All the windows were shattered. But there were no completely burned-down buildings yet. There were definitely no gas pipes, so I think they were shelled with artillery.

On March 8, 2022, I went to celebrate International Women's Day with my colleague. On the way back, I visited an acquaintance. If I hadn't stayed there, I would have died because there was an airstrike in our area.

On March 8, an airstrike destroyed the building where the Red Cross was located. The windows in my apartment were shattered, and I went to live with my colleague at 195 Nakhimova Avenue (a nine-story building, I'm not sure about the exact number—it no longer exists;

it burned down and will be demolished). Since then, I have been living with him. We chopped firewood and cooked food. By that time, all the shops had already been looted. We woke up, washed, and went for firewood, and by then it was already time for lunch.

I also went to my own home.

On March 8, 2022, a plane flew over Priazovsky University, where my colleague's daughter studied. Most likely, it happened during the same airstrike. I filmed a video of the aftermath on March 9, 2022 when I went home to check on my apartment. Because looters had started breaking into apartments. The police were chasing them away. But that lasted for a week—then it became impossible. It was too cold in the apartment.

We understood that it was an airstrike because we heard the roar of the plane and the explosions. The plane flew once every hour.

Neighbors said that on March 8, 2022, a plane flew by around 3:00 p.m. and 4:00 p.m., and I came home at 4:30 p.m. I wasn't there, but they said that three to four shells were falling each time.

Then, on March 15, 2022, I went back home to check my apartment again. I walked along Nakhimova Street, passing by the Drama Theater and heading toward Peace Avenue. I returned at 1:00 p.m., but my colleague had already left with his family; they were gone.

Everyone was expecting buses. People started gathering in cars because everyone was leaving through the port to Mangush. They saw a convoy and got in and left. And I stayed in his apartment alone from March 15.

There were three field kitchens on one side of the Drama Theater. No one thought it would be hit. There were also many cars near the theater, but on March 14–15, 2022, the cars dispersed, around five hundred of them. Otherwise, there would have been even more casualties. The kitchens were still standing.

On March 16, 2022, I left the Drama Theater, took my things, and tried to stop a car. But there were already fifty people waiting there, women, elderly, children, all throwing themselves at the cars—"take us away from here." I stood there, spat, and went to my colleague on Hretska Street (the next street from Drama, perpendicular to Peace). It was March 16, 2022. Around 12:00 p.m., I went back. And then, on the same day, it was hit again.

From around March 5, 2022, planes started flying every fifty to sixty minutes. Around[11]

HELPLESSNESS AND DETERMINATION: HOW I FAILED

One of the first witnesses I speak with tells me a story of his abduction and torture. He sits next to me in our minivan, the yellow one, called Fishy, and shows me the black bruises, which are hard even to look at.

WHO NEEDS THE TRUTH?

I needed the truth, but perhaps the relatives of the victims did not. I knew the truth.

Postmortem Fame as a Form of Justice? Prisoners Killed in Combat[12]

A VILLAGE THAT FITS INTO DORMITORY

They cannot teach you at war crimes research training that you can see an entire village crammed into a dormitory in a big city.

The village of Ivanivka suddenly fits into the dormitory in one of the districts of Kryvyi Rih. We came to the dormitory to

[11] Editors' note: This fragment was left unfinished.

[12] Editors' note: This unfinished section was meant to discuss one of the unexpected lessons of war crimes investigation work. One of the older drafts of the manuscript contains the testimony of witnesses revealing that, while the relatives believed that their loved ones were killed in action, Victoria Amelina learned of their death in captivity after several weeks of torture .

research a woman's very recent death. Her husband is an eyewitness, so we expect the meeting to be an emotionally difficult one. Casanova doubts that is a good idea to record the testimony; perhaps we should let him have some time to grieve?

TWO KALASHNIKOV BULLETS IN MY HAND, THE ONE THAT went through Stanislav's leg and a berry pie from Ivanivka

we look for a man who just lost his wife; he might be a witness in a case of shooting at a civilian

cherry pie
kids playing
ringtone
two bullets

Two former prisoners and one survivor of WWII
The money I wanted to give them instead of justice
11/08/2022

One hot summer day in Kryvyi Rih I documented testimonies of two civilian prisoners who were lucky to escape captivity.

The Death of Roman Ratushny and the Crime of Aggression

There is a definition of combatant in the [Geneva Conventions]. Combatants may be intentionally targeted by an adverse party for their participation in the conflict, says international humanitarian law, in particular article 43(2) of Additional Protocol I (AP1) to the Geneva Conventions of 1949. It states that ". . . combatants, as a rule, are legal targets themselves for the opposite side regardless of the specific circumstances at hand, in other words, they can be attacked regardless of the specific circumstances

simply due to their status, so as to deprive their side of their support."[13]

On June 9, 2022, Kyiv finally seemed safe enough for a writer to sit in a cafe and try to write.

I had attempted to keep a war diary since February 24, but my notes were as chaotic and scattered as my life had been since the full-scale Russian invasion of my country.

I ordered a cappuccino and opened my laptop when my phone started ringing. Again and again. My colleagues were all calling me to ask the same things: "Is it true? Did he die? Does his mother know?"

They were all referring to Roman Ratushny, a twenty-four-year-old Ukrainian civil activist turned soldier, the son of an outstanding Ukrainian poet, and my dear friend, Svitlana Povalyaeva.

I shook my head and muttered something in response. I didn't want to believe the news, and I wasn't going to be the one to ask the mother. So I sat numb and unable to write, think, or breathe normally. Roman's death would be the ultimate manifestation of injustice in Ukraine for the past five months, or eight years since the initial invasion in 2014, or even perhaps all those decades since the Muscovite troops of Peter I captured and destroyed the Ukrainian city of Baturyn in 1708.[14]

I couldn't write. All the crimes from Baturyn to Bucha swirled

---

[13] Roman Ratushny (July 5, 1997–June 9, 2022) was an activist, journalist, and participant in the Revolution of Dignity who voluntarily joined the army at the start of the full-scale invasion (discussed in the chapters "The Angel's Advocate" and "Returning to Kyiv"). On June 9, 2022, he was caught in an enemy ambush on the front line in the Kharkiv region and killed. Victoria Amelina wrote the poem "I Have a Son and She Has a Son" about his death.

[14] Baturyn was the capital of the Hetmanate, an autonomous Cossack state on the territory of Leftbank Ukraine, which flourished under the Hetman Ivan Mazepa between 1687 and 1708. When during the Great Northern War (1700–1721) Mazepa allied with Sweden against Russia, Peter I of Russia ordered to eradicate Baturyn. All of its inhabitants were slaughtered and the city itself razed to the ground by a Russian army under the command of Alexander Menshikov on November 13, 1708.

around me. By afternoon I dared to drop a meaningless message to Roman's mom: ***Hi, I'm in Kyiv, if you need me.*** She suggested that we'd meet on Saturday, July 11.

She didn't know, I concluded, and ordered some wine. Wine didn't help; why would it? Wine helps against an unrequited love, not endless national tragedy.

All the generations of Ukrainians sowed, fought, and died, heroically or not, for a person like Roman to be born. I had imagined he would be Ukraine's president one day. I had told Svitlana and she had laughed at the thought. She, herself, took part in three Ukrainian revolutions in 1990, 2004, and 2014. Roman joined the latter one, of course. He was one of the students severely beaten up by Berkut on the night of Nov 30, 2013. Millions of Ukrainians flooded the streets in response to that brutal beating. Millions of Ukrainians went to the streets to protect people like Roman, young, sincere, uncompromising. The Ukrainian revolution of 2014 was in the name of his generation. Yet in 2022 Russians killed him.

How to Write About Mortals—Zhenia Podobna II

I MET ZHENIA PODOBNA AT THE PARTY IN LVIV. I KNEW ABOUT her precisely because she was the author of a book about women fighters.

Then her heroines started to die.

YANA CHERVONA

On April 2, 2019, in the Luhansk region, the well-known volunteer and soldier from the Donbas-Ukraine battalion Yana Chervona was killed as a result of shelling with heavy artillery.

"Around 1:30 p.m., near the village of Novozvanivka-Popasna, as a result of enemy shelling of our positions with 152mm howitzers by Russian terrorist forces, two soldiers of the Separate Assault Battalion 'Donbas-Ukraine,' Senior Soldier Yana Mykhaylivna Chervona (call sign 'Vidma,' or 'Witch') and Junior Sergeant Oleksandr Anatoliyovych Milyutin (call sign 'Deda,' or 'Grandpa'), heroically died," wrote the battalion commander Viacheslav Vlasenko (Fylynn, meaning "Eagle-Owl") on Facebook.

Yana Chervona was a machine gunner. She served in the 54th Brigade and later in the 46th Special Purpose Battalion "Donbas-Ukraine," which is currently stationed on the front line in the Luhansk region.

OLHA NIKISHYNA

On May 10, [2020], the military servicewoman Olha Nikishyna died of heart disease in the area of the Joint Forces Operation. She served in the 58th Separate Motorized Infantry Brigade named after the hetman Ivan Vyhovsky. This was reported on the Facebook page "Women's Veteran Movement."

Olha Nikishyna initially served in the Volunteer Ukrainian Corps "Right Sector." Later, the Poltava native joined the 16th Separate Motorized Infantry Battalion, which is part of the 58th Brigade.

IRYNA TSVILA

On February 25, [2022], she died in battle defending Kyiv. As the Ukrainian activist, veteran, and fighter Oleh Sobchenko noted, a local resident had informed him about the grave of two unknown soldiers [one of whom was Tsvila] in a forest between Lyutizh and Demydiv, Vyshhorod district.

OLHA SIMONOVA

Olha Simonova didn't like pathos. She saved animals. She was from Chelyabinsk, Russia.

With the call sign Simba, she served in the 24th Separate Mechanized Brigade, named after King Danylo,[15] and was killed in action [on September 13, 2022]. She had renounced her Russian citizenship and was defending Ukraine as part of the Armed Forces of Ukraine. The news was announced by the volunteer Diana Makarova.

TAIRA

Taira was a prisoner and came back.[16]

OLHA FILIPOVYCH

Olha Filipovych is missing or a prisoner of war.

The Lost Sheep of Ryszard Kapuściński—Vira Kuryko II

[15] King Danylo (Daniel) of Galicia (1201–1264) was the ruler of the principalities of Galicia and Volhynia, who became one of the most powerful princes in east-central Europe. 24th Separate Mechanized Brigade named after King Danylo is one of the prominent mechanized brigades of the Ukrainian Armed Forces.

[16] Yuliia Paievska, call sign Taira, is a Ukrainian medic and volunteer. She served as a volunteer medic during the Revolution of Dignity, then as a tactical medicine trainer on the front lines of the Russian invasion between 2014 and 2018, where she founded the volunteer ambulance corps Taira's Angels. Between 2018 and 2020, she was the head of the military hospital in Mariupol. She continued to work as a volunteer medic after her demobilization in 2020. During the Russian siege of Mariupol, Taira filmed her work with a body camera. The recordings were smuggled out of the city on March 15, 2022, by the last team of international reporters. On March 16, Taira and her ambulance driver were captured by the Russian forces. She was released from captivity on June 17, 2022.

When I told Vira Kuryko I'd like to write about her work documenting Russian war crimes in her native Chernihiv region, she tried to talk me out of it. "I don't do anything interesting," Vira warned me, explaining that she was now working on a story about a seventy-five-year-old man who lost all his animals in a besieged village. The Russians had killed them all: Marta the horse, a cow, and a flock of sheep.

We were in the middle of the bloodiest war in recent European history; our Messenger apps were full of stories that would get more clicks than the killing of sheep. Yet Vira chose for her subject an old man who lost his domestic animals. Why? I decided to go to Chernihiv to see her and the man she's writing about to find out the answer.

Vira meets me at the door and apologizes for the chaos caused by her two cats and yellow lab, who cavort freely around her cozy apartment. There's also the potential for rather more severe chaos affecting the building as a result of a Russian missile strike.

There's a big shell hole on that side, Vira tells me, showing me the crack in the wall, which is so thin that the wallpaper is still intact. However, it's an illusion that the damage is minor, construction experts say; if the residents do not act fast, the building will fall apart in two years or so. I'm afraid even to run a finger along the crack, as if my touch might hasten the building's collapse.

We'll fix it, says Vira, putting a plate of cookies on the table next to a book, *War Diaries 1939–1945*, by Astrid Lindgren. Lindgren is of course best known for her children's books, including *Pippi Longstocking*. But in Ukraine her account of World War Two has been the most popular of her books recently.

One of the cats, the white one, swishes between the book and the cookies. The labrador, Sagan, also tries to get my attention, but I'm preoccupied with the book. The Swedish author smiles at me from the yellow cover of the Ukrainian edition of *War*

Diaries as though trying to cheer us up by suggesting there will come a time when Chernihiv will be as safe as Stockholm, and someone elsewhere will read the diaries recounting the present war we have yet to win and survive. Vira finished reading the book the day before the full-scale Russian-Ukrainian war began, on February 23, 2022. It's like a soldier finishing boot camp right in time to enter the first battle.

Now Vira, like Astrid Lindgren, is keeping a diary. She's doing it daily—a discipline I haven't been able to achieve since February. I wonder aloud if she has perhaps missed a day or two. Why not? Some days in Chernihiv must have been tough enough for a reasonable excuse. But Vira shakes her head; she has the discipline.

Vira and I first met in Lviv at the end of March 2022. I was catching up on work in a bookshop café, one of the few open at the time. Space was tight—not just in this cafe but across the entire city, which was flooded with refugees. Almost overnight Lviv's population had nearly doubled. I felt guilty occupying my oversize table alone. So when a girl wearing a red sweater entered the cafe, I suggested she sit next to me.

It turned out to be Vira, who had escaped from Chernihiv during the hardest days of its siege.

"You're Victoria, right?" she asked, recognizing me, although we'd never met in person.

I have a terrible memory for faces, but I should have recognized her from her red sweater at least. I had read about that sweater in Vira's published report about her days in Chernihiv during Russia's assault on that thousand-year-old Ukrainian city.

At the beginning of the report, Vira makes a reader see the heroine, herself, a girl wearing the same red sweater for twenty-two days in a row. She then describes all the horrors of the siege, and the reader has no choice but to follow the girl in red.

So there she was in the café, the actual author, relatively safe in Lviv, yet still wearing her sweater as if it was her new home. I told her then that I loved the essay, and Vira shook her head, saying she had utterly failed as a reporter. She blamed herself for leaving Chernihiv after only ten days of the siege.

"All my life I wanted to be like Ryszard Kapuściński, and here was my war, and I left," she told me.

"To become a new Ryszard Kapuściński, one first has to survive," I replied.

We laughed.

There were no reasons to feel cheerful. Vira's husband and her father had been at the front lines since the beginning of the full-scale invasion. She wore the same sweater for the whole month, not having time for anything but the survival of her loved ones and herself and keeping a diary. She missed her dog, whom she'd brought to the Ivano-Frankivsk region on the first day of the full-scale war. Yet I began calling her Kapuściński, and here we were, giggling in the middle of Lviv, and people looked at us as if it was wrong for Ukrainian women to laugh in March 2022. But it wasn't.

It is striking how much we all laugh during this horrible war. We may not do it that much in front of the foreign reporters, who mostly expect to see Ukrainian women's despair or heroism. The truth is, sometimes, tired of crying or of being unable to cry, we laugh like crazy as if proving that here we are, Ukrainians, still alive.

In the middle of June, when Vira tried to talk me out of writing about her, I remembered our jokes. "I remember you're no Kapuściński, and this is exactly what I have in mind for the title," I reassured her.

The difference between brave writers like Ryszard Kapuściński- and Vira was evident: Vira didn't go to war in order to write; instead, the war came to her, with murderous intent. This simple truth is even more apparent in her apartment, which is slowly falling apart thanks to the missile strike. We only seem to be okay; we, like this building, need help.

On the wall, the one without a crack, next to a bookcase packed with books, including the ones by Kapuściński, Vira has a poster showing a photograph of the planet Earth. Above it is a quote by the scientist Carl Sagan. "Look again at that dot. That's here. That's home," the poster reads.

Waiting outside for an Uber, I have the chance to observe the shell hole in Vira's actual home.

If we were to take the long view and look at the planet from the vantage point proposed by Sagan (the astrophysicist, not the labrador) how might it appear to us? As beautiful as ever? Or irreparably broken?

Don't humans who name their dog Sagan after a pioneering astronomer deserve to live happily ever after? Their happiness must be a part of the ultimate justice I'm trying to at least define by traveling around my war-torn country and talking to all the survivors, lawyers, war correspondents, and human rights activists. Instead, Vira is going from her damaged home to the bombed-out remnants of the village of Novoselivka to finish her report about Mykola, a seventy-five-year-old man who lost his animals to Russian offenders. With the animals went his sense of purpose in life.

The driver drops us off near a checkpoint, one of those shielding Chernihiv from a quite probable second Russian offensive. The Chernihiv region borders both Russia and Belarus. They are so close that when Vira was a village kid, she just ran through the surrounding meadows to announce proudly that she had been abroad. She used to watch Belarusian TV and had to play the role of a cheerful defender of Moscow in World War Two in her Ukrainian school theater. However, the latter role was one forced on children all over Ukraine; it had nothing to do with the proximity to the Russian border but with the outdated Russia-centric education system.

We walk through the blackened ruins of what's left of Novoselivka, surrounded by bright green bushes and flowers. Vira has been here numerous times, so she walks confidently and calmly as if she were taking her dog for a stroll during the apocalypse. The street ends at the edge of the field she described to me while we were drinking coffee and eating cookies in her kitchen. Here, in this field, the man we're about to visit has buried his horse, his cow, and his sixteen sheep.

Vira heads to one of the few houses that look almost unscathed. "Mykola! Mykola!" she calls out to the character in her story. We wait, and I cannot help but turn around and look at the field. It could be full of mines, so we do not let Sagan go there.

Mykola turns out to be a tall, gray-haired man with good posture. He is glad to see us but forgot about his promise to allow Vira to photograph him. "I should have shaved for the picture!" he says, worried about his face in a newspaper. We tell him he's still handsome, and the seventy-five-year-old agrees to sit on a chair in the middle of his garden. Vira takes pictures of Mykola, and I take pictures of Vira taking pictures. Then there's a sheep Vira wants to photograph too, the only one left.

Vira takes a photograph and asks if this last sheep has a name. It doesn't. Mykola didn't name his sheep. The horse that died here in the yard was named Marta, but the sheep remained unnamed. It is always the case with the sheep, I think. I try to remember if the sheep in Antoine de Saint-Exupéry's *The Little Prince* had a name. Mary had a little lamb, but did it have a name? What about the Lost Sheep in the Bible? No, it was just "the Lost Sheep." Yet, doomed to anonymity, even a nameless sheep deserves to be saved.

We sit near the rose bushes to go over Mykola's story again.

I watch him talking, Vira listening, and Sagan trying to eat the roses. I try to imagine how Mykola lived in the house for decades. His kids grew up with the garden and ran in the field, and helped to take care of the animals. Mykola tells Vira how he had to let his animals go one day, so they would not burn alive in the barn. Mykola is no vegan saint but an old farmer used to the sight of dying animals. However, he believes animals should never suffer. He went to his relatives in the nearby village for a little while to save his life because Russian shells had already killed his neighbors. He came home as soon as the shelling grew less intense, only to find his animals' bodies, a wounded dying horse, and one lucky sheep.

"They were here, and here, and there." Mykola shows the places where he found his animals. They were around his house with broken windows, in the garden, and farther, in the field behind the gate.

Then Mykola's daughter calls us inside for lunch. She came to Novoselivka to take Mykola to the Carpathian Mountains in western Ukraine so he could rest a little while. He had been on vacation there long ago, so he agreed to go.

We talk, drink, and flip through their family albums, and it becomes clear that his daughter has arrived to take Mykola away for good. His children won't let him come back home. After lunch, Mykola has to pack his belongings. They will leave tomorrow. Mykola cannot take the last sheep with him, so there is no point in naming it.

Vira visited Mykola numerous times but had never taken down his cell phone number. This time she does. We hug him and leave. We walk past the field and the ruins without really seeing them.

"They're leaving forever, and he doesn't realize that," Vira tells me, her voice trembling.

"I think he knows and just pretends not to know," I say, and Vira seems to like this idea.

Back at Vira's apartment, we look at her family photo albums too. Vira shows me her books. She didn't evacuate them in March because she couldn't choose which ones to take. Vira shows me her dresses. There's one with a floral pattern that was the cause of her divorce from her first husband.

"He said, choose me or the dress," she laughs, remembering. Vira chose her freedom and the dress. She loves her dresses, but she couldn't evacuate them in March either. She became the girl in jeans and a red sweater, trying to survive, no Kapuściński. She had to leave.

Now Vira seems confident that she's not leaving her home, which is invisibly falling apart, again. There is a good chance that the repair will stop the destruction; the residents expect the government will prop the building up before it's too late. Vira brought Sagan back from Ivano-Frankivsk. She even adopted two cats abandoned by someone during the siege; Izyum and Yonsi are their names.

The rumors of the upcoming offensive through the Belarusian border are all over the internet. However, Vira and I don't talk about that. We know but pretend not to know.

I ask Vira again why, of all the people she met in Novoselivka, she chose to write about Mykola. She explains that it's because he is not a hero but an ordinary man in the ruins of his life, the embodiment of regular Ukrainians like us, those who cannot fight but run.

"I hate those stories that end with a false positivity, where people say that the main thing is they are alive. No, I wouldn't want to live if my husband didn't live. Mykola, too, lives, but he has lost everything," she adds. She uses the money she earns from her articles to buy ammunition for her husband on the front line. This is perhaps how she will use the money for Mykola's story as well.

Vira Kuryko is also training to research war crimes. She is joining the Reckoning Project, an initiative run by the prominent Ukrainian journalist Natalya Gumenyik and Janine di Giovanni, a war correspondent who witnessed so many war crimes that she finally embarked on the quest for justice herself. Connected by the Ukrainian-British writer and activist Peter Pomerantsev, Janine and Natalya quickly organized a team that combined Ukrainian journalists and international lawyers, so the stories of horror would be heard by the public and eventually by the courts too. Vira Kuryko is one of twelve journalists being extensively trained to gather evidence of war crimes.

My next destination is Brussels, where the lawyer and human rights defender Oleksandra Matviichuk and I are to talk about justice and accountability for all of Russia's international crimes. But leaving Chernihiv, I think that no court will bring justice to Ukrainians like Mykola. Or like Vira and myself. However, at least we can tell our stories. This story is not about animals, obviously. It's about humanity, about one Ukrainian's ruined home, but also about that home Carl Sagan implored us to notice, that pale blue dot adrift among the stars.

How to Be a Human in Brussels and in London—Oleksandra Matviichuk II

The airspace over Ukraine is closed for civilian aviation; I learned that all too well on February 24 in the small airport of Marsa Alam in the desert. So the way to Brussels isn't simple. Oleksandra and I are to take a train ride from Kyiv to the Polish town of Khelm, catch a train from Khelm to Warsaw, stay there overnight, and only then fly to Brussels early in the morning.

Oleksandra is the last one to enter the train compartment in which we will spend the next thirteen hours on our way to Khelm. We are four in the narrow space with four bunk beds, and Oleksandra recognizes one of the other women. When she was still a student at the Taras Shevchenko National University of Kyiv and a head of the student government, she once attended fundraising training by our fellow traveler. Oleksandra met her future husband at that training, so the encounter might have been brief but quite memorable. The three of us started chatting, remembering this romantic story, and somehow, of course, went on to discuss human rights violations, accountability, and the lack of weapons on the front line. The fourth woman just sits silently, pretending to look out the window and not quite listening to us. I look at her from time to time, as I don't buy it: she is, in fact, listening to us with great interest. But after a couple of hours, she finally talks to us:

"I'm sorry to interrupt you," she says. "I am from Alchevsk."[17]

[Editors' note: The following unedited note in the last working copy of the manuscript is written in Ukrainian. The note appears to refer to the case of another human rights defender, Maksym Butkevych.[18]]

There was no contact with him for the first few months that summer. He was taken prisoner some time between June 20 and 30. After that Russian media showed propaganda themes twice. But at the beginning of autumn there was some contact with him. And once Maksym was able to talk with his parents.

---

[17] A town in the Luhansk region of Ukraine that has been occupied since the first year of the Russian invasion in 2014.

[18] Maksym Butkevych (b. 1977) is a human rights advocate, journalist, and cofounder of the Human Rights Center ZMINA, the project Without Borders, and Hromadske Radio. He took up arms when Russia launched its full-scale invasion of Ukraine; he was captured by the Russian occupiers in June 2022 and remains in captivity in Russia at the time of editing.

Olena and Olenivka

IRYNA DOVHAN SAYS THAT, INEXPLICABLY, MANY UKRAINIANS in Donetsk were busy renovating their homes before the initial Russian invasion in 2014. My friend Olena [Stiazhkina], a prominent historian and writer, is one of those who just moved into a new apartment before the war. I met her when she had already found her new home in a cozy flat in downtown Kyiv. Yet it always seemed to me that she has moved but never really moved on: it only looks like she is in Kyiv, but, in fact, she holds Donetsk in her thoughts.

The full-scale invasion changed that: Kyiv was under attack, so she had to be here and now. For a time, the loss of one home ached less because of the threat to another.

Olena Stiazhkina told me the news in Musafir. In 2014, she was the first from whom I heard a simple and obvious thought: the Ukrainian citizens who supported the ideas of the so-called DPR and LPR weren't separatists but collaborators.[19] They supported the idea suggested to them by the aggressor, the Russian Federation. A minority of the collaborators hoped to join Russia, like Crimea, in the illusion that Russian wealth would somehow help them prosper personally. The rest were just part of a usual phenomenon: where there is occupation, there is collaborationism. Fortunately, there is heroism as well. And the majority of the population just tries to survive the war.

I wanted to talk to her about how it is to be a historian in the middle of history.

I didn't sleep well before the interview. By now, I didn't think it was possible to shock me.

---

19 "DPR" and "LPR" stand for the so-called Donetsk and Luhansk People's Republics, the Russia-controlled self-proclaimed entities created in the occupied regions of Ukraine in spring 2014.

Image 16

Photo of Olena Stiazhkina

[Editors' note: This chapter was not finished. What follows is notes from the last working copy of the manuscript]

CASTRATION JULY 28 2022

On July 28, I woke up to the air raid sirens. It was . . . am.

Later in the day the Russian celebration continued

Late at night I tweeted,

"Russians are proudly sharing their video of their soldiers castrating a Ukrainian soldier, a POW.[20]

Russians have been committing horrible crimes for all these years, from Chechnya in the 90s to Ukraine since 2014.

#Russians enjoy impunity.

Europe enjoys their ballet and gas."

July 29, 2022

[20] On July 28, 2022, a video was posted on a Russian Telegram page showing the torture, castration, and murder of a Ukrainian prisoner of war in the Pryvillia sanatorium by Russian servicemen.

"They executed Azov defenders in Olenivka, you know that?" I didn't. I also didn't know how to react to the news. It is always easier when you read such news all by yourself. You don't have to think over your reaction then. You can swear, or hit the table, or cry, or in disbelief just keep scrolling the newsfeed without any visible reaction.

"No, I didn't know," I replied. I didn't check the news in the morning but rushed to our meeting in Musafir. I took out my phone.

"What are you doing? You want to check? But I'm telling you they did."

"Yes, I understand but I need to see," I replied, though obviously what I really needed was a place to hide for a moment, and this place was my phone. I needed some time to understand how I felt. There was no time for that. There was a sunny day in Kyiv, uniquely delicious coffee in Musafir, and a woman to whom I wanted to talk about justice.

I told her about the project.

"I'm writing a book with the working title *Looking at Women Looking at War: A War and Justice Diary*," I said. "I've worked with a group documenting war crimes here, in the Kyiv region. I went to the Chernihiv region with Vira Kuryko. I advocated for justice with Oleksandra Matviichuk in Brussels and London. I plan to come back to Kharkiv to finish the chapter about the literature museum director Tetyana Pylypchuk and, hopefully, talk to Evhenia Zakrevska, a Euromaidan lawyer turned soldier. But I need a historian too," I concluded and looked at her.

"No, you don't. Why would you need a historian?" she said defensively.

Like all the other women, she didn't think she would make a good heroine for the book.

But what happened in Olenivka that day had happened before,

many times. And Olena, of course, knew it too well. She was not only a historian but a refugee from Donetsk.

[Editors' note: The following excerpt is taken from the book *Martyred Village: Commemorating the 1944 Massacre at Oradour-sur-Glane*, by Sarah Farmer (1999). This book was recommended to Victoria Amelina by Olena Stiazhkina when they discussed what had to be done to the collaborators after the war referring to the European experience of World War Two. Victoria Amelina did not develop the connection between the war crimes committed by the Russian army in Ukraine and the German army in France which she had in mind.]

> Among German crimes of the Second World War, the massacre of 642 women, children, and men of Oradour-sur-Glane by SS soldiers on 10 June 1944 is one of the most notorious. On that Saturday afternoon, four days after the Allied landings in Normandy, SS troops encircled the town of Oradour. . . . The men were marched off to barns nearby and shot. The soldiers locked the women and children in the church, shot them, and set the building (and then the rest of the town) on fire. . . .
>
> In 1946 the French state expropriated and preserved the entire ruins of Oradour. The forty acres of crumbling houses, farms, and shops became France's village martyr . . .

[Editors' note: here the annotation excerpt ends; it is followed by the Victoria Amelina commentary.]

(martyred village), in the Limousin region the most traumatic wartime event in the region: the massacre of the women, children, and men of the town of Oradour-sur-Glane by SS soldiers on 10 June 1944.

Taking History to Court—Evhenia Zakrevska III

I'm waiting for Evhenia in one of the Kharkiv cafes, called Warehouse #7, near the Architect Beketov subway station. I come earlier, afraid to be late and lose precious time. Evhenia's time doesn't belong to her anymore; she's in the army now, exactly like in that song by Status Quo that was popular when we were kids.

Waiting, I first walk around and take pictures of bombed McDonald's, and then sit in the café, trying to write. But I'm too nervous to concentrate. Besides, I start hearing explosions; they are somewhere far away, but perhaps in the city. In front of me, on a lawn in the inner yard of the café, two men are playing Ping-Pong. With each new explosion, I pick up my head and look at them: the men keep playing. So I stopped reacting to the explosions too. It is much easier to concentrate on the regular rhythmic hits of a Ping-Pong ball.

<<She didn't close her eyes and dared "to look up," like only a few characters did in the *Don't Look Up* movie we all watched in January, hoping it was not about Ukraine, and definitely not about us. At least it wasn't about Evhenia Zarkrevska. She knows what to do; she's trained and prepared. On February 24, 2022, her main worry standing in line to the Military Commissariat was: what if they run out of guns before it's her turn, and she ends up unarmed. But she didn't. Already on the first day of the full-scale war she got her gun in Kyiv, and hasn't been unarmed ever since. Unlike me, she can also write. And I mean, not my helpless diary entities, which I don't dare to show anyone, but insightful articles she publishes in Ukrainian media. For example, on March 10, 2022, she already addresses the Russians via [the online media platform] *Ukrainska Pravda.*>>

[Editors' note: The following three sentences were quoted from Evhenia Zakrevska's opinion piece, written in Russian.]

> The author of this phrase, who served in the National Guard, was wonderful, direct, just like the boy from the tale about the emperor and his new clothes. You hear that? Your emperor is naked.

Despite all that, she doesn't feel useful enough, yet she knows that soon she'll be on the front line in the east.

When she's finally deployed to Kharkiv, her unit has to live in the basement of the numerous damaged apartment buildings in the Saltivka [city district]. It's a weird place, full of abandoned dogs and cats, their owners have died or fled the war, flowers that start to bloom, and black burned windows in sixteen-story buildings, which stand but aren't livable anymore. The basement is dark and wet. Evhenia isn't afraid of anything, but she misses fresh air. At this time of the year, she usually walks and hikes a lot. She loves mountains and vast open spaces. But she can only see a wide world now through the drone she operates. In Saltivka, she keeps learning to fly and becomes great at it.

She finally fully understands how crucial her mission of aerial reconnaissance, when her unit moves further east. Ukrainians are outnumbered and outgunned, and every projectile counts. The Russians on the other hand can fire without precision. Besides, the Ukrainian army cares about not hitting civilian objects. Evhenia cares a lot. Not only is she an honest, kind person, she is also a lawyer with substantial knowledge of international law. And isn't it ironic that the army has such a prominent lawyer helping to target military objects, vehicles, and troops?

Her mission is to find and give coordinates, quantity and type of military equipment to M777 [howitzer].

International journalists keep calling the Russian-Ukrainian war a war of drones. Certainly the drone pilots are crucial for making history. But, after all, Evhenia is always where the history is to be made.

Evhenia Zakrevska arrived at Maidan before Berkut beat the students. She arrived in Crimea before Russia annexed it. She joined the Ukrainian Armed Forces before I was able to enter the country on February 26, coming back from an untimely vacation.

If you want to be where history is, you have to follow Evhenia Zakrevska. She walks away and I cannot stop looking at her delicate figure in military uniform until she disappears behind Kharkiv's green trees.

The men keep playing Ping-Pong.

The Keepers of a Ruined Museum

<< We arrive at the ruined Museum of Skovoroda, and its director, Nataliya Mitsay, says she cannot meet with me. Her subordinate Hanna is ready to show me what's left of the museum and the park around it. I know why Nataliya doesn't want to meet me; she is exhausted from talking to journalists. But this is the reason I wanted to interview her. I wanted to see this other side of war journalism: being a person everyone suddenly wants to feature in their articles not because of all the work you've done but because all your work is in ruins.

Just give me a minute with Nataliya and I will explain why I need to talk specifically to her, I say. Hanna calls her boss, and Nataliya comes to see me.

I WANT TO KNOW ABOUT YOUR WORK

We're friends with one of the museum workers and with her

The case of Skovorodynivka was

My first question for Nataliya isn't about the tragedy or even the museum, which is now a ruin, but about her background. And she finally starts smiling, telling me that she majored in Ukrainian language and literature.

Justice, Not Cash—Zolotar Torture Case I

I WORKED WITH THYMUS BORYSTHENICUS ON THE ZOLOTAR case, which is absolutely hopeless in terms of prosecution and so absolutely important to describe. Of course, that is not his real name, not even a real call sign known to others on the Truth Hounds team, like Casanova or Marusya.[21] Thymus Borysthenicus is what he bitterly asked me to call him in the book; the name stands for a plant that grows near his native village. The village is still occupied by the Russian forces. And Thymus's family still remains there, unable to leave.

The fear for his loved ones makes it almost impossible to write about Thymus as a person, and it's a shame because he is an incredible one. But he will remain a plant in this story, an endemic that grows in the fields of southern Ukraine, from Zaporizhzhya to where the Dnipro River flows into the Black Sea.

Instead, I will tell the story of the Zolotar family, which we are researching together.

"I was born in the village of Sadove in the Kherson region. At the

[21] Marusya is Victoria Amelina's callsign in Truth Hounds.

time of the full-scale invasion, I had been living with my husband, Yan Zolotar, and our two children, ages four and one and a half, in the village of Mala Oleksandrivka on 65 Myru Street" [says Victoria Zolotar].[22]

The occupation of Mala Oleksandrivka in the Kherson region began on March 9, 2022. Robberies of stores, searches, and detentions began.

In the village, there were two protests on March 13 and 14. Vika filmed the protest on her smartphone. On March 13, between seventy and eighty people gathered in Velyka Oleksandrivka with Ukrainian flags near the House of Culture. The protest lasted about an hour and a half. The occupiers first fired warning shots about ten meters away from us. They threatened to shoot us.

On the second day, March 14, people gathered for the protest again. The occupiers said, "If you don't get off the stairs by the house of culture, we will shoot." Some people were already scared, so there were fewer protesters than on March 13. They took our passports and demanded that we go with them to the police station, but one of the occupiers told us to give the passports back to the people.

The villagers also brought out a portable speaker and played the Ukrainian anthem, singing on the streets. After March 14, everyone was already afraid to gather for protests.

"I had a car, a purple Zhiguli[23] with a white roof", [notes Victoria Zolotar]. "When I drove for food, our military was not on the road at first. But then the Armed Forces of Ukraine appeared in Bereznehuvate, and I gave them information about the location of the Russian military. The head of the village of Mala

[22] From this point, the author includes the testimony of Yan Zolotar's wife, Victoria (Vika) Zolotar.

[23] Zhiguli was a car based on the Italian Fiat 124 manufactured in Russia and the Soviet Union from 1970 to 2012. For export markets the cars were sold under the Lada brand.

Oleksandrivka, Kramarenko Zoya Pavlivna, remains in the occupation."[24]

The first search in the Zolotar family's home took place in March, but I cannot recall the exact date. Russian soldiers in balaclavas came to the house. I asked if they had an accent, but they spoke pure Russian. They entered the house despite Vika's pleas not to scare the children. They were searching for weapons, but the Zolotar family had never owned any. They asked for the husband's whereabouts; six other soldiers were waiting outside on the street.

"On March 27, 2022, after 11:00 a.m., my husband and I were preparing to leave with the children from the occupation in the village of Velyka Oleksandrivka. My husband, Yan, went to pick up his friend and disappeared. This is what happened." Vika [Zolotar] had already packed the children's things. Her husband said he would pick up his friend and be back in fifteen minutes. But he hadn't returned after thirty minutes, and Vika began calling him. Someone was cutting off all of Vika's calls. Finally, her husband answered the phone. She asked him, "Where are you?" He asked, "What is my password for hidden files?" Vika replied that she didn't know because she didn't know about any hidden files. In fact, there were none. She asked him what she should do now. Her husband replied, "Everything's fine, let's talk later," which was uncharacteristic of their usual conversation. Vika's husband's friend, whom he was supposed to pick up, also called her repeatedly. She told him that she suspected her husband had been detained. She continued to call her husband, but her calls were blocked. Then she sent a text message saying, "Where are

[24] The head of the village stayed under occupation because of her old mother who could not be evacuated.

you? We're worried about you and the children." She didn't receive a reply.

"It was getting late, around 5:30 p.m., and I called my husband's brother Oleh", [Victoria Zolotar continues]. "I told him I suspected that my husband had been taken. A few minutes later, a friend of ours came by on his scooter and said he had just been in the area and saw our car, a purple Lada with a white roof, still parked at the intersection near the Russian checkpoint by the district hospital in Velyka Oleksandrivka. He also saw Russian soldiers talking to my husband there earlier in the day."

I called Oleh again and we grabbed our marriage and children's birth certificates and drove to the checkpoint. As we approached, the Russian soldiers came toward us and started waving their hands to slow down. They had already dumped gravel on the road to make cars swerve back and forth as the Russians were renovating the checkpoint near the hospital.

I told them I was Victoria Zolotar and came to look for my husband, Yan. I showed them our documents. The Russian soldiers at the checkpoint confirmed that my husband had been detained and taken to the police station.

At first, they wouldn't let us go to the police station, but I convinced them to let us through. Oleh parked his car near the police station where the occupiers had forbidden parking. They aimed their guns at us for this. I explained that my husband was missing and I was looking for him, and our little children were waiting for us at home. The Russian soldiers replied in Russian, "Oh, that's the one we took from the cards game, that wild one."

One of the occupiers also said to me, literally: "If you come here again, we'll shoot you in the head, and believe me, we won't miss."

They also told me that my husband had already been taken to Nova Kakhovka and if he didn't do anything wrong, they would release him and return him to where they took him from. We had to leave the police station.

We drove back to the checkpoint near the hospital. I asked one of the occupiers there, who was standing near the Tatiana store, about my husband. He replied, "I didn't take him." We drove back to the checkpoint near the district hospital but from a different direction. There was already a BMP [IFV, infantry fighting vehicle] there, buried in the ground. One of the Russian soldiers (tall, thin, fair-haired, in his twenties) said that they were leaving soon and that I should go home."

Vika [Zolotar] continued to wait for her husband, watching to see if he would come, because the occupiers in the police told her they would release him. Vika kept faith. But I don't write about faith, only facts: they told her, she waited. Meanwhile, the shelling in the village intensified. From the yard, Vika could see the Bila Krynytsya railway station. She saw that from where the Orlyonok [children's] camp was, the Russians were firing rockets toward Bila Krynytsya. The Russian rocket launchers were located about a kilometer from the residential area. Later, the Ukrainian Armed Forces were able to bomb this firing position. On March 28, 2022, Vika started calling the Ukrainian hotlines for missing persons. But her husband was not there, no matter what she did. After four days, Vika began looking for someone to take her out of the occupied village. She had two small children with her, Yan's children. Vika had already packed her bags; she wrote CHILDREN on notes to stick on the car window. At night, around 11:00 p.m., the head of the village, Zoya, called and said: "Don't go, the Russians started digging trenches across the dam at the entrance to Mala Oleksandrivka and the Russians won't let civilians out." But Vika still persuaded Oleh to take her away. They could hear strong shelling. Oleh lives near the dam and saw that the Russians were indeed above the dam and had a good view of the road. He wanted to see if any civilians would be allowed on this road, or shot. On the morning of April 2, 2022, Oleh called and said he had seen one civilian car drive through without being shot or stopped, so he could risk driving past the dam across the Inhulets [River].

"Our car had sheets with the word 'children' written on them. We drove down along the Inhulets. Another car was following us. When we crossed the dam, I was very afraid that we would be shot. Vika saw how Russian automatic rifles were aimed at us from above. The BMP barrel was also aimed at the dam. When Oleh took me to Nova Pavlivka, he returned to his wife Inna and their child, and he left. And somewhere within an hour and a half on April 2, 2022, the dam was partially destroyed" [narrates Victoria Zolotar].

"On the night of April 3, 2022, at around 11:30 p.m., a woman from Nova Kakhovka called me. She had seen our advertisement and spoke with me in a mixture of Ukrainian and Russian. We spoke for about half an hour, during which I asked her to relay the message that we were going to the Kirovohrad Oblast. She said she would try to help so that they would release my husband."

"Former prisoner Vitaliy also called. He told me that he and his wife were in the ATO,[25] and the occupiers had detained them along with Yan, and that my husband was being held in detention in Nova Kakhovka."

[25] Anti-Terrorist Operation zone, or Joint Forces Operation zone, is the term used to indicate the parts of the Luhansk and Donetsk regions under Russian occupation. The term was used before the start of the Russian full-scale invasion in February 2022.

"Two former cellmates of my husband from Nova Kakhovka also contacted her. They had been released for 10,000 hryvnias each."

"Then, on April 9, 2022, around 12:30 p.m. before lunch, I received a call from an unknown MTS[26] number, and I heard my husband's voice. He said that he had been released and was near the village of Urozhayne in the Bereslavsky district. He asked me to call someone to pick him up and bring him home. But no one could pick him up, as all of our friends with cars had already left the occupied village."

"I immediately called the head of the village, Zoya. Here I must add that Zoya is still under occupation. Zoya was overjoyed to hear the news of my husband's release, and even cried tears of joy as she started preparing food for him. Then, Vika called her husband's old number again. Someone else answered and said in Russian with an accent: 'We've already cut his head off.'"

[blank]What was happening to Yan during all this time?

"Occupiers detained me on March 27, 2022 (my wife called me at 11:00 a.m., but the calls were rejected). On that day, I wanted to take my wife, two children—a four-year-old daughter and a two-year-old son—and their godmother out of the occupied territory. My family had already gathered, and around noon, I left to pick up the godmother who lived in Velyka Oleksandrivka."[27]

"At the intersection near the district hospital of Velyka Oleksandrivka, the 'kadyrivtsi stopped me.[28] One of them had Slavic

---

[26] MTS was a mobile network operator, rebranded as Vodafone in 2015 but still remembered under the old name.

[27] From this point, the author includes the testimony of Yan Zolotar.

[28] "'Kadyrivtsi" refers to the Kadyrovites, a paramilitary organization in the Chechen Republic, Russian Federation, that serves the purpose of protecting the Head of the Chechen Republic. The term is also used to refer to any armed, ethnically Chechen

appearance and a covered face. There were about ten people, and a BTR and a Ural were parked there.[29] They stopped my car, removed the tinting film from it, and found a phone in my armrest. They began to examine the phone."

"The farmer I work for sent me a map on the phone, showing how to get to Kryvyi Rih via the steppe roads. One of the occupiers saw this map and accidentally opened a video, a song about the Bayraktar.[30] The occupiers also realized that I was helping people leave for Kryvyi Rih, which made them angry. People called me and asked if we were going to Kryvyi Rih, which also angered the occupiers."

"The farmer called and asked, 'Yan, are you going to leave?' I said no, and he realized that something was wrong and hung up."

"Then the occupiers forced my car off the road to their BTR, parked it, and called someone to report a suspicious person, which was me. Then three Slavic-looking soldiers on Tigers arrived and took me to the police station in Velyka Oleksandrivka.[31]"

"The police station in Velyka Oleksandrivka is located near the prosecutor's office, and the prosecutor's office is across from the pharmacy. They took me to a small room on the first floor of the police station. The occupiers were young and had Slavic

---

men under the control of the head of the Chechen Republic, Ramzan Kadyrov. The Kadyrovites have been involved in the Syrian Civil War and in the Russian invasion of Ukraine.

[29] Ural is a truck produced at the Ural Automative Plant in Russia.

[30] "Bayraktar" is a Ukrainian patriotic song written by the Ukrainian soldier Taras Borovok and released on March 1, 2022, during the Russian invasion of Ukraine. It is dedicated to the Baykar Bayraktar TB2 combat drone, successfully used against Russian troops and equipment by the Ukrainian Armed Forces.

[31] "Tigers" are Russian armored vehicles.

appearance. They began to interrogate me about the video (with the Bayraktar).

"A young, russet-haired occupier, around twenty-five years old, started hitting me on the head with a thick book (probably some sort of code). He hit me five or six times. Another occupier with darker hair did not hit me, but kept going in and out."

"Then they threw me into the basement for half an hour. They took me to the basement blindfolded and with a hat on my head, and the hat was taped. I heard that there were other people in the basement."

"I was taken from the police station with my hands tied tightly behind my back (my hands were fixed with handcuffs) and with closed eyes (with a hat and tape). Additionally, there was probably a bag over my head."

"They put me in a car, where there were three to four convoy men with me. They didn't beat me, but they forced me down and forbade me to raise my head, otherwise they would shoot me.

"When we were still driving around the area, I recognized every pothole, and then I got lost. They drove me for an hour, no less. They scared me, threatened to shoot me. The occupiers spoke Russian without an accent.

"We arrived somewhere where we could hear explosions. They pushed me out of the car, and the shooting began. They gave me a shovel and said, "Dig in, or your own people will kill you." I kicked the shovel away with my foot because my hands were handcuffed behind my back.

"They told me to lie down and not get up. I could hear the occupiers nearby, but I couldn't see anything. So for about the first day, I lay on the ground. It was very cold at night.

"The night passed. I no longer felt my hands, which were still handcuffed high up behind my back.

"The next day they took me to the first floor of the building (judging from the echo, it was not a one-story building, but rather an abandoned building). The wooden floor was rotting.

"They sat me in a chair. The first Russian military men who entered this building (there were three of them) threw me to the floor and beat me cruelly for ten minutes. They interrogated me about why I was there. I said, 'I don't know, probably because of the video.' They spoke Russian without an accent.

"Every hour, the Russian military changed, and a new group came in.

"I felt like I was sitting with my back to the window, heard gunfire, and understood that they could accidentally shoot me.

"The second shift did not beat me. They asked me why I was there. I said I didn't know. They gave me a cigarette (lifted the bag and put a cigarette in my mouth) and allowed me to sit further away from the window, leaning against the wall. They began to question me about our government, saying that Ukrainian soldiers castrate Russian soldiers. I asked if he had seen it himself, but the occupier did not answer.

"I had a nickname there—'Bayraktar.'

"They didn't give me any food or water.

"On the second day on the front line, in the evening, they started to mock and beat me harder.

"In the morning, at the beginning of the third day, I was thrown into a car—judging by the sounds, it was a Ural—and driven back to Velyka Oleksandrivka. At some point on the road, I realized it because I know all the roads well and can feel the potholes. It was still cold, it was morning. We drove for about an hour."

"When they dropped me off the Ural, I realized that I was near our police station. My eyes were still closed."

"One of the occupants asked, 'Where are you taking him?'"

"And another said, 'No, take him there.'"

"It was unclear where exactly."

"We got back in the Ural and drove for two hours. I heard us stopping two or three times to let convoys of heavy equipment pass. And they dropped me off in Nova Kakhovka—although I didn't know that at the time."

"There they took me, as it turned out later, to a police station. They hit me hard in the chest three times. There, they finally took off my handcuffs and threw me into a cell on the same first floor. They spoke without an accent, so I guessed they were Russians. There was another person in the cell."

"He started knocking on the door and asking if he could untie me. My cellmate removed the tape that had been on my head the whole time."

"The room had a window, but it was in a grille and too high up."

"My cellmate was chubby, about 1.78 meters tall. He said he was from Nova Kakhovka and had just been walking his dog when he was taken here. The two of us spent two hours together."

"Then they started periodically throwing others in with us. They let drug addicts go within a day."

"There was also a man, about sixty years old, with gray hair and bald spots, who was the elder of some village in the Kherson region on the left bank of the Dnipro River, but I can't remember the name of the village. They promised to release him on the same day as me. They were supposed to send us to Crimea on April ninth, as far as I could tell.

"There was also a military medic, a young man, thirty to thirty-five years old, tall and thin, from Odesa. He had already been brought back from Crimea. They caught him when he was evacuating the wounded."

"Sitting with the medic was a young man, twenty-five years old, a police officer from Mykolaiv. They were taken to Crimea together before they were put in the cell with me.

"There was a participant of the ATO in 2014 from a village near Kakhovka, Vitaliy Kuznetsov. He told me that when they arrived at the base, the military police didn't let them out, but took them to the commandant's office instead. There, they made them sign some papers, after which they were put on a bus and taken to another location, and from there they were taken to the border. They crossed the border and ended up in Crimea."

"We were fed very poorly. When one of the military personnel gave me some biscuits for everyone, he told me not to tell anyone else about it. We slept on the floor in a cell, with not enough space for everyone, and there were usually seventeen to eighteen people in the cell. The size of the cell was about three by four meters."

"We helped the police move furniture. For this task, they took me, the elder, and the person who was in the cell when I first arrived in Nova Kakhovka. That's when I met Nina, and I started asking to be taken outside, because it was very stuffy in the cell."

"Early on the morning of April 9, 2022, when we were taken out to the street, Nina told me that my wife was looking for me everywhere. I asked Nina to let me call my wife. She replied that she would try to reach my wife through the internet and tell her that I was alive. She also said that she would try to get me a certificate from the military commandant's office to release me. I no longer have this certificate, I gave it to our military personnel later at one of the Ukrainian checkpoints."

"A woman, apparently, worked and had a relationship with Serhiy Tomko from Nova Kakhovka, a former Ukrainian policeman who was later blown up in Nova Kakhovka. This woman said, 'They will take you out to the HES.'"[32]

"A woman from Nova Kakhovka helped get a certificate at the Russian military commandant's office."

"Two other civilians were taken with me, each about fifty years old. There were soldiers behind the wheel. I asked them to take me at least to Beryslav, and they did."

"From Beryslav to Urozhaine, some woman drove me. This woman gave me a phone to call my wife.[33]"

"At every checkpoint from Urozhaine to Bruskynske, they checked me, undressed me, looked for tattoos, and so on. In Bruskynske, there were already 'DPR-ites,' something like a check-

---

[32] HES is the acronym for the [Kakhovka] Hydroelectric Power station, which was destroyed by the Russian occupying forces on June 6, 2023.

[33] Editors' note: as we remember from [PAGE], Yan's wife called her husband's old number at about this time. The telephone was in the hands of Yan's captors. They used a widespread terror technique when they lied to her that they had already cut off the head of her husband.

point.[34] They offered to let me sleep there because I wouldn't make it ahead of curfew.

"They took me to a local woman to spend the night, but the woman was afraid to let me in, and the 'DPR-ites' took me to Davydiv Brid. These 'DPR-ites' (one of whom was bald and bearded without a mustache) let me call my wife, who was already in the Kirovohrad region. A photo of the 'DPR-ites' who provided assistance can be found on the Facebook page Vika Zolotar."

"These 'DPR-ites' expressed outrage at the behavior and crimes of Russian troops in villages (quote: 'They do such things in villages, dogs'). They also called their combatant, tall, gray, short haircut, and told him that Russian troops were abusing me, and I needed to be taken home. He was thinking about how to help me and looking for gasoline for this purpose. As a result, they drove me home on a cargo van. The 'DPR-ites' were also afraid to go where Russian troops were."

"I stayed home for two days in Velyka Oleksandrivka. Then I called Eduard Kovalevych, my employer, from someone else's phone."

"Eduard Volodymyrovych Kovalevych, a farmer, volunteer. He may have the contact information for a young policeman who was held in Nova Kakhovka with Yan Zolotar and a photo of a note."

When Yan Zolotar was released from captivity in Nova Kakhovka, the policeman gave Yan a note with the contact information for

[34] Fighters affiliated with the so-called Donetsk People's Republic (DPR).

his relatives so that Yan could inform them where he was. Later Eduard passed on the note.

"Eduard arranged for me to be smuggled out. I had a certificate from the Russian military command saying who I was and my Ukrainian passport, which my wife had hidden. Edik advised me not to show this passport to anyone while I was still under occupation after liberation. I drove into the controlled territory through Kazanka, showing my Ukrainian passport. In Kryvyi Rih, I was met by my employer, Kovalevych Eduard Volodymyrovych, and I brought my family from Kirovohrad Oblast to Kryvyi Rih on April 13, 2022."

"A month after I arrived in Kryvyi Rih, representatives of law enforcement agencies came to Kolachevsky Street. They were interested in whether I could identify collaborators from the police in Nova Kakhovka. Then they did not contact me again. The story of my captivity did not interest them."

Do Not Become a Torturer

<<Before meeting Hanna, I listen to her interview on the radio. She says, she no longer thinks of those who torture and kill us as humans. This is what changed for her after Feb 24. Previously, she tried to rationalize their behavior, now she gave up her attempts to understand.>>

Her earrings swing, her [hair?] blows in the wind. I say she looks like a mermaid.

"Mavka," Casanova corrects me.

"Right," I agree, because after all, Anya is definitely a Ukrainian character.

Mavka is a creature from Lesia Ukrainka's play *The Forest Song*. Anya keeps telling us about how she dreams about finally getting into nature after the victory. Maybe she'll live in a tree house, or just live for a couple of weeks in a tent. She would sleep and wake to drink coffee and then sleep again. Serhiy, her boyfriend, would probably be the one making the coffee. They are going to get married in September, she says, and then pauses to explain, "Not really marry, but just to register our marriage because of the war."

I ask what the difference is, and we inevitably get into this discussion.

"Documenting airstrikes is worse than documenting torture," Anya says. Both Vika and I stare at her.

"But it is," she insists, "when there's torture, there's a torturer. There's this person to hate and punish. It's different with airstrikes. You see all the mess, all the suffering and death. But who's guilty? Whom do you hate? The one who fired the artillery doesn't see all the pain. Perhaps he was following orders. The one who gave the order doesn't see all this pain either, he's probably following orders too."

I come back home and continue listening to the radio program from May 2022.

"Tell me about how Ukrainian Luhansk fights for Ukrainian Luhansk" [the journalist says].

She says she cannot help but try—because of hope. She finally has hope for Luhansk to be free.

"As one guy, a former prisoner from Luhansk, said, I'm tired of being a former prisoner, I'm tired of being a victim, and finally

I can fight for getting back." She says she will go back to her home in Luhansk, say farewell and then return to live in Kyiv. She'll remain in Kyiv then—not as a refugee but by choice.

[Editors' note: Victoria Amelina did not finish this chapter. What follows is her unedited notes.]

TRAINING ON TRAUMATIC MEMORY

Training on interviewing the traumatized

She begins the training on psychology by offering us water, coffee, and cookies to the meeting room. Then

Eyewitnesses are traumatized as well

Seen, heard, felt with my body

Because during the traumatic event people often

He tells what happened and then you check what you have seen, heard and felt

At some point you ask

Involvement

People want to be involved. They might not be eyewitnesses, but they will tell you they are. It is important

It's not a lie; it's how the memory of the traumatized works. That is why you always have to ask open-ended questions.

Hanna asks which category of the

-Family of the prisoners
-Family of the missing
-Victims and eyewitnesses of gender-based violence

Casanova adds a separate category: parents of murdered children.

We do not interview people younger than sixteen years old.

Family of the prisoners

One person talks to the witness, and the other records.

It is important

In the occupied territories relatives could not look for their missing relatives, yet understand that they missed a lot of time.

Their world is broken

First they go to the occupation administration and encounter something they are not used to

If they have a connection they google

If there is no connection, they hear rumors: prisoners get tortured

Stabilize the witness's condition before talking to them. How?

First you say you want to ensure if the person has fulfilled all the steps

You start counting

1. National Information Buro 1648
2. Police

You talk about the person's actions, not feelings. You ask them to write them down. You ensure that the person knows she has done or will do whatever she could.

Before the interview, ask for water and do not drink it. In fact, that is water for the one who is bringing it; she will need it, she just doesn't know it yet.

The interview should take place where a person can

First you talk to the person about her, her background, where she grew up,

Be attentive, and notice what is important for the person. Her work? Her garden? Her grandchildren? Remember those things as they give her strength. You will use these when necessary.

Our witnesses have to breathe. This might sound absurd, but it is important to monitor that they are breathing, and how. This will help you notice if

What do you do if there is nothing that gives you strength? Or maybe you haven't found it?

You never leave a witness who is panicking, hysterical, or crying. If you have promised to talk, you talk. This talk might not be that useful for the research, but you have to keep talking.

Between humanity and research, you choose humanity.

If you cannot see how she breathes, you are already too close to her trauma. She freezes from time to time.

Check that you feel your own body. If you yourself cannot feel the ground, you will not be able to help the witness. You ask for water. If you have a second glass of water, you drink with little sips.

it's not happening to me, derealization
You don't feel your body,

You may ask your colleague to finish the interview

She says she is

I want to ask her for an interview and I really want to hug her. But I know that she is a former prisoner of one of the Luhansk torture chambers too. I shouldn't be another torturer, she just taught me. So, of course, I don't hug Hanna. But I also don't ask her for an interview for the book. She taught me well. And she allows me to publish this chapter about her training for the novice war crimes researchers.

If Life Gives You Grenades, Not Lemons

Coming back from one of the missions, we stop to buy watermelons on the roadside. Casanova runs to the lady selling them, leaving us in the car. I am not sure I want a watermelon at all while Kherson is still occupied and my sister is there as a human shield.

We learn of Vitalik's death[35]

War Researchers' Hugs, War Researchers' Sense of Humor

[35] See the chapter "Evacuating New York."

I am on my way from the field mission, somewhere in the Dnipro region, when my phone rings and I freeze from the name on the screen. My sister-in-law, Iryna, is calling me from occupied Kherson. We talk often but she never calls without messaging me first. Besides, I've been just recording story after story about detention and torture[36]

Just a Local Producer at War

ON AUGUST 28, I JOIN A SMALL TEAM WORKING ON BODY IDENtification in Bucha. I am invited by Evhen Spirin, a well-known Ukrainian journalist, who before creating his own media used to work in a mortuary and so was able to volunteer in the Bucha morgue when all hands were needed to cope with the unprecedented number of bodies from the mass grave. Spirin is also my colleague, a writer: he described his work in the Luhansk morgue in a novel. I bet he now has so many stories that he could write a dozen novels. However, he doesn't seem to be able to write fiction now, just like me.

We meet in the Bucha city council building. It's a weekend, so the building is empty, but the security lets us in. The deputy mayor comes with her little son. He plays in the same room where we discuss the bodies and look at the big pile of papers containing names and photos. The photos are black-and-white, quite small and poorly printed, but I still worry every time the boy runs to his mother. Other participant[37]

The building, like Bucha itself, looks almost normal now as if nothing has happened. But it has.

[36] This sentence was left unfinished.

[37] This sentence was left unfinished.

Ilovaisk Memory

When foreign journalists helped Iryna Dovhan get out of Russian captivity in Donetsk, she had one question for them: "Does my Ukraine still exist?" The five days that she spent in the hell of Russian captivity in 2014 were hell for the Ukrainian soldiers and their families too. These were the last days of August, the days of the Ilovaisk tragedy.

Svitlana [Povalyaeva] and I agreed to meet at eleven o'clock on August 29, officially the Day of Remembrance of the Defenders of Ukraine. The day was chosen because August 29, 2014, was the day of the greatest Ukrainian losses during the Battle of Ilovaisk. Perhaps it is no longer the deadliest. Yet we are used to commemorating the fallen on that date. My meeting with Svitlana wasn't an interview but a meeting of friends. Yet with her permission I write about it.

I look through Svitlana's page to find her post about her son's body's extraction but run into an interview with a judge of the Ukrainian Supreme Court turned soldier. I think he might be an interesting character for my diary and start reading the interview. They call him Judge Dredd at war, just like the British character; it is his call sign. Roman Ratushny came up with it. Judge Dredd, the judge turned soldier, was Roman's commander. I close the article. Somehow it's easier to look for the pragmatic information on the dead bodies than to read this and realize once again what a beautiful person Svitlana's younger son was.

When I arrive at St. Michael's Cathedral, I don't see Svitlana, and I panic a bit. I feel out of place there among the women in black, who obviously came to honor their dead sons and husbands. There is no word to describe a feeling of shame for the fact that your family is alive, and there shouldn't be. Yet I have this unnamed feeling a lot.

"Where are you?" I ask Svitlana on the phone.

She's already waiting for me at the cafe table opposite the Cathedral and Wall of Remembrance.[38]

"Look, Roma is here. I kind of sit here with him," she says and nods in the direction of the wall.

I turn around to see her son's beautiful smiling face is in the center of a new composition of photos. I don't know what to say, I just look at the Wall of Remembrance. Svitlana looks too and smiles.

"I knew that he would be here. I know the guy who's responsible for the Wall and he asked which photo I'd like him to use. But can you imagine, they won't have space for all the dead here, will they?"

"No, they probably won't. But it's good that you can sit here near Roma."

"Yes, we are drinking coffee with Roma."

She thanks me for not being afraid to meet with her as she hears a lot that people don't know how to talk to a mother who has just lost a child.

"Why would I be afraid?" I pretend not to understand, though I do. The pain inside her is so strong; it's just that she is greater than the pain. She is able not just to live but to love, to give love despite suffering. But not everyone near her is equally strong.

She disappears inside the café to buy us coffee. So I sit there with Roman on the wall. Women come and go; there must be a long line in the café.

I wonder if I can ask Svitlana for a favor. Anna doesn't have

---

[38] The Wall of Remembrance of the Fallen for Ukraine is the wall of the Mykhailivsky Golden-Domed Monastery, which is covered with photos of the servicemen and women killed in action while defending Ukraine.

her husband's body to bury.[39] So maybe she would be glad to at least find his photo on this wall. However, they won't have space for all the dead here, will they? They probably won't. Who am I to influence who'll be here? Maybe Anna doesn't need it. What does she need? The body? A funeral? A grave to come to?

Svitlana comes back with two coffees. We chat about Buddhism and war. She tells me the stories of her retreats and I tell her how I was in Tibet and in the Himalaya temple made a wish on the day Euromaidan started.

"What did you wish for?" she asks

I didn't know what to wish for in 2013. I kind of had everything. I wanted to write books, but it would be stupid to ask Buddha about that; it was up to me to write. So I used a quote from *Roadside Picnic* by the Strugatsky brothers: "Happiness for everyone, free, and no one will go away unsatisfied."

I wonder how Svitlana feels about me quoting Soviet writers here and now. But she said that this is actually the perfect formula. I don't ask if she knows how the novel ends: a boy has to die as a sacrifice for the wish fulfillment.

We agree to go to Tibet together someday. Then Monika joins us. From Poland, she was a journalist until she became a war crimes researcher like me. Only she works for the Polish General Prosecutor's Office. She's just back from the front lines in the Donetsk region. She looks beautiful and talks quickly. She tells me how in March she decided to evacuate people from Irpin instead of just interviewing them where they were in cold and danger under the bridge. I think I should interview her for the book. This was the turning point for her: she decided to intervene, not to record. And now she is pursuing justice in Ukraine, like so many others.

---

[39] Anna has been featured above in the chapter "Evacuating New York"; she is the mother of the girl named Yasya, whom Victoria Amelina helped to evacuate to Ireland, and the wife of Vitaliy, featured in the previous chapter.

We don't set a date for the interview as we're both busy. And I don't ask Svitlana about adding Anna's husband to the Wall of Remembrance. I sip my coffee and do not dare to ask. The summer is over for me that day, just like it was for many Ukrainians on August 29, 2014.

PART III

Living the War

Shevchenko Liberated

It becomes clear that this is really happening only when, on September 10, I see a short video shot by the Ukrainian soldiers in Balakliya. They want to film the process of tearing down Russian propaganda from a billboard, something about Russia and Ukraine being united. But when the soldiers remove the Russian layer, it's not empty underneath. Underneath it is not some random advertisement. Underneath it is a portrait of the greatest Ukrainian poet, Taras Shevchenko, and one of his poems.[1] And what a poem it is. Here I quote it in translation by John Weir:

And glory, mountains blue, to you,
In ageless ice encased!
And glory, freedom's knights, to you,
Whom God will not forsake.
Keep fighting—you are sure to win!
God helps you in your fight!
For fame and freedom march with you,
And right is on your side!

Destroyed Bridges and Greek Cheese

[Editors' note: The editorial group found a more detailed description of the events below in an older version of the manuscript. This fuller draft is included

[1] Taras Shevchenko (1814–1864) is the poet at the top of the Ukrainian literary canon, an artist, and a key figure of Ukrainian national revival. Born a serf, he was bought out in his early twenties but enjoyed freedom for less than a decade. In 1847, he was jailed, sentenced to exile and compulsory military service for his inflammatory poetry which criticized the Russian Empire.

below. The abridged fragments saved in the last working copy of the manuscript are in fragment B of appendix I.]

<<The Ukrainian Army liberated Izyum on [September 10, 2022]. On the same day, Casanova wrote in the work chat: "Who wants to join the mission to the liberated Izyum?" Damn, I think, as I'm going to be at the book fair in Gothenburg, Sweden, speaking on an amazing panel with my fellow Ukrainian writers Oksana Zabuzhko, Natalka Sniadanko, and the former political prisoner and writer Stanislav Aseyev. But more than anything I want to be on the first Truth Hounds mission to the liberated town of Izyum. What if I cancel my participation in the book fair? Would the organizers and colleagues understand? I write to one of the co-organizers, Sofia Cheliak, and get back a video message I'm afraid to open: it seems like she might be yelling at me. But Sofia isn't yelling at me—or maybe she is, exclaiming with a remarkable passion: "Of course you should go to Izyum. This might be the most important thing you do!"

I smile. It feels so good to be understood. I cancel my trip to Gothenburg, Sweden, and plan my trip to Izyum, Ukraine.

The elegant suitcase and dresses will have to wait. I pack the backpack I bought for hiking but have used for my trips to the war zone since 2014, first as a writer and now as a war crimes researcher. I know there is no electricity, running water, or heating in Izyum yet. So I pack snacks, candies for kids, warm clothes, a sleeping bag, and three power banks. I'm ready to face both the horror of what I might see, and the expected discomfort of the trip to a war zone. We put our helmets and body armor into the trunk of Cucumber, the green Volkswagen Transporter, and another Truth Hounds car, a Subaru, which oddly seems not to have a nickname, and set off. I'm in the passenger seat next to Casanova, hoping to talk or, rather, to listen to her talking on the way to the Kharkiv region.

But she isn't talkative.

"Have you been to Izyum before?" I ask.

Yes, she has been in Izyum a lot: she had a family there, and used to visit every summer as a kid.

"Do you know how they are? The family . . ."

No, she doesn't. I write down the street where she lived.

In the afternoon, we stop in Kharkiv to meet with the prosecutors. They are glad to get our help. There are too many war crimes. The corridors in the building in which we meet are empty: all the prosecutors are in the field in Izyum. He cannot help us coordinate with them as there is still no connection. He wishes us good luck. We drive through the equally empty Kharkiv streets farther east.

After the hectic driving[2]

As soon as we turn off the car headlights, the darkness around us is complete, one of the most perfect darknesses I have ever seen. And while no one can see me in it, I take a moment to look up and realize: I still see the same stars that were there on February 24 when it all began, but I'm east of Kharkiv, and the Ukrainian army is in the middle of a counteroffensive.

"Is there a chance we can have dinner in your restaurant?" I ask, feeling that the question might sound weird and out of place.

"Yes. I'll see what we have in the kitchen, but yes, of course you can," the man replies, as if realizing that he now has customers, regular customers, not hungry refugees fleeing the war.

We enter the restaurant which creates an impression of a dining room in a private mansion belonging to a happy family with good taste. Everything from the black-and-white drawings on the walls to the books on a shelf seem to be in its place.

---

[2] This sentence was left unfinished.

The host disappears into a kitchen and comes back with the news rather than amenu:

"We can offer you our Greek salad, but only four portions, unfortunately." We look at each other as there are six of us, and then we all nod. Four portions of salad are better than none. But the host keeps talking about the salad: the feta and the olives are directly from Greece, imported specially for this restaurant before the full-scale invasion. These are the last Greek olives he has, and the last Greek feta. The olive oil is also from Greece, of course. How about wine? He still has some wine, not the very last bottle, but one of the last ones. And how about red wine? He only has red. But tomorrow, he can cook us fish. They will just go fishing, and so their signature trout from the Dinets River will be ready for tomorrow's dinner.

All this gourmand chatter sounds surreal in this place that we hardly found amid the burned houses, destroyed bridges, and dark woods full of soldiers. But as the four portions of the Greek salad arrive and the host joins us at the table for a glass of wine, I realize what this chattering was about. Bila Khata, or White House, used to be no ordinary place, but a sincere attempt to enjoy every bit of life in the most exquisite human ways: by watching the Ukrainian sunsets, tasting the trout from Dinets, feta cheese from Greece, and wine from Italy, fishing, listening to bird songs, and discussing art with friends. Then the full-scale war started.

I leave the table hungry, but sure that I just have eaten the best Greek salad in my life. I'll come back after the war, when the import from Greece to the Kharkiv region is resumed, to order a portion of salad for myself. Heading to my room through the yard, I stop and turn off the flashlight to look at the stars. The world is connected and eternal, with olives and argonauts from Athens, with wine from vineyards in Italy, with the stone scarab somewhere in Luxor, Egypt, fulfilling the wish of my son, slowly and yet inevitably. I turn the flashlight back on. Dogs bark somewhere in the distance, and I suddenly feel insecure in the dark. Can the lost Russian soldiers be in this dark? Well, perhaps they could. In the Chernihiv region, people kept running into them, dirty, disoriented but aggressive, months after deoccupation.

I got a separate room, choosing it randomly. To my surprise, it is a two-floor suite with a huge bed and a view of a small private pool. It's completely dark outside, but I see the pool in the light of my small headlamp.

"I'm fine. Staying in a luxury hotel with a pool," I message my mom, who is always worried about me, and fall asleep, too exhausted to read or write anything down for my diary.

I wake up to the birds singing outside, go downstairs and pull aside the curtain to see the view in the daylight. The terrace is dirty, the white fabric of the deck chairs has turned gray, and there is a dead frog in the swimming pool.>>

We planned the mission hastily, and I'll quote part of the mission plan here:

Preliminary Mission Plan: Izyum, Balakliya, Sviatohirsk
September 20–27, 2022

Team	Casanova Roman Avramenko (Fisher) Victoria Amelina (Marusya) Anastasia Kryshtanovych (Bulka) Oleksandr Volchansky (Quiet) Oleksiy Starynets (Olstar)
Numbers of Mission Phones	XXX XXX XXX XXX XXX XXX XXX XXX
Location	Kharkiv Oblast: Izyum city, Balakliya city, Verbyvka village, Kapytolivka village
Mission Goals	Initial screening of the situation regarding possible war crimes: a) extrajudicial executions, forced disappearances, civilian capture/kidnapping, torture, sexual and gender-based violence

Mission Goals	b) regarding shelling: the death and injury of civilians during shelling, destruction of civilian infrastructure and specially protected objects, use of human shields, etc. c) destruction of cultural heritage Search for information on potential victims and survivors, contact with witnesses, etc. Documentation of violations of international humanitarian law with a focus on identifying potential perpetrators: units that exercised control in the occupied territory, leaders, individuals; determining the location of military units, equipment; location of places of detention, mass graves, etc., following the Truth Hounds methodology Meeting with representatives of law enforcement and investigative agencies in Kharkiv Preparation of a narrative report based on the mission's findings
Priority Cases	**IZYUM** Russian occupiers shelled Kremenets Hill in Izyum and damaged monumental stone sculptures, stone babas, which date back to the ninth through thirteenth centuries.[1] **BALAKLIYA** On February 26 and 27, an airstrike targeted the city hospital in Balakliya. Torture chambers. **VERBIVKA** Verbivka, Balakliya district, Kharkiv region. Balakliya City Council's Verbivka School, located at 68 Tsentralna Street. On September 14, information appeared on the website Suspilne Kharkiv stating that the Russian army, upon leaving Balakliya (around September 7 to 9, 2022), destroyed a school in the neighboring village of Verbivka. **KAPYTOLIVKA** The abduction of Volodymyr Vakulenko.
Background	On February 26, 2022, in Volokhiv Yar, there was a shooting at a civilian bus resulting in eight deaths and fourteen survivors. The driver was killed by the Russians. **IZYUM** February 27, 2022—Shelling February 28, 2022—Airstrike on residential buildings

[1] Stone babas, also called kurgan stelae, are anthropomorphic stone statues found in the steppe belt of Europe and Asia. Ukrainian stone babas were erected by Scythian and Sarmatian tribes between the seventh and fourth centuries BCE and by Turkic peoples between the sixth and thirteenth centuries CE.

Background	March 3, 2022—Stepan Maselsky, the head of the Izyum District State Administration, stated: "Rocket and aerial strikes are constantly being carried out on cities and villages in the Izyum district! After Balakliya, Kunye, Vesele, Volokhiv Yar, overnight and now during the day, airstrikes are being conducted on Izyum, and a school in Horokhovatka has been bombed. During the past night, we had 9 casualties, including 2 children." March 29, 2022—Report of thirty-plus people trapped under the rubble of a multistory building. Photos show a large crater in the schoolyard and the destroyed part of the hospital opposite the school. April 3, 2022—In Balakliya, the driver of one of the evacuation buses for patients and staff from the hospital was killed in shelling. According to preliminary information, there were no patients or staff on the buses as they had not reached the hospital yet. March 26, 2022—In Balakliya, Russians detained the deputy mayor, Serhiy Poltorak, and the head of the Civil Protection and Interaction with Law Enforcement Agencies Department, Oleh Bludov. **KAPYTOLIVKA** According to Iryna Novitska as of September 18, 2022: "My ex-husband, Volodymyr Vakulenko, was arrested twice. Later, he was allegedly taken to Belgorod (his elder son mentioned the date of April 12), and since then, nothing is known for certain. At the commandant's office, the parents were told to 'look for him in the ground.' Volodymyr's elder son tried to find his father in the Belgorod prison, but he was driven away, and they threatened to arrest him."

Our plan for the Izyum area is too big:

Shelling of the Polovetsky Babas complex after March 15, 2022[3]
Shelling of the World War Two memorial during the period from March 1 to an unknown date in 2022
Shelling of the obelisk
Shelling of the chapel
Interview with the chief paramedic of the ambulance service
Remote mining, shelling, cluster munitions
Filming of the destruction around the central square
And last but not least, Vakulenko's disappearance

In Izyum, Fisher and Bulka talk to a local ambulance doctor. We talk less and less with the owner [of the resort].[4] Our mood changes.

During March 2022, the emergency medical workers faced challenging conditions. Because they could not use vehicles on the roads filled with debris, they resorted to carrying and transporting the wounded on stretchers. As time passed, they began repairing the vehicles to resume their operations. The roads were heavily littered with shrapnel, making it nearly impossible to navigate. Despite the difficulties, they made efforts to document and record information about all the injured and sick individuals they attended to, although most of these records were kept in the main

[3] This is a reference to the stone babas near the city of Izyum on Mount Kremenets, which were shelled by the Russian forces in spring 2022. One of the eight statues was completely destroyed, others damaged. Polovtsi is the Ukrainian name of the Cumans, the Turkic nomadic people which lived in the steppes of Asia and Europe between the ninth and fourteenth centuries.

[4] During the next week (September 20 to 27, 2022), the Truth Hounds team documented war crimes in the Kharkiv region and returned to the resort in the evenings using it as their base.

hospital department. The team worked tirelessly; it consisted of three workers, one trauma specialist, three to four nurses, several paramedics, and some support staff, totaling around ten people.[5]

"Around March 15, 2022, I arrived at the hospital premises with a patient who had suffered a severe open head injury caused by a mine explosion. As I was about to leave, I noticed a drone hovering over the hospital. Suddenly, an explosion occurred at the spot where I had been standing, followed by another explosion as I was moving away. When I returned home, I discovered that all four tires of my vehicle had been deflated.

The trauma specialist, Yuriy Yevhenovych Kuznetsov, worked tirelessly without rest, displaying true heroism. I stayed behind because, firstly, there was nowhere to escape, as volunteer buses only accommodated women and children. Secondly, at that time, there were only three of us, and others would come and help as well.

Toward the end of April and the beginning of May 2022, we climbed up Kremenets Hill to identify the locations where the injured had been. There were instances where Russian Federation cluster munitions hit the ambulance vehicles. The river crossing over the Siverskyi Dinets River was established in May 2022, but it took some time for emergency vehicles to be allowed through the established crossing. In the meantime, we had to rely on bicycles for transportation. Civilians were not permitted to cross the river through the designated crossing for about a month.

The number of people with traumatic amputations was so high that they eventually stopped counting. There was a shortage of personnel available to work, and there was nowhere else for me

[5] Below the author includes the testimony of a medical professional from Izyum.

to go. I did not want to go to Russia, so I continued to assist people on this side of the city. During the occupation, I lost twenty-four kilograms due to the lack of food and water."

Torture Chambers in Balakliya—Casanova III

TO GO ON THIS MISSION, I CANCELED MY PARTICIPATION IN the Gothenburg Book Fair.

Oleksandr Kharlats was short and stout, and limped on one leg; he walked with a cane. He had a short haircut and was around forty-five to forty-seven years old. He had already been in the cell for seven days. The reason for his arrest was that his son serves/served in the armed forces.

Before his arrest, he used to drink heavily. Only in the cell did his hands stop trembling.

"We had a clock in our cell," [says Oleksandr]. "It was left behind by someone who was there before us. It was an electronic clock. We could look at the corridor through the screen, like a mirror. There were also clocks in the third cell. No one knew about our clocks. There were two cigarette butts. We had lighters and a box of matches. The lid from a can could be used for something."

He was told that a man from Savyntsi, who at that time had been in custody longer than anyone else, would come out, "and we will leave you as a talisman." According to Oleksandr, the previous "talisman" spent over ninety days in the police station.

"To my left, there was a person who hit me with a police baton. They put a wire in my hand and said, 'If you drop it, we will hit you.' Then came another shock with electricity. The wire fell, no questions asked, and I was struck with a stick in the chest area. They wrapped the wire around my hand so I wouldn't drop it. They applied a ten-to-fifteen-second electric shock. They started asking questions, just like when they detained me near the car and took me to the police station.

What is the general mood in the unit?
Who is Loboda?
What connections do you have with the Armed Forces or "TRO"?[6]
Who did you call?

"They were interested in why we didn't take the Russian humanitarian aid and who gave the order not to accept help from them."

Oleh Hyrya is from Balakliya, the 110th district. He loved reading. There was a book by Lev Tolstoy in his cell, which he read in three days. He was arrested near the railway tracks, where he went to download an e-book because he could "catch" the internet there. He was spotted by the military. After inspecting the content of his phone, they found a video with a Russian column, and that's why they took it away. Initially, he was held in the commandant's office, on the premises of the Baldruk printing house, 14 Zhovtneva Street, Balakliya, Kharkiv Oblast, coordinates 49.4522256, 36.8427841. In the commandant's office, both men and women were held together. Everyone used a bucket as a toilet. After that, Oleh was transferred to the cell in the police station. When they took Oleh out of the com-

[6] TRO is the abbreviation for the Ukrainian term "terytorialna oborona" (territorial defense forces).

mandant's office, they put a mask on his head and drove him around the city in a van. He thought they were taking him for execution and was very surprised when they brought him into the cell in the police station, which was located across the street from Baldruk.

[Editors' note: The following excerpt was pasted by Victoria Amelina into the last working copy of the manuscript from the narrative report of the mission.]

During the period 20–26 September, 2022 the Truth Hounds mission visited the Kharkiv region.

Collected: 29 signed testimonies
Kilometers covered during the mission: 2700_
Days of documenting: 6
Documenters (nicknames): Fisher, Marusya, Casanova, Quiet, Bulka, Olstar
Vehicles: Dovhonosyk [Weevil], Cucumber

During the mission field team documented the following alleged war crimes all happened in settlements: Izyum, Kapytolivka, Balakliya, Verbivka, Ivanivka, Vyshneva, Bryhadyrivka, Savyntsi.

Indiscriminate attacks:
Izyum, March 2 to 10, 2022. High intensity continuous Russian shelling and airial bombing of the right-bank part of the city. Many dozens killed, many buildings destroyed. City hospital's two surgeries severely damaged, policlinics burned down. City center severely damaged;
Izyum, April 4, 2022, cluster attack;
Izyum, July 28, 2022, cluster attack, seven people wounded;
Izyum, distant anti-personnel mines planting.

Attack on cultural heritage:
Izyum, March 2022—shelling the World War Two memorial;
Izyum, July 2022—shelling the polovets idols at the Kremenets Mountain.[7]

Enforced disappearance: Balakliya, March to April 2022. Four witnesses testified that their relatives were captured by Russian forces at the time and disappeared.

Unlawful detaining: Balakliya, March to August 2022. Thirteen witnesses testified about at least seventy-six persons who were captured and detained or captured and disappeared in Balakliya OTH[8] during the occupation. Two of the witnesses were also victims detained and tortured in the basement of "Avtopark" (autobase in Balakliya 49.457086,36.903966); four of them were detained in the building that had formerly housed the police department in Balakliya ROVD[9] (Balakliya, Zhovtneva-str., 33) and testified about the another one place of captivity: the basement of Baldruk, local typography (Balakliya, Zhovtneva-str., 14).

Verbivka, March to August 2022. Due to three witness statements in Verbivka, Russian forces used the children's cloakroom in the Verbivsky Lyceum (Verbivka, Tsentralna-str., 68) as a place of detention and captured there at least five persons.

Kapytolivka, March 24, 2022. The Ukrainian writer Volody-

[7] See note 62.

[8] OTH stands for *obiednana terytorialna hromada* in Ukrainian, meaning a united territorial community, a special unit of administrative division in Ukraine from 2015 to 2020.

[9] "ROVD" is the abbreviation for rayonnyi otdel vnutrennikh del (in Russian), meaning a district police department.

myr Vakulenko was captured by representatives of Russian forces and disappeared, probably was murdered.

Izyum, September 1, 2022. One person was captured by representatives of Russian forces and was detained with two other persons in the former police building.

-Willful killing:

-Izyum, May 7, 2022. One person, a pathologist, was shot near morgue by a Russian combatant, who represented himself as Akhmet, Kadyrov's nephew.[10]

-Balakliya, April 3, 2022. One person, the driver, who had to take part in the evacuation of Balakliya central hospital, was shot near the checkpoint by Russian combatants, probably representatives of so-called LPR forces.

Tortures and inhuman treatment:

Balakliya: Four persons testified that people detained in the former police building in Balakliya ROVD (Balakliya, Zhovtneva-str., 33) and Baldruk, local typographers (Balakliya, Zhovtneva-str., 14) were tortured (beaten with baseball bats, tortured with the use of electricity, making cuts in their skin, etc.), treated in inhuman conditions of detention

Two persons testified that people detained in the basement at the territory of "Avtopark" (autobase in Balakliya 49.457086,36.903966) were tortured (beaten), suffered from hunger, dehydration, cold temperature and long-term binding of limbs.

[Editors' note: The following two paragraphs present the translation into English of an excerpt from a witness interview that was pasted into the manuscript.]

[10] Ramzan Kadyrov (b. 1976) is the current head of the Chechen Republic.

Then the russian soldiers came three days later to my house, to agree about typesetting, they came in to drink some water and I later gave the glass to the local authorities for the prints.

The russians planned to print 60,000 newspapers a month. They wanted me to help them with typesetting. They had already set up barracks where there used to be rolls of paper.

They wanted to fix the risograph printer and print something. I fixed it, but we needed ink and printing drums, but in the first days of the war we had already taken them home and hidden them. Therefore, I told them that they should find whoever stole the drums and ink and then I could launch the work. Everything was turned upside down, they believed that one of them had done it. They asked me what was needed and then said they would go find it. But they didn't come back after that and didn't ask anything. I was in Balakliya until the end of the occupation and had no more contact after that with russian soldiers.

(Not) Buried in Izyum

[Editors' note: This section is based on the testimony of the deputy director of a funeral agency in Izyum. It was found by the editors in the older versions of the manuscript. The original testimony is in fragment C of appendix I.]

<<*So I put the recorder on the coffin.*

"There were days when we buried nineteen people.
There were days when we buried seven or only three.
There were even days when no one died."

Izyum was occupied for 163 days, from April 1 till September 10, 2022.

Tamara had lived in Izyum since 1982. And since the beginning of the invasion she had been acting director of this funeral agency. She and her team had to be in the Shakespeare cemetery everyday at noon. Then, when there were more deaths, they started meeting at 9:00 a.m. near the administration building. It was their duty.

Besides their agency there was a team of volunteers, organized by the occupiers; these were called 200s[11] and they collected bodies around town. People would bury their relatives and neighbors in their yards and the 200s would rebury them. Only Tamara's team and the 200s were allowed on the other side of the Dinets River. At first, they had to carry the bodies, as the bridge was ruined, but then the occupiers built a crossing over the river, so it became easier. Both teams, Tamara's and the 200s, collected notes about the deceased. They buried the body under a number and entered the number and the name of the deceased into a journal. They tried to do a good job, although they weren't paid; that was not the point. The investigators have her laptop with the journal now.

Three bodies with gunshot wounds to the head were found in Kapytolivka in June. The perpetrators tried to burn and hide them; Tamara's team then had to rebury those victims at the Shakespeare Cemetery.

A drunk Chechen killed a forensic expert, a friend of Tamara's. She didn't get to bury him, as the body was taken to Belgorod, Russia. No one has seen it since then. She says Valya might know, as she lives near the mortuary where it all happened. We'll find Valya, but she knows nothing. We hug her, as she has lost her son. Valya will give me a bag full of walnuts.

---

[11] Cargo 200 (Ukrainian: *dvokhsoti*, two-hundreds) is a Soviet code phrase used for the transportation of military casualties. In post-Soviet states, "200s" has become a euphemism for killed in action.

Russians shot at a car with civilians, including her friend Tetyana. All Tetyana's family died, and Tetyana is in Russia.

Her nephew was arrested, held, and beaten.

Russian soldiers shot a girl. Her last name is in the journal, but the journal is with the investigators, so she can't tell us.

She names all the bases of Russians in Izyum: the schools, the kindergartens, and the city administration.

"I'm Russian," she says, as if challenging us.

"No, you sound like someone who chose to be a Ukrainian. We are a political nation, so it is your choice."

She names all the food she bought in the last eight weeks before the deoccupation as thoroughly as she listed the bases: one kilo of rice, one and a half kilos of sugar, two cans of stew, one canned fish.

She was questioned by law enforcement, but only about the mass grave, not about other things that happened. She doesn't call it a mass grave, of course.>>

[Editors' note: The following section was found in the older version of the manuscript. What follows is the testimony of Valentyna, who used to work in the Izyum morgue.]

If you find a woman who has worked in Izyum's only morgue for the last forty-one years, what war crime would you ask her about? Valentyna stayed in Izyum during the occupation. She didn't always come to work during that time, but she tried to survive, cooking on a fire near her apartment building like many others in town. But since April 20, she has been told she has to appear at work as usual. Too many were dying, so the occupation authorities needed all hands on deck. They weren't going to pay her, though, but to give her some food from time to time. However, she wasn't in position to negotiate. Walking to work for the first time in a while, she saw human bodies scattered on the streets; they died from shelling, she thinks. Although Valentyna is not a doctor, but a laboratory assistant, she still has a great deal of experience with death.

Before she was summoned to work in April, only the funeral agency on Kyivska Street buried people.

"Without any expertise," Valentyna emphasizes.

To her, it seems quite obvious, why after the liberation all the bodies buried during the occupation should be exhumed. One of the foundations of peaceful lives is knowing the reason for each and every death. Registering birth and death properly, we gain a sense of control over life and death matters. But also, in the case of violence, we have a chance to react properly.

[Editors' note: What follows is the translation into English of Valentyna's testimony.]

Fedir Havrylovych Zdebsky, born 1951, was not on duty; he was home, as there were no ferries running since the bridge over the Siverskyi Dinets had been destroyed.

On May 5, we were working with the pathologist Serhii Valentynovych Mazhukhin, age sixty-three, born 1959, when Fedir Havrylovych Zdebsky came in. As it happened, the Russian soldiers had brought in the bodies of Ukrainian soldiers, and the characteristic smell was already coming from the bodies.

Zdebsky came as soon as a bridge had been erected, at 10:00 or 11:00 a.m. on May 5. He said that he wanted to discharge certificates for the Ukrainian soldiers. Six of the bodies had no documents on them. There were seventeen soldiers in total. Blast injuries.

He took all the Ukrainian soldiers' documents and the morgue log. He said that he would note them all down in the postmortem report. The head of the Russian mortuary, who declined to give his surname, said "Ivanov." When the certificates are ready, we will bury them in a mass grave and then turn your certificates over to the Ukrainians.

We arranged it with Zdebsky for May 7 at 12:00, here at the morgue at 2 Zalikarniana Street.

Zdebsky arrived at 12:00 in a car, a black-and-gray Volkswagen (more black, and shiny); he drove up and stopped in the parking lot as usual. He parked his car and walked in the entrance of the pathology building. I put out a chair for him and the three of us sat there: me, Fedir Havrylovych Zdebsky, and Serhii Valentynovych Mazhukhin.

This "Ivanov" came by, took the certificates, and left. As soon as he left, a Russian soldier of Chechen ethnicity came running in.

He introduced himself in Russian: "My name is Akhmet and I'm from Chechnya. I'm related to Kadyrov. Whose is this Volkswagen? I'm twenty-six, I've been at war all my life, I've nearly died four times, but I've always been lucky. Hand over the car."

Zdebsky said he would not hand it over since he was disabled (he has a prosthesis instead of a left leg); his car had special manual control since he couldn't pump with his feet.

I explained that Zdebsky was in the process of finishing up the log. Zdebsky offered to Akhmet, the Russian soldier, a lift when he finished work so that he wouldn't take away his car.

Akhmet started telling us that they had come to free us.

I said that we had been living a good life before this, whereas now I had spent two months sheltering underground, cooking over an open fire; that the radiators at home had now frozen; and that my grandson was sixteen years old.

In response, Akhmet said that he had been sleeping on the soggy ground because of us, and then said the following: "I see that these three are from *that* side. We'll take these three away for processing." Obviously, he meant that we weren't pro-Russia, but pro-Ukraine, and so all of us had to be punished.

I said that we had a peaceful life before the invasion, we worked hard, and everything was absolutely fine.

Akhmet asked: "So who's to blame for me having to sleep on the damp ground?" Obviously, he was referring to having to stay in the trenches.

In response, Fedir Havrylovych Zdebsky answered him in Ukrainian: "You're to blame. You're the one who came to my land, you came and occupied my Izyum."

Akhmet threatened him, boasting that he was carrying the rifle of the deputy police chief.

All this took place in the pathology building.

Then Akhmet started having a go at us, complaining about how bad his life was in Izyum.

I saw Akhmet fire two shots into the ceiling. Then one of his comrades, another Chechen, ran over and pushed Akhmet away from the door, which gave me the chance to clamber out onto the street and run toward the maternity hospital to call the other Russian soldiers to get them to stop their colleague, perhaps. But the Russian soldiers did not agree to come with me to the pathology building, saying that they would go and report this to their superiors. These soldiers had the Russian flag on their sleeve. They ran over to the medical college where the Russian leadership was then based.

Then I heard many shots. It was only later that I saw Akhmet shoot four times at the ceiling and four times at Fedir Havrylovych Zdebsky.

I saw our chief doctor, Oleksandr Andriiovych Bozhkov, born in 1950, coming over.

Bozhkov grabbed the soldiers, saying, "Let's go, something's happening in the morgue." I also returned with them to the pathology building. Akhmet sent Mazhukhin to get me, saying, "Where's that woman, the one talking about the smashed windows and frozen radiators. Go and bring her here." He probably wanted to kill me as well.

I returned to the pathology department with two Russian soldiers, O. A. Bozhkov, and S. V. Mazhukhin, but by then there was nobody in the building, except the murdered Zdebsky.

About twenty minutes later, Russian "investigators" arrived; they were based on the crossroads in the traffic police building. They were young men, around forty years old. There were two of these "investigators"; one of them said he was from the St. Petersburg region and worked in the military prosecutor's office there and had two sons aged eleven and twelve. The other one was called Sasha; he was the younger of the two. There were wearing their "mottled" uniform.

The investigators said that he would "be held responsible," that people "had already been sent for him and they will arrest him."

Akhmet also took Mazhukhin's documents—his military ID and passport. Mazhukhin had been given those documents that same day.

Their car, a big BMW, had MILITARY COMMANDANT'S OFFICE written on it. As you drive, it goes very smoothly (high ground clearance—documenter's note).

Mazhukhin said to me: "Akhmet sent me to Illichna Street; he took the documents too. I didn't see him kill Zdebsky." Later Mazhukhin said that after examining Zdebsky's body, he had been shot twice in the stomach and twice in the neck.

Mazhukhin was still there when Akhmet started brutally beating Zdebsky, especially with his rifle butt. First, he hit him around the back of the head, then punched him in the face, and then did the same with his rifle butt. Finally, he kicked him in the face.

The murdered Fedir Havrylovych Zdebsky had worked his

whole life as a forensic medical expert. He was seventy years old. Time of death: around 1 p.m.

The investigators wrote everything down and took us back in their Military Commandant's Office car at about 21:00.

The murdered Zdebsky's body lay in our morgue on May 8 and 9, and on the tenth it was taken away by the Russians. A mobile refrigerator came and took away his body to Belgorod, Russia, I was informed by the same investigators from the military commandant's office.

Valentyna Ivanivna Solovyova later told me how he also terrorized people in the basement of the police department. Valentyna fed the people who lived in the basement.

The occupying commandant's office took away all of Fedir Havrylovych's documents and cards and then said they would take them all to Belgorod.

Fedir Havrylovych Zdebsky, born May 29, 1951, resided at 6 Vasnietsova Street, Izyum. His first wife and daughter lived in Kharkiv. His daughter was severely disabled.

Vitalii Viktorovych Borchan phoned her from Mount Kremenets. She picked up the phone and said, "Oh, Fedya, you haven't phoned in a while!" At which Vitalii said, "I'm sorry, Alla Ivanovna," which is how we informed her of Fedir's death.

Valentyna Kurylo, the victim's partner, left Izyum on April 13, 2022.

Consequences suffered by the interviewee:

After what I had experienced, the first nights following I would wake up and not fall back asleep until about 5:00 a.m. I cried at night. Fedir Havrylovych and I had worked together for forty years. He always helped everyone. I cannot forget how he was killed.

There were bodies in the morgue showing signs of violent death, but no blast wounds.

We had a tied-up corpse in the morgue, a drowning victim,

his arms and legs tied together. He was about forty years old. His last name began with B.

Then there were three corpses in the forest, gunshot wounds to the head and one to the chest (blunt trauma to the chest, broken ribs). They were buried in Shakespeare Cemetery. On March 22, 2022, their relatives came and identified them. One of them, a younger man, was not identified.

I did not examine the bodies; they were examined by Dr. Mazhukhin. As I'm a nurse, I only took notes that the doctor asked me to in the reports.

When I was sheltering underground, my joints became inflamed because of the cold. People were not receiving their pensions and there were no working cash machines. There were people who somehow would cross the checkpoints to withdraw their pensions, although with a commission: they would come back with 7,000 instead of 10,000 [hryvnia], for instance.

Among the 420 we saw, I estimate that about three hundred people died of natural causes (from illness or old age). And the other 120 died violent deaths, including those with blast wounds.[12]

While I talk to Valentyna, Roman [Avramenko] films the building exterior and interior, including the four bullet holes in the ceiling.

Looking for Vakulenko

So this is it, Kapytolivka, the letter "K" in my colleague's name. I have never been here before but I've already

[12] As a result of her mission to Izyum, Victoria Amelina wrote the poem "Testimonies."

looked at pictures: we passed what friends called Volodymyr's little garden, "sadok," several trees he planted along the roadside. The trees are thin, just like Volodya's body was. A couple of them got damaged, run over by a Russian military convoy perhaps. Who cares about trees in a war? We pass Volodymyr's house, not recognizing it. We look for the address of Volodymyr's mother, which [Volodymyr's ex-wife] Iryna [Novitska] has given me. Olena, or rather Lena—people in the village all know her by the Russian variant of her name—lives in one of the few five-story buildings in Kapytolivka. People call this small area "little houses," or "domiki," although these are the tallest buildings in the village.

"It's the twenty-fourth, exactly half a year after Vovka is no more. I have it recorded, a black day," he [Volodymyr Vakulenko Sr.] says, pointing at the wall calendar, a bizarre one with a tiger and dollars perhaps symbolizing awaited prosperity in 2022. Two dates are in black pen.

He was born in 1949 in Russia. His parents were both sent to Tula. His father was guilty of being a POW in the Winter War. His mother was guilty of being[13]

AS HIS FATHER WAS BECAME A PRISONER OF WAR IN 1939, IN the POW in Finnish war in 1939 and he st

He lived in Tula, then in

Mother was born in Lyubotyn, Kharkiv region, taken by Germans as an ostarbeiter, and was punished for that.

Since 1958 he lives in the same house

Till March 5,

---

[13] This sentence was left unfinished.

Five people came. He calls Bes "gestapo." He took away his smartphones.

Two of them had pistols.

slippers, sweater, jeans

On March 22 he was interrogated in the houses on Luhova. Everyone knows these houses in Kapytolivka now: Russian occupiers from LPR lived there. He calls these houses gestapo.

He had a ringtone, "Putin Khuylo,"[14] but Volodymyr Senior is reluctant to pronounce the second word; he says "Putin KH." He worries that he doesn't remember well as too much time has passed, half a year. Others will interview him even later. He will start

On March 24, they woke up and started cooking outside the house for [Volodymyr's son] Vital'ka.

On April 4, the house where Volodymyr Senior has lived since 1958 was hit.

[Editors' note: What follows is a rough draft of the intended section on the recovery of Volodymyr Vakulenko's diary.]

I was not afraid to walk in his garden, although the land near Izyum was full of landmines. But I was terrified of not being able to find his diary. Too many Ukrainian manuscripts have been destroyed for us to lose even one more. But Volodymyr's father and I did find the diary that day. So now, I can quote Volodymyr's words, his last note, made on March 21, 2022:

> Sometimes, dropping off for an hour or two, I have dreams. During the first period, I dreamed of numbers, old calendars, friends, I also dreamed of our boys fighting, dreamed I was

[14] "Putin Is a Dickhead" ("Putin Khuylo") is a mocking song popularized in Ukraine by football fans at the start of Russia's invasion in 2014.

> hugging them, greeting them. I am scared to think of how they are. During the first days of occupation I gave up a little, then due to my half-starved state—totally. Now I've pulled myself together, even raking the garden a little bit and I dug up potatoes to take into the house. The birds only sing in the morning; in the afternoon you won't hear even a caw from the crows. In the end, I am saved by the music on my mobile phone. I recorded it before the war: Joryj Kłoc, Plach Yeremii, Gorgisheli, etc. And today, on Poetry Day, I was greeted by a small sedge of cranes in the sky, and through their "curlee" calls one could almost make out, "Ukraine will be well again! I believe in victory!"

I imagined that one day I would join the army too. But it appears it is so hard to dig, and how would I dig a trench then? Everyone knows that digging, not shooting or anything else that is romantic, is, in fact, the most crucial skill to survive. If you want to live, dig, they say on the frontline.

I found it. I found it. I said[15]

Types of war crimes: enforced disappearance, captivity, execution of a civilian (bus driver).

Stay in Kharkiv.

Meeting with the Security Service of Ukraine (SBU) in Kharkiv. The team goes to Skovorodynivka to collect missile fragments for examination at the request of our lawyer. I head to the museum alone.

---

[15] Victoria Amelina visited Kapytolivka during her Truth Hounds field mission. Volodymyr Vakulenko's father told her about his son's diary buried in the garden. They decided to look for it together. It was Victoria who found the diary and dug it up with her own hands. She delivered the pages, carefully wrapped with plastic film, to the Kharkiv Literary Museum where the work of deciphering and digitizing unfolded. In June 2023, Volodymyr Vakulenko's diary was published by Kharkiv's Vivat press (destroyed by the Russian missile strike in May 2024). The publication included Victoria Amelina's foreword with the story of the diary. With her colleagues and Volodymyr Vakulenko's family, Victoria presented the book at the Book Arsenal festival on June 22, 2023.

The Diaries of Kapytolivka—Yulia Kakulya-Danylyuk II

[Editors' note: The following excerpt is the translation into English of Volodymyr Vakulenko's diary entry pasted into the manuscript by Victoria.]

AND SO, EVERY NIGHT THE ENEMY APC, ITS HUGE GOB-LIKE fuel tanks full to the gullet with diesel, rumbles all night. The small fence next to which I had sown flowers was half-crushed, and blotches of russian waste started appearing on the patch that till recently was always tidy.

After the roadblocks were taken down in the residential area, we went outside and had a short walk around the village. I saw the traitors, who practically embraced the enemy. On our first day out, I cleared up some of the occupiers' junk left on the street. Miraculously, my saplings had survived. But to tell the truth, I didn't go where the row of bird-cherries stood. The occupier had changed the colors of our flags on the fence, and corrected the graffiti "Glory to the heroes!" to "Salo to the zeroes!" The occupier was offended that it had been weeks and they were still being scorned. As soon as they leave the village, their mocking of us will get painted over.

A neighbor on my street tried to provoke me into a sincere conversation, tried to justify herself and say that she had no links with the occupiers, just that the russian fascists saved her life by shooting down a Ukrainian drone in her yard. You're a trustworthy witness, I thought, whereas out loud I said, it's your business. I don't argue with people now—it arouses suspicion. A "souvenir from the 'DPR'" packaged in muddy camo told me off for not wearing a white armband. It rattles them that they bowed down to the occupiers long ago, but there are people here who still don't acquiesce; I couldn't stand this guy and fought back, but from then on, the road to the village center was once again closed to me.

[Editors' note: The following excerpt, from the book *Repressed Diaries: The Holodomor in Ukraine 1932–33*, by Yaroslav Fayzulin (2018), was pasted into the last working copy of the manuscript by Victoria Amelina.]

". . . mentioning it, even in private diaries, was prohibited. An entry like that could ruin one's life, turning into decades spent in the Gulag camp network. Yet despite this, even in the hardest of times there were people who could not stay silent and attempted to leave behind testimony for future generations. In particular the terrible times of 1932 to 1933. Among the hundreds of thousands of criminal cases stored in the archives of the former soviet intelligence services, seven diaries (or copied excerpts of them) of witnesses of the Holodomor were preserved among the physical evidence. These diaries belonged to: Oleksandra Radchenko, a teacher from Kharkiv region; Dmytro Zavoloka, a party member and head of the department of culture and propaganda in Kyiv's Leninskii district party committee; Nestor Bilous, a villager from the district of Lebiazhii-Pechenihy (now Chuhuiv) of Kharkiv Oblast; Oleksii Nalyvaiko, a village schoolteacher and student at the Kharkiv Professional Educational Institute's literature faculty; Dorota Federbush, political émigré and literary editor of Ukrderzhnatsmenvydav ("State Publisher of the Ethnic Minorities of the Ukrainian SSR"); Yurii (Georgii) Sambros, professor and head of practical pedagogy at the All-Ukrainian People's Education Institute; and Mykhail Sinkov, lector at the Kirov Kharkiv Chemical Technological Institute.

The Soviet "bodies" in charge considered keeping such diaries "counterrevolutionary activity." People were arrested and tried for keeping them. As a rule, during the investigations and trial these entries featured as part of the main evidence. All seven of these authors survived the Holodomor, but not all of them managed to survive the Great Terror, a time when, for some, all trace of them disappeared forever. The diaries of witnesses to the Holodomor are a view from inside of the crime committed by the communist regime, from the epicenter of events and people who were its victims, witnesses, or at times collaborators. Among the victims were the villager Nestor Bilous, the teachers Oleksandra Radchenko and Oleksii Nalyvaiko, who recorded the course of forced collectivisation and grain procurement, the robbery of village homesteads and the lawlessness/mayhem wrought by the authorities, the feelings of the people, the seizure of the peasants' agricultural production and the result—mass starvation. The political émigré Dorota Federbush, pedagogue Yurii Sambros and lector Mykhailo Sinkov were witnesses to this crime. All three of them lives in Kharkiv, back then the capital of Soviet Ukraine, and in their diaries they described the atmosphere of terror in the city, the starving and dying peasants on the streets, at the markets and stations. Hearsay and stories from friends and acquaintances informed the bulk of their knowledge about the terrible starvation in the Ukrainian villages. The party member Dmytro Zavoloka could be conditionally included among the number of collaborators, since he was within the Orgburo of the central committee of the communist party of the Ukrainian SSR and worked in Soviet monitoring bodies that ensured the fulfillment of top-down directives. In his private notes the party member wrote about how the party erred in its politics toward the village, blamed the Communist Party leadership and Joseph Stalin himself for the starvation and suffering of the peasants, including his own relatives who lived in Boryspil, near Kyiv. However, out of anxiety about his career—or life—he did not dare to declare this publicly.

The Woman Who Wrote Poems on the Mariupol Walls and a Nobel Prize

[Editors' note: This section was moved here by the editors from an older version of the manuscript. The excerpt below is a transcript of the conversation "Women and War," which took place at Lviv BookForum 2022 on October 7, 2022. Participants: Victoria Amelina, Emma Graham-Harrison, Lydia Cacho, Diana Berg, Yaryna Chornohuz, and Janine di Giovanni.]

We were introduced in a bar in Lviv, at the opening party for the wartime Lviv Book Forum festival. Diana [Berg] is to chair the panel discussion on "Women and War."

Berg was displaced twice: "When Donetsk, my hometown, was actually occupied in 2014 and now in Mariupol after it was completely destroyed during the siege . . . It was not my desire to go, to move; indeed, it's very difficult to accept this. And there are so many women who are, again, twice displaced, but even once it's already a trauma."

[Addressing Janine di Giovanni, Diana Berg said:]

> I just want to comment on your memories of the siege in Sarajevo, because I survived the siege of Mariupol. And it really is something that you remember forever. So I can relate to that very much. And you brought up the wide spectrum of roles women can play and are playing within the war. It's not only women combatants, but also women like mothers, women in captivity, women who become victims of rape, of torture, of trafficking—we saw so many cases of women and children deported to Russia, from Mariupol, violently—and also roles like refugee mothers who go abroad and so on. We women of Ukraine are experiencing so many different emerging roles.

In a couple of months, talking to a man who survived more than a month of Mariupol siege,[16] I will remember the poem on the city's wall. Trying to identify the exact location of the wall with the poem, I'll start looking at the city map and remember where I lived and walked. I'll end up devastated and numb looking at the streets I walked and comparing them to the images of the ruined city from the news.

"Do you by any chance know the people who wrote Zhadan's poem about the refugees from the city of stone and iron on the wall in Mariupol?" I will finally ask Diana, thinking that I want to find out about the people more than about the wall.

"I did. That was my project," Diana replied.

Talking to Philippe Sands in Raphael Lemkin City

[Editors' note: The transcript of the discussion was pasted into the manuscript by the author. See appendix II.]

Not Today in Shevchenko Park—
Massive Attack on October 10, 2022

At least 514 cultural objects in Ukraine were destroyed or damaged by Russia after February 24. Today this list became longer.[17]

---

[16] See the chapter "The Map of Mariupol."

[17] On October 10, 2022, Russia launched its mass bombings of Ukrainian energy and water supply infrastructure. In one day, it damaged not only 30 percent of Ukraine's power grid but also multiple cultural sites and residential buildings in Kyiv and eight other regions. The mass bombings of energy infrastructure continued throughout the autumn and winter of 2022, causing blackouts and electricity shortages during the coldest months in Ukraine.

Cultural objects that were damaged in Kyiv this morning: Taras Shevchenko National University of Kyiv, the Bohdan and Varvara Khanenko National Museum of Arts, Kyiv Picture Gallery, the concert hall of the National Philharmonic of Ukraine, Maksymovych Scientific Library, Kyiv City Teacher's House, [National Museum of Natural History at the National Academy of Sciences of Ukraine, and others.]

Some say that one of the targets of the occupiers was the Taras Shevchenko monument in front of the university.

I plug my phone in to get it fully charged; there might be a power outage soon. Then, sitting on the corridor floor, I text and call my friends: Oleksandra, Evhenia, Tetyana, Sofia:

"Are you okay?"

They're all okay. They worry if anyone got killed in the explosions and about the Khanenko art museum: is it damaged? And what about the historic university buildings? The Shevchenko monument?

I hear the sound of another explosion and rush to my balcony with the phone in my hand. A dense black blast cloud tries to swallow the sky, but the sky is too big and too bright to swallow.

"The Russians just hit something again. Sorry, I'll call you later," I say to Sofia when another missile hits the same area near the railways. I shoot a video and then just stand there on the balcony and watch the sky. I know the air defense guys are watching it now, so I'm not alone. "In air defense we trust," I whisper.

It is sunny, and apart from the black clouds on the horizon, Kyiv looks as beautiful as always. I know why Russians want it and why they will never have it.

I pour myself a glass of wine. It's certainly too early for alcohol, but I feel like it's almost the end of the story, and I should mark it. The neighbors won't judge me. The city is under attack again, but the heroines of my diary are not scared at all. One of them just received a Nobel Peace Prize. Another is finishing her book about Irpin and Bucha. All of them are winning a fight. For a moment, it seems that justice is not only possible but inevitable simply because I can eventually define it. I feel it. Standing there, defenseless but fearless, I know what justice is. I simply don't have the time to write about this yet. I leave my glass half-full in the kitchen, put an additional first aid kit into my backpack and head back to the street.

I call all the women I love. I don't call Evhenia Zakrevska; she is in constant danger in the war zone.

Oleksandra Matviichuk doesn't pick up, but messages me: I'm safe.

In the evening I find myself frozen in the shower. I remember what Oleksandra told me, you should put cream on your face just to start feeling something, at least the cream on your face, its coldness, softness, and its smell. I find a moisturizing mask on the shelf and slowly put it on my face, trying to feel. It's cold, soft and it smells of clay. I'm alive, I have a face, fingers white from the clayish substance, a life, which is here and now, a life that didn't end this morning.

In a week, the Russians will try to target the same heat supply station on Zhylyanska Street. They miss. Instead of destroying the station, they kill three people: a fifty-nine-year-old woman and a young couple. The young woman was six months pregnant. She worked as a sommelier in a local wine store. Her name was Victoria; friends called her Vika.

The Ministry of Justice

Almost everyone leaves, but we still have John Lee Anderson and Peter Pomeranstev with us, so we go to the Ukraine Ministry of Justice as planned.[18] There I meet Marharyta Sokorenko [Ukraine's commissioner for the European Court of Human Rights].

She has worked here since 2012. Like Evhenia Zakrevska, Marharyta remembers that her life changed on the night of November 31, 2013. She stayed up late at work, and woke up to realize that in less than hundred meters from her,[19]

[Editors' note: What follows is a rough draft of the section that includes notes originally written in Ukrainian.]

No, it has to be justified

I spent the whole night that night sitting and reading the European Court of Human Rights' decisions on the protests in Turkey

and made a compilation of why that would be a violation

the ECHR is still against it, I'm sorry to say

belief

2014

Everything was good with a belief in rights

On 13 March 2014, on her birthday, the first submission was put to the ECHR

the decision from 14 January 2021 the ECHR announced the decision about the eligibility in Ukraine's case against Russia

[18] After BookForum 2022 in Lviv, participants went to Kyiv. Their visit to the capital coincided with the start of Russia's mass bombings of civilian infrastructure on October 10, 2022. One of the participants, Henry Marsh, reflected on the experience in his article "I Thought It Would Be Safe in Kyiv. Then the Bombing Started" for *The Times* (October 17, 2022).

[19] This sentence was left unfinished.

about Crimea, saying that Russia took over Crimea, and had effective control from 27 February (the parliament was taken over on the night of 26–27) and the blocked connection between Turkey and Cyprus has been in litigation for 40 years.

The Security Services of Ukraine, the chief prosecution, and police gave info on what was happening in the east and we understood that the next stop would be the east, so we started gathering materials

On 12 April the anti-terrorist operation was launched

And we added to it

And have been adding to it

In 2016 the ECHR separated the case into two

Ukraine v Russia re Crimea

Ukraine v Eastern Ukraine

We did not like this

But it was their decision

For a month from 26 January 2022 we were in Strasbourg at oral hearings

Hundreds of thousands of ru forces on the border and every day we were under threat of real invasion as a result of the ongoing act of aggression from the ru federation

26 January 2023—we went according to the decisions about the eligibility of the Donbas case

On 12–13 June 2014 were the first notifications of children and orphans being taken into Russia—from Valeriya Lutkovska

The carers at the childrens' home were taken out of Snizhne to Dnipro

They were able to notify the guardianship bodies

The ministry of international affairs was Involved

Lists

And within an hour and a half we had prepared submissions to the ECHR

That children were currently being transported out of the

country into Russian territory and we asked to give the admonitions from the Rus Fed

Evening of 13 June the ECHR had already given the indication to allow Ukr consuls (the children were already on Rus Fed territory) and on the night of 13–14 the children had landed in Dnipro

there were underage minors and teenagers.

21 February independence of the so-called Luhansk and Donetsk People's Republic declared

That night they held meetings in f-ing Russia Security Council

I could not sleep that night and watched

The deputy head of the secretariat

That morning we starting monitoring

Chronology of events

Real time we added information from both the OSINT and law enforcement

We initiated a briefing on the 22 February we held a briefing with the defense minister, the Security Service of Ukraine, and General Staff, with the agenda of coordinating collaboration.

About information communications

24 February

The phone exploded with hundreds of notifications

An hour before it I woke up in front of my turned-on laptop and had missed putin

I woke up at 5-something because my phone was vibrating nonstop

In Obolon district in Kyiv

The first of my colleague

"Margot wake up, the war's started" and I hear an explosion in the background

My first thought was to wake up everyone working at "Piranha"

Of the cases against Russia—from the very beginning the chat avatar was of the Defender of the Motherland monument holding putin's head

now he called

Put a thumbs up anyone who is awake, who is in what situation

Everyone reacted, apart from one colleague. She had also slept through it

Gunman Who Killed Seventeen in Parkland Is Spared the Death Penalty

ON OCTOBER 14, 2022, I OPEN THE *NEW YORK TIMES* TO READ what they have on the recent attacks in Ukraine. Instead, I see another article at the top of the one of the most influential newspapers in the world. The piece is not about Ukraine, but it's clearly on the topic of justice for mass murderers.

"The victims' families were horrified and baffled at the decision that gave Nikolas Cruz[20] life in prison without the possibility of parole," the leading line says. I click on it to learn about the feelings of people who lost their loved ones, mostly children, during peace time in their country. They expected the jurors to sentence the mass murder to death. They are outraged with the decision to spare his life.

I try to find out the name of the Ukrainian eleven-year-old

[20] On February 14, 2018, Nikolas Cruz opened fire on students and staff at Marjory Stoneman Douglas High School in the town of Parkland, Florida, United States, killing seventeen people.

who spent six hours under the rubble of his home yesterday, got rescued but died in a hospital. And I cannot find his name. He is nameless. His grieving parents are nameless. His murderer is nameless. I can go to Mykolaiv and try to find out the boy's name, talk to his parents or, rather, hug them silently, because what would I tell them? Nikolaz Cruz is sentenced to life in prison, and the victims' families are outraged. The boy's murderers are free, some of them, if we follow the chain of command right to the top table, powerful and wealthy. "I know nothing about the inevitability of penance," Serhiy Zhadan wrote in a poem, in the one quoted on Peace Avenue in Mariupol.[21] I know nothing about the inevitability of penance either. Yet I can[22]

The victims, the heroes, and the murderers shall all have names again one day.

There's no guarantee, but so many Ukrainians and friends of Ukraine fight for that day. It will come, won't it?

The Nobel Peace Prize—Oleksandra Matviichuk III

MANY UKRAINIANS WERE OUTRAGED AT THE NOBEL COMMITtee's decision to award the prize to human rights advocates in Russia, Ukraine, and Belarus.

Many believed this evoked the old Soviet myth of "brotherly nations." Some people even demanded that Ukraine decline the Nobel.

Few people in Ukraine regarded the Nobel Committee's decision as an anti-Putin maneuver or a celebration of the resistance

[21] The line is taken from Serhiy Zhadan's poem "Where Are You Coming From?," translated by Victoria Amelina.

[22] This sentence was left unfinished.

against the forces of evil shown by human rights advocates. These are people who have spent years talking about war crimes committed by the Russian army in Chechnya and Ukraine.

PARIS (2 NOVEMBER 2022)

She advocated for changing article 124

Macron

She tells him about Yuriy Kerpatenko[23]

impunity

helplessness of the

security council, France

tribunal—open for talk; ICC doesn't support that

radbez

ICC Georgia—just small fish, 5 days war, war crimes. Charges to 3 people in ten years, no top leadership. Chain of command wasn't proven

They have to show results, we won't wait for ten years, we're Ukrainians.

Eat oysters.

We walk to Louvre to see the Mona Lisa in an empty room, and this feels surreal. I think about how I will write about the experience as something very different from the story of *Lady with an Ermine*, a much less well-known but equally masterful painting by Leonardo da Vinci, stolen by the high-ranking Nazi criminal Hans Frank during the Nazi occupation of Poland.

---

[23] Yuriy Kerpatenko (1976–2022) was the chief conductor of the Hileia chamber orchestra of the Kherson Regional Philharmonic. On September 27, 2022, Russian occupiers killed Yuriy Kerpatenko for refusing to collaborate with them. His wife, who was with him at that moment, was wounded. Victoria Amelina visited and interviewed her in Kherson in June 2022. It was one of her last field missions.

Yet it appears that there is a misunderstanding about the time, and so we're late, the Louvre is already closing. And on the one hand, I feel disappointed. On the other hand, perhaps, it is just not right to have such a beautiful painting just to yourself, even for a moment. I'll come back to Paris later, when I have enough time to spend it in the line to see the Louvre. After all, Janine di Giovanni invited me to be her guest in Paris. And wouldn't that be wonderful, to meet in Paris and not talk to her about the thirty-seven wars and three genocides she has seen, but only talk about art and beauty? I try to imagine this happy time while walking the Paris streets with Oleksandra.

A Ukrainian in Courtroom 600

November 4

While the kids sleep, I sneak out to get myself a cup of coffee. Or perhaps coffee is just an excuse; I want to be one on one with Nuremberg whatever the word would mean to me from now on.

The morning is chilly, and the streets are empty. I listen to the birds chirping and the sound of my own steps on the Jakobs market square.

I wander the city and the word Nuremberg transforms for me as I walk.

We buy the tickets, and I ask for the audio guides for the kids.

"Where are you from?" the ticket man asks.

"Ukraine," I say.

"So Russian?"

"English and Polish please," I reply, as my son prefers English and my niece prefers Polish. Russian used to be their first language. But now they refuse to use it. "You don't have Ukrainian, I assume?"

THE COURTROOM 600 IS ON THE SECOND FLOOR. WE

The room is divided in half. The part where the defendants sat is closed to visitors. A guard is sitting there, reading a book, not looking at anyone. What is he reading?

I hear my son explaining to my niece: this room is important. We'll try Russians like that one day.

The man is rea

I sent Vakulenko's diary to his [older] son [Vladyslav]. I don't know if it's lawful or wise but it was human.

It was proven here in Nuremberg.

In fact, I'm not sure if this was the main thing that was proven.

Electricity November 23

[Editors' note: the following excerpt is the translation into English of a message from the Truth Hounds work chat pasted into the last working copy of the manuscript by VA.]

😞DEAR ALL, THE TRAINING TOMORROW AND THE DAY AFTER has been canceled:'(we don't know when the electricity and water will come back on mothafcknrussia

Graves in Chernihiv, Dancing in Kherson—Vira Kuryko III

ON AUGUST 23, I TALK TO VIRA ABOUT GOING TOGETHER TO Volodymyrivka, her home village on the border of Russia and Belarus, to research what happened there during the Russian occupation. Vira thinks some of the towns in the Chernihiv region get attention; the best known of them is Yahidne, where Russians forced the entire population of 367 people, into a school basement, with not enough space or air, for almost a month. Yahidne's story, which ended with the death of eleven villagers, even hit the cover of *Time*. Still, many other villages, Vira says, the ones closer to the Russian border and unaccessible right after the liberation due to destroyed bridges, remain largely unexplored. I check in the folder for Truth Hounds and see that about twenty villages have been investigated, yet Volodymyrivka is not among them. Besides, I'm eager to see Vira's childhood home and work together.

On the phone, my friend sounds desperate, too worried for her husband, Serhiy, a man she loves more than life, who is on the front line but tries to work and not think about the worst. It seems it would be a miracle for him to survive as we receive more and more news about our friends and colleagues killed in action. Yet Vira believes in miracles, and I cannot sleep thinking how I wish there were miracles for these two. The next day we get the news: he was hit by an armored fighting vehicle. The car she bought for him, raising money on social networks and writing articles, is gone. But he is alive.

"He has no major visible injuries, so he can be sent back into battle," she cries on the phone. "His fingers are broken, so how will he shoot? How will he dig quickly enough?"

I know what she means. Everyone who has been to the front

line or has friends there knows the main rule for survival: if you want to live, dig.

Vira's fear does not come true. Serhiy is sent to a hospital, and I cannot help but think that the accident was perhaps the answer to our inept prayers. Now he will not be on the front line: this is his chance to live.

Our plan to go to the border between Ukraine, Russia, and Belarus together is ruined, but who cares? Vira rushes to the hospital and then spends a month with her husband as he recovers from internal injuries in their cozy apartment in Chernihiv. For the first time since March 3, the day of the first airstrike of Chernihiv and Serhiy joining the army, they are together for more than a day. I do not disturb Vira, imagining how happy those three must be: Vira, Serhiy, and Sagan, their dog named after an astrophysicist.

I will finally go to visit Vira only on November 28, 2022.

IN MY SLEEP I HEAR PEOPLE DISCUSSING CHERNIHIV, SAYING something about Rokosovsky [Street]. I contemplate correcting them[24]

We dare taking an elevator despite the risk of the power outage

The whole in the building looked completely fixed now.

N Testimonies

She draws the schemes on a lined piece of paper and tells me: "Here they lived. Here the bombs fell."

She knows every move, although she doesn't know the perpetrator. As if she investigated not just this crime but chance itself:

[24] The Rokosovsky Street (after Konstantin Rokossovsky, the Marshal of the Soviet Union) in Chernihiv was renamed Levko Lukyanenko Avenue (after the Ukrainian politician and dissident).

why some survived, and others didn't? Where was the turning point for each of them?

[One of the residents of the bombed building] Iryna didn't make it into the final draft by Vira; yet, Vira passionately evaluates all over again if she had a slightest chance of[25]

March 3 is a turning point for Vira too. On March 3, she and her husband came back to Chernihiv. On that day Serhiy headed to the military recruiting center to volunteer for the territorial defense; this will lead to him fighting in the most dangerous places in the east, like Lysychansk and Sievierodonetsk. On that day Vira headed to the city to see the results of bombing; this appeared to become her project for the next eight months.

Cemetery
Chornovil [Street]

Vira wants me to meet her new friends in the Chornovola building. But she doesn't want to introduce me as someone writing about the war; people in the building are tired of journalists, bloggers, and war crimes researchers asking the same questions. Vira herself is a different case: she spent so much time in the building that she feels like a neighbor, not someone hunting for a story.

"I promised she can finally see Sagan, so let's just go to her together," Vira says about one of the heroines in her report.

Last time I saw the building it looked almost unrepairable, but this was my emotional perception, perhaps. Now the complex is surrounded by a new fence and construction is in progress. A lot of walls and windows are intact again, and a crane is in operation, promising more progress. The site of the tragedy

[25] This sentence was left unfinished.

that happened more than half a year ago looks hopeful now. Yet a couple of burned cars are still there. Some local kids walk past them not even looking, ordinary neatly dressed boys and girls with backpacks on their way back home from school. Then two boys stop for a couple of moments to look for something in the grass. Perhaps they habitually sneak around every day on their way home.

"It's still possible to find something peculiar here," Vira explains.

"Like what?"

The boys seem to find nothing today.

We walk around the building.

They are joking about how they all suddenly started coliving: the airstrike ruined the walls between the apartments, so their separate living spaces became one common ruined home. The walls have now been restored, but it seems the feeling of having one home for all remained.

While I'm heading back from Chernihiv to Kyiv, my sister is already dancing on the streets of Kherson waving her blue-and-yellow flag.[26] I keep looking for her face on numerous videos but with no success. This party is hard to get into: you had to either survive half a year of occupation or fight your way to Kherson. I didn't earn my way in. But the main thing is my sister is fine.

This evening I suddenly collapsed on the floor and wake up with a horrible headache and vomiting. When the ambulance comes, about ten minutes after my call, they measure my cardiogram, put a drip to my vein, and talk to me like they care.

"Oh, so your sister is in Kherson? So this is the reason, perhaps. You stressed too much over it."

[26] Kherson was liberated on November 11, 2022.

Late for the Funeral, on Time for Blue-And-Yellow Heart—Iryna Novitska III

When we leave from Kyiv by bus, it is still dark. I spent the night at Tetyana Teren's place, as I did not want to climb the stairs to my cold and dark apartment. The apartment Tetyana rents is equally dark and cold, but it is seventeen floors lower than mine.

Funerals should not look like press conferences, but Volodymyr Vakulenko's does.

In the crowd, just two of us look in the same direction: not at the coffin covered with a wrinkled flag, not at the bent father, not at the mother's trembling shoulders, not at the priests doing their job, not at the correspondents with all their cameras, but at the sky watching us from the higher windows of [St. Demetrius Church]. Or perhaps, now this isn't even true as I'm no longer looking at the sky, but at her, Svitlana [Povalyaeva]. She doesn't notice I'm looking at her; her gaze is fixed up above. She doesn't notice, yet I know myself that I am no better than all these photographers and cameramen trying to film the ultimate grief from the finest angle. I, too, came not only to mourn but to finish the story.

The priest, Father Vasyl, is talking about justice. . . . I chuckle. During the last . . . days I've heard many assurances that justice will come. Father Vasyl makes it easy. Maybe we should't have bothered documenting all these war crimes fitting in like a kids' puzzle patterns for crimes against humanity and the definition of genocide. God got us covered anyways, or so Father Vasyl believes. And I like Father Vasyl, he says all the right things for the grieving family: he promises justice, he says farewells, he forgives and asks to forgive on behalf of all parties but perpetrators.

I see how Volodymyr's dad straightens his back, and Volodymyr's mother's shoulders stop trembling.

Bombed Festival in Vysokopillya, and Ecologist at War

<<FEBRUARY 23, 2023: ONE MORE RUINED FESTIVAL, VYSOKOPILLYA

Oksana [Pasichnyk], the director of the cultural center, is glad to show us around. Unlike people in Kyiv region, here, in the south, people aren't tired of journalists and researchers; we are the first ones to come to ask for her story. She shows us the decorations damaged by the explosion: the huge banner is now hanging twisted under the broken roof, but it's intact and I can see the wheat, the words about the holidays, and the Ukrainian state symbol, trident

"Here we celebrated the Day of Unity of Ukraine," Oksana explains, and clearly waits for me to react.

Maybe I am supposed to say that the banner is beautiful, or ask about the details of the celebration. But I just gasp. The story of Unity Day in Ukraine has already been too moving, and this ripped off Unity Day decoration in a recently liberated village seems surreal.

The history of Unity Day began in a rail car in 1918. A century ago, Ukraine was perhaps the only country whose leaders' headquarters was on a train; hence the train of Symon Petlyura[27] could even be called Ukraine's temporary capital. Of course, the

---

[27] Symon Petlyura (1879–1926) was a Ukrainian politician, journalist, and military commander who led the Ukrainian People's Republic during the Ukrainian War of Independence (1917–1921).

reason for having commanders on a train wasn't fun: Ukraine faced a problematic internal political situation and had to fight for independence. So the Directorate of Ukraine, a collegiate state committee of the Ukrainian Republic, was always on the move. That is why it was on a train at the small Ukrainian railway station that the leaders of West Ukrainian People's Republic, a state created by Ukrainians of the former Austro-Hungarian empire, and the Ukrainian People's Republic[28], a democracy created by Ukrainians of the Russian Empire, agreed on the Unification Act. The historic agreement between two integral parts of Ukraine was later signed solemnly on St. Sophia Square in Kyiv on January 22, 2019. And the celebration of unity was as joyful in 1919 as the celebration of Kherson's liberation in November 2022. This story was never forgotten. In 1990, when the Soviet regime was still in power, Ukrainians dared to resist by celebrating the anniversary of unity. Almost three million people linked arms, forming the longest chain of 770 kilometers, connecting Lviv to Kyiv as a symbol of solidarity. I try to imagine three million people preparing to create a human chain in a totalitarian state in a pre-internet era, sewing forbidden blue-and-yellow flags, deciding on who's going to be where on the frozen winter Ukrainian roads. Would I join them if I was an adult back then in 1990? I was four at the time. Since 1999, Ukraine has celebrated the Day of Unity on January 22 every year to mark the signing of the treaty.[29]>>

[28] The Ukrainian People's Republic was a state established on the territory of central Ukraine. It declared its independence from the Russian Empire in 1918 and existed until 1921. The West Ukrainian People's Republic was a nation-state established on the Ukrainian ethnic territory of the former Austria-Hungary on November 9, 1918.

[29] On the Day of Unity 2024, Victoria Amelina was posthumously awarded by the President of Ukraine with the Order of Merit (Third Class). Among the cultural figures awarded alongside her were Maksym Kryvtsov, Vasyl Kukharskyi, and Volodymyr Vakulenko.

The Justice of Street Names: Ratushny and Vakulenko Streets

[Editors' note: This section was not completed by the author. An older draft contains the list of streets named after the figures and events of Soviet history which were renamed in 2022. In particular, Victoria Amelina noted that Lomonosov Street in Kyiv was renamed after Roman Ratushny, and that a street named after Volodymyr Vakulenko appeared in Izyum.]

PART IV

Answers and Victories

Christmas in Times of War, and the Death of a Survivor

2022 MUST COME TO AN END, BUT IT SEEMS IMPOSSIBLE. No year can end in February, and we are all still in February. It's the morning of February 24, 2022. Casanova is driving Birdy, evacuating kids from the Kharkiv region, thinking she has to find time to make a call about returning to the Truth Hounds team. Zhenia is knocking on the neighbors' doors; the doors are still intact, and the apartments aren't burned and empty. All twenty-five heroines in her book about female soldiers are still alive. Oleksandra . . . [1] Vira still wears her red sweater; her husband has not yet joined the army. Maria still gives interviews about the beginning of the Russian invasion (which is happening, by the way). Evhenia still persuades herself that, despite the bombing, she will go to the courtroom to fight for justice as a lawyer. I still tell my son to look for the constellations in the sky, and he keeps looking outside the window into the starry sky over the eternal desert, not knowing missiles are already flying above his country and his identity is a target. "I see it now!" he says joyfully, over and over again. And missiles are still in the sky over Ukraine, never landing, never killing anyone on the ground, just hanging above us like Ursa Major, like a reminder of how easily a fragile and phantasmal peace can end. On the third day of 2023, my fellow war crimes researcher, the one whom we call Thymus Borysphenicus, like a plant that grows near his occupied village, writes me a message: <<Yan "Bayraktar," the lucky one who survived Russian roulette and miraculously got home in the Kherson region, died. His car set off a landmine near his now liberated village. It's against the rules to get involved with

[1] This sentence was left unfinished.

the witnesses, to make it personal. Casanova wrote in the team chat that she is sharing the information not as a head of field missions.[2]>>

The Art Museum, Philharmonic, and Library in Kherson

[Editors' note: This section was meant to reflect on Victoria Amelina's trip to Kherson. The city was the only regional capital the Russian army managed to capture at the beginning of the full-scale invasion. It was liberated by the Ukrainian Armed Forces on November 11, 2022. These notes are from the PEN Ukraine volunteer trip to the city on December 27, 2022. On that day, the group of Ukrainian writers and journalists visited the Kherson Regional Academic Music and Drama Theater named after Mykola Kulish, the local editorial office of the public Suspilne Media, Oles Honchar Kherson Regional Library, and Oleksiy Shovkunenko Kherson Regional Art Museum.]

KHERSON MUSEUM
Center

we got some info at the beginning of dec
Hanna Mamonova

Ivan Antypenko video up online
roughly November 4 or 5 when

the article is from November 4

10400

Around 2500 left

---

[2] For the story of Yan "Bayraktar," see the section Justice, Not Cash—Zolotar Torture Case I'.

13902 were left (almost 14000 works)

Molhin 10000

Not confident that the entire collection got to Crimea

From the permanent exhibition—Aivazovsky and Kramsky, Pokhitonov (on the first photographs from the Taurida museum), Bogolyubov, Rozhdestvensky, Makovsky

2 weeks after it started

On the newspaper *Izvestia's* resources a big article came out, they sampled subjects of art that the russians considered would be part of

our 18 c—icons and Aivazovsky

5 loaded lorries

2 buses

from their neighbors at the local history museum—the weapons collection was loaded onto a private car

photos letter—part 1

on the 1 April the rus-occupied Kherson oblast signed an agreement with the directorate of Henichesk and the museum in Tavrida about storing the works there

this info was released on 2 April

there was an edit that it was not the local history museum—which they'd started working with

ministry for culture Kherson oblast, Henichesk

vga

was also in the local history museum

We had a graphic work by Burlyuk

Rural landscape from 1930, he painted it in America

Soberly

Head of the information department
Since December 2019 I have been working
of journalism

Odesa
I am not in Kherson
One colleague is among the collaborators

Someone appeared
I am just starting this work
The fact that
I am using a photo database
And these photographs on facebook
Anna Skrypka—most often
Vlada Dyachenko—she recognized this work which I had not looked at
Sometimes we see a fragment and you can see that it's a master work from the fragment
The worker a stripe on the side—along the stripe

The prosecutors received all this information and the pages
ICOM released a red list
The ministry for culture
A landscape by Chornenko

The Posthumous Victory of Roman Ratushny

[Editors' note: This section was not finalized. The older drafts show that it was meant to discuss the victory of the NGO established by Roman Ratushny, Protect Protasiv Yar, in the case against influential construction companies that intended to raise new buildings in the park.]

Last Year's Angels on Instytutska Street

I CAME TO INSTYTUTSKA STREET LOOKING FOR THE RAINBOW I saw last year in the photos by Evhenia Zakrevska. A year ago, that unexpected rainbow and phantasmal light in the sky on February 18, the anniversary of the massacre of Maidan protesters, gave hope to many. The sky seemed to bless us for resistance.

On February 18, 2023, the weather and the sky are very different from last year. There are also no new origami angels made of colored paper. Of course, there aren't. Schools in Kyiv are mostly closed and education is happening online in a wartime, just like in the time of pandemics; maybe it is the reason the children didn't make new paper angels. Or perhaps there is no more capacity to honor all the heroes.

It's too windy today.

A man in a gray hat lights and gives out candles to everyone who wants to put a candle to the monument of the Heavenly Hundred. I take a candle and walk among the few who came to Instytutska on this day I look at them trying to guess why they are here: have they lost loved ones? Have they risked their lives here and suffered from the survivor's guilt since February 2014? Are they lawyers working on one of the many Maidan cases like Evegenia Zakrevska? Are they like me, no one, just a passerby? Too much curiosity on my part: the candle blows out when I reach the monument with the portraits and names of those to whom I owe the ability to live in a democracy for the past eight years. I sign and come back to the man in gray hat.

He understands without me saying:

"It went out, sure," he signs, lighting my candle again.

"Thank you. I'll try to protect the fire better," I say.

He doesn't reply, turning to someone else to give out one of the last candles.

I don't look at anything but the candle, still it goes out. It's too windy today. There's no chance to see the rainbow in the sky, like Evhenia Zakrevska saw on February 18, 2022, a few days before she joined the army. Last year we hoped the rainbow over Kyiv was a good sign or a blessing before the fight. Maybe it was. We did need faith back then. Now we just have to keep working. I take a picture of the gray serious sky over Instytutska and send it to Evhenia.

"You cannot be here today, so here is Instytutska."

She is somewhere in the Kharkiv region, busy operating a drone, looking at the map attentively like she looked at legal cases before, driving fast along the dangerous road, or just petting Bobby in the blindage. She doesn't reply till late at night when I'm already on the train to Kryvyj Rih to see Iryna Novitska for the first time since Vakulenko's funeral.

[Editors' note: The following fragment contains an excerpt from the collection *Bykivnya: From the Territory of Death to the Memorial Site*, pasted in the manuscript by Victoria Amelina. It was meant to draw a parallel between the sites of mass shooting during the Revolution of Dignity in Kyiv and a mass execution which happened in the same place during the Soviet period and was investigated by the Sixtiers (see the chapter "Among the Guiding Stars—Oleksandra Matviichuk I").]

One more site of mass shootings in Kyiv during the years 1934–1938 was the internal prison of the NKVD of the Ukrainian SSR, located in the buildings of the former Kyiv Institute for Noble Maidens (later known as the October Palace after World War II). The secret NKVD site in Bykivnia was one of the most classified facilities in the Soviet Union, where secret burials of victims of mass political repressions took place from 1937 to 1941, including those executed in Kyiv prisons.

The actual area of the "facility" was 5.3 hectares. The territory was enclosed with a high solid wooden fence, and an observation tower and a building were constructed. It had round-the-clock armed security. Several access roads were built from the Chernihiv Highway. Trucks such as the GAZ-AA (commonly known as "Polutorka")[3] would bring the bodies of those executed to the site during the night. The bodies were dumped into prepared pits and covered with lime and soil.

To conceal the true purpose of the site, a legend was spread among the local population about an artillery depot supposedly located on the premises. It was a successful legend, as prior to 1923, there was an artillery range belonging to the Kyiv state-owned Arsenal plant in that area (from Brovary to the outskirts of old Darnytsia).

The Anniversary of the Invasion

IT'S WEIRD HOW WE ARE ALL WAITING FOR THE ANNIVERSARY of the full-scale invasion. The date, February 24, is cursed, feared, hated, and perhaps should be marked black in calendars, like Volodymyr Vakulenko's father marked it and the day of his son's abduction black on his funny calendar featuring a tiger and a dollar.

On the night of February 23, I'm trying to fall asleep in the weirdest place, on the second bunk of a double bunk bed in a stranger's cold house in a half-ruined village in the Kherson region. I chose the upper bunk in the hope that it would be warmer there. It might be warmer, but I'm in a sleeping bag

[3] "Polutorka" means "one-and-a-halfer." It is a common name for the truck (the Soviet copy of the Ford model AA) lifting 1.5 tons of weight.

which is slippery, and the upper bunk has no barrier to prevent me from sliding off to the floor. It would stupid to die like that in the Kherson region on the anniversary of the invasion. But this is not the main reason why, exhausted, I cannot fall asleep. It's like I am waiting for something to happen. The forecasts are gloomy again, but a rain of Russian missiles is not what I'm waiting for. I need this year of war to end as if knowing that we have survived a year of full-scale war would make me stronger, more resilient and thus more fit for my tasks. But a sleepless night can only make you weaker. So the next day when we head to the village of Starosillya, I sleep in the Fishy, the yellow minivan of Truth Hounds, and miss the beautiful views of the Inhulets River.

The Holodomor and the Fields of Mines in the Kherson Region

[Editors' note: This section was left unfinished. It was meant to recount the Truth Hounds mission to the Kherson region. The draft contains the beginning of the section, a witness account found in older drafts, and a quote from Vakulenko's diary. It was meant to reflect on the weaponisation of hunger by the Soviet Union and Russia, past and present.]

THERE IS NO PHYSICAL ACCESS TO PLACES WHERE THE GREATEST number of atrocities were committed. The evidence there was being destroyed just as I was documenting war crimes where possible and writing this book. Mariupol is not only a mass grave now but also a crime scene. Yet the perpetrators did everything in their power to destroy all the evidence there. Yet it is impo[4]

[4] This sentence was left unfinished.

"Do you know why the village is called Bilohirka?[5] Because every time during hunger my ancestors would add white clay into food, and survive like this," the witness says.

Suddenly he starts talking about his grandma, though obviously her story has nothing to do with the war crimes committed in this village. Unless I want to find justice for those who suffered in the Holodomor. And I do. I'm writing it all down: Pelahiya Avramivna Minska-Hozholovska told her grandson, the eyewitness of the atrocities in 2022, that the harvest of 1932–33 was good, more than enough to feed every Ukrainian in the region. But all the food was taken away, and her house was searched to make sure she would die from hunger. But she didn't. She survived and had children, and made sure that the truth is told.

"I'm writing it down. Perhaps the prosecutors will be quite surprised to read the testimony about your grandma, but I'm writing it down, because telling her story is the ultimate justice."

The witness chuckles, looking somewhere beyond the ruined village, somewhere beyond the sky, somewhere Pelahiya, whose father's name was Avram, is waiting for long overdue justice, her story. It is finally coming, isn't it?

[Editors' note: What follows is a translation into English of an excerpt from Vakulenko's diary pasted by Victoria into the manuscript.]

It was the last of the bread procured for the village, and I divided the last loaf into five pieces, just for my son. By two weeks of occupation I had already forgotten the taste of bread, and I gathered the crumbs left on the table by the little one into a handful and ate them greedily, just to have the slightest taste of bread.

[5] Bilohirka is a village in the Kherson region with a population of about 135.

Russian Books and Newspapers from Kherson and Izyum

I HAVE A PILE OF NEWSPAPERS IN MY APARTMENT IN KYIV. THE ones from Kherson are clean and almost not crumpled. The ones from Izyum are mostly dirty, crumpled, and stained. In these newspapers, published in Russia or in occupied Donetsk, Luhansk, or Crimea, are the reasons for thousands of war crimes, crimes against humanity, and uneven Russian attempts to destroy Ukrainians as a group, political nation, i.e., commit genocide. I also have school books from Kherson borrowed from one of the witnesses who survived the occupation, the book about Stalin found in a place where civilians were killed and tortured, and letters to the "unknown soldier" from Russian children.

The One Who Won in Hostomel—Zhenia Podobna III

:) [ZHENIA PODOBNA:] "TODAY I SAW THE MONSTERS WHO scared me so much that day. Three of them. Completely destroyed. Because there's nothing to scare me and fly near my house anymore :) I wanted to feel satisfaction. I didn't feel anything. Except for love and boundless gratitude to those who held the sky back then and continue to hold it now. I know the name of the person who shot down that same first helicopter and restored my faith. He was wounded this year, healed, and returned to the front line; he's now fighting on the Bakhmut front. I will definitely thank him personally, finish this project, and finally turn the page."

Iryna Dovhan in New York

THE STORY IS REPEATED AGAIN AND AGAIN. FOUR YEARS BEfore the invasion, Iryna founded an organization uniting[6]

About twenty women joined with the goal of helping each other. They had a lot in common: they came from the Donetsk region, supported Ukraine, and were horribly punished by occupiers and their accomplices. Most of them had an experience in the isolation camp their fellow former political prisoner Stanysav Aseyev described in his book *The Torture Camp on Paradise Street*. But February changed everything.

The Birth of a Festival and the Birth of a Girl on Women's Day

LARYSA [DENYSENKO] AND I MEET IN A CAFÉ IN PODIL. WE are both feminists, so we mark International Women's Day with hugs and small presents. Larysa gives me a colorful scarf, I give her fancy earrings, and we start talking about gender-based violence in the occupied territories.

Eva is born. She is born to live.[7]

<< Svitlana [Povalyaeva]: "We [all] want the war to end. After victory, we can hold a great festival. [But] when is this 'after'? We don't know if 'after the victory' even exists. We have to do it now."[8]

---

[6] This sentence was left unfinished.

[7] Eva Zolotar was born after the death of her father.

[8] The note relates to the first meeting of the organizational committee of the festival

And others have nothing to answer or add. I have nothing to add either.>>

If It Feels like a Victory—Kateryna Rashevska III

UKRAINIANS BEHIND THE PUTIN ARREST WARRANT

"It feels like victory," but this is not it, Kateryna says. "The victory for me is not the arrest warrant but having all Ukrainian children back in Ukraine."

[Editors' note: What follows is the translation into English of unedited notes.]

IN FEBRUARY 2023 I SAW CHILDREN WHO HAD ARRIVED

There was one girl who said that she cried every day because she wanted to see her mom so badly, she was 11 years old

Every time she sent me, I

Sometime in November 2022 I started talking online with parents from Kharkiv Oblast whose children were returned from the camps

One boy's mum doesn't fully understand what happened

We were able to talk to him on the phone

We talked about ways of getting compensation

In February a group of children from Kherson Oblast were returned

An 11-year-old girl

I monitored open sources and collected stories, that

Protasiv Yar in Memory of Roman Ratushny. Victoria Amelina was a member of the committee.

Documents about rus families who took in children

Before October no one was interested
Then foreign media
Got interested

Philippe
she openly announced in October

The move could take place in July, he had already received a passport

It became more active after the de-occupation of Kharkiv region, since the children had not returned yet

We need to file a report with the ICC about Lvova-Byelova
Older sister, niece aged 7

February 14 Yale Conflict Observatory Nathaniel Raymond

March 17 Arrest Warrant Putin & Lvova-Belova

That day

I instigated on *October 25 2022 a report to the ICC*

A description of the episodes—how many, where, when, a justification of why this is a genocide, the locations

April 2022

I started searching 57 locations
4 locations were on Belarusian territory

Arresting Putin Is Nothing

Poetry Day in the Kharkiv Literature Museum

On March 21, 2023, the sky is clear and my friend drives me from Balakliya to Kharkiv so I can open Poetry Day at the Kharkiv Literature Museum. Today, for the first time since the full-scale invasion, the museum opens for visitors with a new exhibition. There is only one object on display in a small room with dim lights. I will be talking about finding Vakulenko's diary and reading a couple of poems.

Over the last year I've seen a lot of museums. At first, the Kharkiv Literary Museum was empty; Russians constantly shelled the city, so Tetyana Pylypchuk evacuated the collection dedicated to the Executed Renaissance and the Sixtiers. Then the museum reopened with only one object, the diary of Volodymyr Vakulenko, on display. The museum in Skovorodynivka near Kharkiv was ruined by a Russian missile, and I wandered between its burned walls trying to comprehend the reality of destruction.

The Kherson Art Museum was empty; the Russian authorities had stolen almost everything. The museum in Vysokopillya, in the Kherson region, stood with broken windows behind the equally damaged German school and the church that had been turned into a cultural center.

I saw how a Russian missile hit Shevchenko park in downtown Kyiv, damaging the Khanenko Art Museum.

I also visited one museum in Poland, the Princes Czartoryski Museum, where I always sit in front of *Lady with an Ermine* by Leonardo da Vinci. After looking at it for half an hour or so, I usually leave, trying not to look at the other paintings so they don't blur my impression of Leonardo's work. This painting is not only at the center of art history but also at the center of history of justice. As Philippe Sands writes in *East West Street*, Hans Frank, the head of the General Government in Nazi-occupied Poland, hung the painting in his chambers. It is hard to acknowledge that you have anything in common with a war criminal, but we did share two things: we were both humans, and we appreciated *Lady with an Ermine*.

The German former governor-general of Poland was found guilty of war crimes and crimes against humanity on October 1, 1946. His death sentence was carried out at Nuremberg Prison about two weeks after the trial.

[Editors' note: The following paragraphs present unedited and unfinished notes]

Sixtiers museum Lubov Panchenko

Bucha And the Sixtiers

I am aware that I'm not the first crime researcher among Ukrainian writers. The Sixtiers, the generation of writers that is between the Executed Generation of the 1930s and myself, spent a lot of time trying to find out what happened to their predecessors. Bykivnia[9]

Creative Youth Club, in 1962–63 she was a member of the commission for checking rumors about the mass executions of political prisoners. Together with her friends, the best poets of the generation, she [Alla Horska] visited dozens of villages in the vicinity of Kyiv, interviewing local residents and searching for mass graves of prisoners shot dead and buried by the NKVD. Just like we stood at the places of mass burial in Bucha and Izyum, those writers and artists of the sixties stood over the

---

[9] This sentence was left unfinished.

graveyards of their predecessors. History moved in circles, and I should only be grateful that this time Russian regime didn't get a chance to kill as many of us as it wished. On the basis of indisputable physical evidence, they opened the previously secret burials of victims of Stalinism at the Lukyaniv and Vasylkiv cemeteries and in Bykivnia. An appeal was prepared and submitted to the Kyiv City Council with the demand to turn burial sites into national memorials (Memorandum No. 2). The City Council ignored this appeal. [Vasyl] Symonenko found himself on a special account with the relevant state authorities. Soon he was brutally beaten by the police, which led to his premature death.

The Library, Not the Courtroom—
Yulia Kakulya-Danylyuk III

We arrive in Kapytolivka before ten, but the crowd is already waiting next to the administration building. People always gather well in advance for humanitarian aid. We take out the boxes with clothes and tell the villagers to pick what they need. Yulia, the librarian, doesn't take anything. She says she works and can buy everything she needs, so why take aid? She gets into our minivan to show us the way to her library. When we're almost there she asks the driver to be careful: there is something that looks like a mine in the ground of the school yard in front of the library marked with a red fire extinguisher, lying next to it on the ground. As soon as we stop and get out of the vehicle, I go to take a picture of the mine and send it into the work chat of the Truth Hounds team.

"Is it a landmine?"

"It looks like it."

I panic a bit.

"How do we make sure that kids do not step on it? I mean, it looks like an anti-tank mine, but it's still a mine."

Yulia tells me not to worry as everyone in the village knows about the mine.

"But these are kids, what if they forget?"

I realize I'm panicking because I'm not used to living my life in an area contaminated by explosives. The Russian war has created a minefield of 250,000[10] square kilometers in Ukraine; demining could take decades. Besides, no one can guarantee that the fighting will not come back here, or even the occupation. The situation is even worse in the Kherson region. Some villages there still do not have electricity restored; the electricians die stepping on mines while trying to restore the grid. But somehow people learn to live next to the danger left behind by the combat. The farmers find mines and mark them with a couple of sticks and a piece of red cloth. Some die exploring their fields, hoping to be ready for the seeding season. The demining teams are stretched thin, exhausted and they lose personnel too.

The library in Kapytolivka is full of light. The main room has just been renovated, and Yulia has even decorated the room with colorful balloons.

The next day I come to the library to take pictures of the documents, which Yulia found in the library. It appears to be a list with call signs for Russian soldiers, a medical card belonging to one of them with a military unit specified. I sign the book for the Kapytolivka library and make a mistake in the date, writing March 24, 2022, when the Izyum region was still occupied and the occupiers searched people's houses for Nazis, weapons,

---

[10] The figure keeps changing. According to EcoAction NGO's, at least 30 percent of the territory of Ukraine needs demining.

and valuables to steal, the day when they abducted Volodymyr Vakulenko.

"That's not even a mistake, as this year still with us," the librarian tells me kindly.

I agree with her, but correct the year, to 2023 as if trying to turn the page finally.

Yesterday I came to the library as a writer and culture manager, but today I'm a war crimes researcher again.

Last Mission with Casanova

[Editors' note: The following report was pasted into the manuscript in Ukrainian.]

REPORT ON THE RESULTS OF THE MISSION TO BALAKLIYA AMALGAMATED TERRITORIAL COMMUNITY, KHARKIV OBLAST

1.

Date report filed: March 29, 2023
Report authors:—,—,—,—,—
Mission dates: March 20–26, 2023
Mission task: investigation of detention sites in Balakliya ATC

The mission documented incidents that occurred in the following settlements: Balakliya city, Brihadyrivka village (within Balakliya urban community, Izyum district). Savyntsi urban-type settlement and Savyntsi settlement community, Izyum district: Morozivka village, Dovhalivka village, Rakivka village,

Zaliman village, Vesele village, Kuniye village (Kuniye community), Izyum city, Kapytolivka village.

Husarivka village missing?

The following incidents were documented during the mission:

- Attacks directed against civilians, especially protected facilities and critical infrastructure:
- Vesele, 27.02.23. SMERCH MLRS attack committed by unspecified armed forces, most likely RF. A school and a residential workers' accommodation were damaged, 1 person was killed.
- Vesele, summer 2023. Strike by RF AF. 1 wounded, 1 dead.
- Kuniye, 26.02.23. Rocket attack, most likely from a SMERSH MLRS by unidentified armed forces, most likely rus fed. A school and residential buildings were damaged, 2 people died during the bombardment, 1 other later died in the hospital.
- Zaliman, early May 2022. Cluster munitions bombing by RF AF. 1 dead.
- Zaliman, 30–31 May 22. 152mm artillery strike by RF AF. Buildings on Tsentralna Street from no. 107 to 129 were destroyed, including the village council (Tsentralna Street, 119a)

LOOTING:

Looting and theft from the RF armed forces was widespread, primarily taking cars, household appliances, tools, and valuables.

- Vesele, robbery from local population, ransacked school
- Kuniye, ransacked school
- Savyntsi, office equipment stolen from school no. 1
- Balakliya, robbery from local population

- Kapytolivka, IT equipment, furniture, and electrical equipment were stolen from the school (Kapytolivka, 2 Peremohy Street)
- Looting of "Light of the Gospel" Evangelical Christian Baptists church property (Balakliya, 22/1 Soborna Street)

DEPORTATION/FORCED RELOCATION/ RELOCATION TO FILTRATION CAMPS:

- Morozivka, removal of child to a "rest and recuperation camp"
- Kapytolivka, removal of child to a "rest and recuperation camp"
- Balakliya, forced deportation of at least three persons to a securely occupied territory

UNLAWFUL DETENTION OR IMPRISONMENT OF CIVILIANS

- Balakliya, March-September 2022, Balakliya district police dept
- Kunie, during occupation (March-September 2022), at least 5 civilians were detained
- Kapytyolivka, during occupation (March-September 2022), at least 9 civilians detained, 2 survived
- Dovhalivka, April 2022, civilians detained on the territory of "Geologiia" (49.3875212,37.0652828)
- Izyum, unidentified number of people detained in an unidentified location during the March-September 2022 occupation
- Balakliya, April 2022, detentions in the Balakliya district police dept and transferal to a Russian prison (confirmed by the ICRC) International Committee of the Red Cross do we make a note of what it is somewhere

- Vesele, detention of unidentified number of persons on the territory of the "tractor brigade" (49.392185, 37.207197). At least 2 civilians who were detained in March and April 2022 for a period of 12–24 hours.
- Vesele, Veselyi Lane, in the basement of Petro Tiutiunnyk's MOT service station.
- Husarivka, March 2022, detention of 3 civilians in an undisclosed cellar
- Balakliya, June 2022, unidentified number of civilian persons (at least 2 persons) in a cellar on Smyrnova street

Inhuman detention conditions, torture

- Balakliya, April 2022, Balakliya district police dept, beatings
- Balakliya, April 2022, at a checkpoint in the Laheri district (49.470017, 36.797074), beatings, threats with shots being fired, forced labor
- Balakliya, May 2022, Balakliya district police dept, inhumane detention conditions, beatings, beatings with a bat, threats of rape on the grounds of accusations of sectarianism (the Baptists)
- Balakliya, May-June 2022, Balakliya district police dept, inhumane detention conditions, beatings with a stick, torture with stun gun
- Balakliya, May-June 2022, Balakliya district police dept, inhumane detention conditions, beatings, forced labor
- Balakliya, June 2022, Balakliya district police dept, inhumane detention conditions, torture with a stungun
- Balakliya, June-Aug 2022, Balakliya district police dept, inhumane detention conditions, threats of being used as a "demining" device for mine fields, torture with stun gun, with electric shocks (with a "tapik" field telephone), beatings with batons
- Balakliya, July 2022, Balakliya district police dept, inhumane detention conditions, torture with stun gun

- Balakliya, Aug 2022, Balakliya district police dept, inhumane detention conditions, 2 persons
- Balakliya, Aug 2022, Balakliya district police dept, inhumane detention conditions, beatings, strangling, SGBV (stripping of a woman)
- Balakliya, Aug 2022, Balakliya district police dept, inhumane detention conditions, beatings, holding person[s] upside down
- Balakliya, Aug 2022, Balakliya district police dept, inhumane detention conditions, beatings with a stick on the knees of detained person[s], electric shock torture for bettering understanding of Russian language
- Balakliya, Aug-Sept 2022, Balakliya district police dept, inhumane detention conditions, beatings, electric shock torture
- Balakliya, Sept 2022, Balakliya district police dept, inhumane detention conditions
- Balakliya, Aug 2022, "Baldruk," inhumane detention conditions
- Balakliya, Aug 2022, "Baldruk," inhumane detention conditions
- Vesele, tractor brigade station, in one of the containers (49.392185, 37.207197), 2 persons, beatings, electric shock and stun gun torture, torture by drownings in a bucket of water, inhuman detention conditions
- Kapytolivka, March 2022, detentions on the territory of a residential building on Luhova St, torture
- Dovhalivka, April 2022, on the territory of "Geologiia" (49.3875212,37.0652828), torture, torture by hanging, beatings, inhumane detention conditions, forced labor
- Izyum, March-April 2022, undetermined location, inhumane detention conditions, torture, beatings, blindfolded detention, torture by drowning, stun gun torture

- Husarivka, March 2022, inhumane detention conditions, beatings, starvation, mock executions

Violent treatment

- Morozivka, July 2022, searches, physical pressure, [reports of] "being taken to a cellar in Savyntsi urban type settlement," and "being taken out to be shot"
- Bruhadyrivka, June 2022, harassment of a female minor by a soldier from the "LPR"
- Izyum, undetermined location, "being taken out to be shot"
- Balakliya, April 2022, rape
- Kapytolivka, sexual relations between rus soldiers with girls under the age of consent
- Balakliya, June 2022, severe beatings during detention
- Balakliya, June 2022, severe beatings during detention, threats of being drowned, shots fired overhead [detainees] during transportation

Murders

- Balakliya, March 2022, a hospital worker was arrested at a checkpoint near Balakliya hospital, some time later his body was discovered with signs of torture.
- Kapytolivka, discovery of at least 7 bodies of persons detained by the rus armed forces. The bodies showed signs of torture, most likely were extrajudicial executions.
- Shooting at an evacuation bus on the exit out of Balakliya, April 2022, the driver was killed.
- Husarivka, murder or execution of 5 civilian persons.

Attacks on cultural heritage, language

- Balakliya, attempt by the occupation authorities to remove books published in Ukrainian after 1991, from the Balakliya

City Council public library (16 Zhovtneva Street, Balakliya, Kharkiv Oblast)

- Savyntsi, September 2022, School No.1 was ordered to remove all Ukrainian textbooks

II

Number of days documentation recorded: *7*
Number of testimonies: 35
Working locations: *Balakliya city, Bryhadyrivka village, Savyntsi urban-type settlement, Morozivka village, Dovhalivka village, Rakivka village, Zalyman village, Vesele village, Kuniye village, Izyum city, Kapytolivka village.*
Number of kilometers covered: *841 km*
Vehicles: *Cucumber*
Mission team setup: *4 documenters + 2 for 1.5 days*

Date, working location	Description of daily activities	Comments, contacts, undocumented incidents identified
20.03.2023 Kyiv-Kharkiv-Balakliya road	x and x went to Amelina's to drink morning coffee, after 9 they were intercepted by x and x. At 12 борт компліт drove to Balakliya. They checked in, called around their contacts, split into 3 pairs: 1. x and x went to x, a doctor, and happened across a rape case. Names, background and other details about the rapists are known. 2. x and x went to the Ukrainian SES to look for the contacts of x and found them 3. x and x went to Savyntsi and asked x and his wife about being detained (district police dept), and took a lot of contacts about the teachers	

21.03.2023	x and x went to Zalyman to speak with the village elder, film, cover the consequences of shelling, took cream?wtf from the House of Culture there. x and x looked for doctors or witnesses of the murder of x, they found his mother in law (x), who reported his disappearance, searches and the body of x found near Husarivka (still occupied). She also gave the contacts of x, a nurse. x, Амеліхххна: they spoke on the phone with a surgeon from Balakliya hospital (x—during the occupation he worked in the outpatient clinic, tel. no. +xxx), who gave them the contacts of x's mother in law and the ENT doctor. He declined to give a witness statement. x, x: interviewed librarians at the central library about the attacks—seizure of Ukrainian-language literature published after 1991. Around 1400, x and x left for Kharkiv region. They phoned x (ambulance nurse): she is now in Kharkiv, in the hospital seeing her husband (AFU soldier). On 22.03.2023 she will return to Dovhalivka. She will check with the head of the ambulance team to see if she can give a witness statement.	
22.03.2023	x and x questioned three victims: x, a judge who was robbed, heavily beaten and temporarily held in the district police dept. x (x and co.) who was held in the district police dept for five days, had electric shock torture. x, who was held in the district police dept and was tortured with a taser gun. x and x found x, who was held in Geologiia, declined to talk with them, and was badly injured. Morozivka, they interviewed a teacher about the pressure put on her and a mock execution. Savyntsi, they interviewed a grandmother, x, abduction, imprisonment,	

22.03.2023	confirmed by rus fed, has contact of son, imprisonment at district police dept Bryhadyrivka, interviewed a postwoman x from x's testimony Volchanskyi: phoned x (the ambulance nurse) from Dovhalivka. Contact acquired from x. She declined to talk after the (lack of) approval from the ambulance management. x: called the wife of x, who is currently a POW, for now she declined; phoned the sister of x (maiden name x), x. x in a very poor psychological state, does not wish to talk to anybody, staying with their children in Kharkiv, being treated by a psychiatrist	
23.03.2023	x, x: Dovhalivka, meeting with the camera operator and filming in Geologiia, questioned x from Savyntsi, age 71 took photos, videos of the school in Vesele that had been shelled and where people were sheltering, the guide was the wife of a guard/сторожа, but it would be better to speak with her husband. They watched a game with the local team, where out of the twelve players three of whom had been tortured, and the fourth was the son of x, who had been questioned. They interviewed the football referee, documented the attack on the school and tortured that happened in Vesele. In the morning x and x interviewed the mother of the boy who had been detained in Husarivka for two weeks. And then they went to Laheri, first by foot, then they got tired and called a taxi. The pastor from the protestant church who had been interviewed, received information about the torture and murder of POWs in Husarivka, they also interviewed x, the brother of a prisoner detained by the occupiers. x got sick with a sore throat, and x with an ear infection.	**x**, detained in Husarivka village
24.03.2023	A rather merciless and pointless trip by the whole team to Izyum, at least we documented the school and the place where, most likely, the video was shot when they took away Volodymyr Vakulenko.	

24.03.2023	We talked to his neighbors, walked around the outskirts of the town, but could not find anyone who might have been held in the No. 2 School, only those who were in the police dept. We went to Kapytolivka, interviewed the married couple who gave us the general context for the events, as well as descriptions and the callsigns for several of the soldiers from the so-called LPR. We went to Vesele, talked with the Vesele school guard, who was on shift during the strike on the school, and showed us the sites of three hits.	
25.03.2023	x and x found and interviewed x and x from Laheri, as well as x. They eventually located both female victims from x's witness statement. The other girl, x, declined to testify, because the Buryat soldier who raped her was identified by the russians and was shot by another one, which many people had told her. x and x went to look for x, found their address on x or x street, but she had left for treatment. They went to Verbivka to look for x who had been detained alongside x in the district police dept but did not find her. They went to Rakivka to look for x, found yet another victim and questioned him (his father had also been taken, but in Kupiansk. They eventually found x as well and arranged a meeting. They made one more trip to Zalyman to take photos and a nice one for the media guys. They called up all possible contacts and were practically told to get f*cked. x and x had lunch and jumped into a taxi heading for Savyntsi, from where the team set off to Vesele to look for bomb craters and other witnesses. In Vesele the team split up, x and x stayed behind to interview one victim, and x and x accompanied by encouraging gestures climbed down to look for two more shell craters. They found one in a vegetable patch next to the soldiers' base and a transformer substation, took a covert photo and quickly nipped off to Kuniye. There they	

25.03.2023	interviewed a witness to the attack on the school in Kuniye village and received the contacts of people from the village who had been taken prisoner in Izyum.	
26.03.2023	The whole team checked out of their apartments and set off toward Rakivka, where a meeting with x had already been planned for that morning. x and x interviewed the victim O. x, after which we all went to the possible place of residence of x , who was not answering his phone. Having knocked at the gate and waited for some time, we did not see anyone and left for Kuniye village to search the address of victims they had found earlier: x , Kuniye village, 31 x St, no. +xxx, but nobody was there. After that we set off to the site of the strike on 26.02.2022, from Kuniye village, x St, x , where the owner died. In pairs, x and x and x and x interviewed two witnesses of the strike. Then we returned once again to Svitla St, where another victim was found: x , with whom we arranged a future meeting. The entire team set off toward Kuniye high school where they documented the shelling that took place on 26.02.2022. When that was completed we left for Kharkiv, from where all us snoops left, dispersing all over Ukraine.	

[Editors' note: The following paragraphs contain expanded excerpts from the witness' testimonies collected during the field mission.]

Then he takes my socks off and screws wires connected to a TA-57 [Soviet army telephone] to my toes. One of them starts twisting the wire, and the other one holds me down. The current went through my whole body. The more he twisted it, the stronger the current shocked my body.

Again, he started asking me: "Do you know which people are in the ATO?" and so on.

And once again they forced my head into a bucket of water.

And then all this was repeated. All three of them beat me with their buttstock, punched and kicked me.

This went on until about 1:00 p.m.

And then one of them said, "See, we know you're a footballer!"

Then he started hitting me with a wooden bar from the hip down. He hit me about six times on my left calf muscle (gastrocnemius muscle). My muscle was pummeled into pulpy flesh.

Then they said, "Get up!"

"I can't."

They picked me up and one of them got out a knife. I thought that this was the end. But instead he cut off a length of tape and told me to lie down there, on the straw.

Detainees and their contacts:

Balakliya:

X, from Morozivka, "Tsarske Selo," taken to the forest for execution, his money taken off him.

X, from Brihadyrivka. He gave his phone to a repair shop, and on it there was a photo of a friend in the Ukrainian military. When he came to pick up his phone, he was arrested. He was found in Kupiansk prison.

X, from Balakliya. She was detained. A technical worker from No. 1 school, Balakliya. Her husband died during the liberation of Kupiansk.

On April 3, 2022, all doctors were gathered in the assembly hall (the pink hall) to coordinate their forced labor for the russians. On that day we left.

The Price: I Will Never Meet the War Crimes Researcher "Swan"

In March 2022, Orest joined the army and fought as an officer in the 53rd Separate Mechanized Brigade of the Armed Forces of Ukraine.

He became a member of our team on March 29, 2016. His first mission was to Stanytsia Luhanska and Tryokhizbenka, in the Luhansk region, where he documented shelling and the shooting of civilians during the battles for these settlements. For six years, he perfectly knew and loved the expanses of Donetsk and Luhansk regions, and was a participant in the hundredth-anniversary Truth Hounds field mission. In April 2019, Orest documented in Bakhmut and its surroundings, where now, four years later, his life ended.

Our database contains more than 200 documents authored by Orest. There are eyewitness accounts, photos, and videos taken at crime scenes.

Lyudmyla Ohnyeva

[Editors' note: The following fragment contains an excerpt from the article "'The Tree of Life' Was Found! The Story of Lyudmyla Ohnyeva on the Search and Recovery of Alla Horska's Mosaic" (*esthete* newspaper, 2022), translated from Ukrainian into English and pasted into the manuscript by Victoria Amelina.]

This panel was created by a team of monumentalists led by Viktor Zaretsky and Alla Horska in 1967. After Horska's death, due to ideological reasons, the artwork was bricked up and remained hidden for almost forty years. It wasn't until July

2008, thanks to the enthusiasm of Lyudmyla Ohnyeva,[11] that the "Tree of Life" was discovered and freed in October. However, circumstances led to the restaurant closing shortly after, and the premises remained locked for many years. As a result, only a few fortunate individuals had the opportunity to see the works of Alla Horska's team with their own eyes.

Not the End—Everyone

OLEKSANDRA AND I MEET AGAIN IN THE OFFICE OF THE Center of Civil Liberties.

She looks less exhausted and more hopeful. We have plans together: we both are invited to the summit of Iranian resistance [2023] which is to take place in Paris this time. Paris is a good destination for sure, but one day we will also meet in Tehran[12], and much sooner, very soon we will all meet in Luhansk, Donetsk, and Bakhchysaray[13].

Casanova is leaving the Truth Hounds team. In the beginning of April, she will start training to be a deminer. She found a plot of land near Kharkiv, with an old, fruitful garden and a little house; before the full-scale invasion she planned to buy a new house in the Poltava region, west of Kharkiv. But now it's important for her to grow her garden near Kharkiv; it's a very Ukrainian stubbornness: growing gardens near the border with Russia is like building a beautiful Pompeii near a volcano.

Casanova says that perhaps it's a good idea to make notes and

---

[11] Lyudmyla Ohnyeva (1936–2022) was a radiophysicist and decorative artist.

[12] Editors' note: Oleksandra Matviichuk could not attend the Free Iran 2022 conference. Victoria Amelina spoke in Tirana on behalf of Ukraine on July 23, 2022 (figure 24).

[13] Reference to the Jewish saying "Next year in Jerusalem." By evoking it, Ukrainians and Crimean Tatars express hope to meet next year on their liberated ancestral lands.

then write a book about how she, a war crimes researcher, turned into a deminer. I hope she writes her deminer's diary soon, and when she does you can look it up. It will be under her pen name, Victoria Yalivets.

Iryna Dovhan invites me to her home near Vasylkiv. It is full of light and new animals. The old shepherd dog Matilda, whom she had evacuated from her house near Donetsk, has already died. But Iryna has Koyot, a dog, whom her daughter saved after he got run over by a car, and countless cats, at least two of which were taken from the war zone as kittens. Iryna talks a lot about the women she helps to be heard, the garden she cherishes, and her husband. Recently, she bought him a vyshyvanka, the embroidered shirt that is a national symbol for all Ukrainians.

"At first, he was surprised as it's so hard now and I spent money on the vyshyvanka, instead of helping the army more. But what if tomorrow it's victory and everyone takes to the streets and you don't have a vyshyvanka to put on during the nation-wide celebration? He listened to me and agreed."

On the second floor of the house, in her daughter's former room, Iryna shows me her treasures, the vyshyvanka shirts the family will wear on the victory day. She believes in that day, just like Vakulenko believed in the day of Izyum liberation a year ago. Their faith makes me a believer too.

In the evening, coming home on the Kyiv subway, I think everyone on the train has their vyshyvanka ready for the day too. I should definitely get a new one for my son. More than a year has passed since our vacation to Egypt—he is eleven now, and has definitely outgrown his old one. But how would I order a shirt for him? I gasp when I realize I don't know his size anymore; I'd have to ask my aunt with whom he is staying in Poland to measure his height.

Since February 24, 2022, I turned from a writer into a war

crimes researcher and then learned to be both to tell you, the world, the story of Ukrainian civil society's quest for justice. Now there should also be a story of me learning to be a mother to my eleven-year-old son. But I'll let him tell this one in the hope that our children and loved ones will understand, respect, and forgive our choices.

In April, the International Publishers Association decided to give a special prize to Volodymyr Vakulenko posthumously. They were looking for someone to accept it and one of Volodymyr's publishers, Marjana Savka, advised them that it should be me. With mixed feelings, I agreed and, on May 22, delivered a short speech, the main part of which was a quote from Volodymyr's diary in translation by Daisy Gibbons.

I am speaking on behalf of my fellow Ukrainian writer Volodymyr Vakulenko who, unlike me, did not survive another attempt of the Russian Empire to erase Ukrainian identity.

This award is unique, meaningful and moving to the Ukrainian literary community, partly because hundreds of Ukrainian writers, publishers, and artists were murdered for choosing to be Ukrainian in the twentieth century, but none of them received such an international prize in Norway posthumously. I am sure that Volodymyr would like to dedicate this award to all of them too.

In September 2022, after the Kharkiv counteroffensive, when Ukrainian forensic experts were uncovering bodies from the mass grave, I uncovered something else, a war diary by Volodymyr Vakulenko. He was writing during occupation in the hope that you, the world, would hear him.

In memory of Volodymyr Vakulenko I would like to read some of the last notes he made in his diary:

I also dreamed of our boys fighting, dreamed I was hugging them, greeting them. I am scared to think of how they are. During the first days of occupation I gave up a little, then due to my half-starved state—totally. Now I've pulled myself together, even raking the garden a bit, and I dug up potatoes to take into the house. The birds only sing in the morning; in the afternoon, you don't hear even a caw from the crows. In the end, I am saved by the music on my mobile phone . . . And today, on Poetry Day, I was greeted by a small sedge of cranes in the sky, and through their "curlee" calls, one could almost make out, "Ukraine will be well again! I believe in victory!"

Volodymyr Vakulenko, March 21, 2022, Kapytolivka.

I brought this diary by Volodymyr to a museum in Kharkiv. And now I promise to bring this award to Kapytolivka, to Volodymyr's parents and son.

And I am sure Volodymyr would want me to finish with these two words: Slava Ukraini!

But I do not travel directly to Kapytolivka. I go back to Kyiv and stay there for several days to be present at the opening of a new literary festival in memory of Roman Ratushny. On that day I will cry a lot, as if returning this ability to process grief to myself. I will cry when I see Evhenia Zakrevska, Roman's lawyer and friend, walking with Bobby, her little brave dog from Kupyansk. I will cry, when Svitlana, Roman's mother, tries not to cry at the opening. I will cry when Marjana Sadovska, a powerful Ukrainian singer, sings Serhiy Zhadan's poem, the one I remember written on Peace Avenue in Mariupol. The hall near Protasiv Yar, where the concert takes place, is reminiscent of a typical Soviet palace of culture, and thus reminds me of all the ruined cultural centers, from Vysokopillya in the Kherson region to Derhachi near Kharkiv. But mainly, of course, it will remind me of the cultural center in the small town called New York in the Bakhmut area, where I used to organize a literary festival and an essay contest for teens.

However, I don't cry and I don't even feel sad when Evhenia

Zakrevska shows me a video tutorial on how to attach a grenade to a drone. We sit on the grass, not listening to a discussion on the festival stage, and watch the video.

"Here, see, there is nothing difficult," she comments when the grenade is finally attached and the drone is ready to start its flight, and I realize she is showing it to me not for this book, but for war.

I am particularly bad at handicrafts and even worse at reading maps, but if the war lasts long enough, my shortcomings won't matter. If the war lasts for years, I will finish my book, my son will grow up, and war crimes research will seem like not doing enough. If I'm being honest, it already seems like not doing enough to me. So then perhaps I will remember Evhenia's lesson just like her friend the journalist Lesya Ganzha remembered her mentioning the very possibility of joining the army in 2014. Then I can finally join, can't I? This thought calms me down, and Evhenia's attitude boosts my self-esteem as a potential soldier: she would not doubt whether I can do her job. This is all a question of whether I'm ready to leave everything behind and do it.

Evhenia stays in Kyiv for training about which she would not talk in detail: she learns to operate bigger, more efficient and obviously more deadly drones. I board the night train to Kharkiv. My backpack is heavy. I have Volodymyr Vakulenko's award from Norway, my laptop and the papers for potential witnesses to sign the power of attorney, some blue cheese for Yulia, the librarian of Kapytolivka, a bottle of good wine to bring to my friend in the Donetsk region, where alcohol is prohibited due to the proximity of the front line, and thirty children's books for the bookcrossing shelf in Kramatorsk humanitarian aid warehouse.

The next day I finally bring the award to Vakulenko's parents in Kapytolivka, they are waiting at the gate in front of the house.

I will enter his room again, the room where I forgot that I am a war crimes researcher and acted like a Ukrainian writer who lost her colleague due to Russian imperial ambitions. I will bring the prize to Kapytolivka; Olena and Volodymyr Senior, Volodymyr's parents, will cry and hug me as if again, we are burying him on a cold winter day in the Kharkiv cemetery. Then we will walk to Volodya's garden: Volodymyr Senior [will plant] despite the danger of mines.

I plant flowers here too. Yulia, the Librarian of Kapytolivka, brought gloves for me.

"And do you have gloves for yourself?" I ask her.

"No, but I am from a village, and you are a city girl; you're not used to putting your hands in the soil."

"No, I searched for Vakulenko's diary without gloves, and I want to plant flowers for him without gloves."

Yulia understands. We plant flowers, take pictures, and even laugh. Volodymyr's parents start smiling too. Just a bit.

[The Kharkiv volunteer] Oksana [Astrakhantseva] and I spend the night at the Librarian's cozy house, sleeping soundly after restless nights in Kyiv and Kharkiv, and then we head to the Donetsk region.

When I leave Kharkiv the huge poster MACLENA GRASA 26/02/22 18:00 is still hanging on the Drama Theater building.

I'm spending loud Kyiv nights writing a foreword to Vakulenko's diary on the floor of the corridor in my apartment, the safest place in my reach; the parcel I found in the black Ukrainian soil in September 2022 is about to become a book. My little mission of delivering Volodymyr's message to the world is almost complete. My own book is almost finished too.

Sometimes when an air raid alarm sounds I go to the balcony and watch air defense rockets rise into black sky over the skyline. I don't have to overcome any fear; I just don't fear death anymore. I imagine even how all the women I write about would finally gather at my funeral: they all are busy fighting for justice, so such an occasion is definitely the only chance. But then I remember I have yet to finish this book, watch my son grow up, and possibly even join the army in several years. So I step away from the magnificent but dangerous view and get back to writing.

A Poem Instead of an Epilogue

In a barren springtime field
Stands a woman dressed in black
Crying her sisters' names
Like a bird in the empty sky

She'll cry them all out of herself

The one that flew away too soon
The one that had begged to die
The one that couldn't stop death
The one that has not stopped waiting
The one that has not stopped believing
The one that still grieves in silence

She'll cry them all into the ground
As though sowing the field with pain

And from pain and the names of the women
Her new sisters will grow from the earth
And again will sing joyfully of life

But what about her, the crow?

She will stay in this field forever
Because only this cry of hers
Holds all those swallows in the air

Do you hear how she calls
Each one by her name?

Afterword: Empty Pages

When Russia began its full-scale invasion of Ukraine, Victoria Amelina was known as the author of two novels and two children's books, as well as the founder of the New York Literary Festival, based in the town of New York in the Donetsk region of Ukraine. However, after February 24, 2022, like many Ukrainians, Victoria tried to find a new role in which she could better serve others. For her, the role of novelist was no longer relevant, for no writer's fantasy could compete with the unimaginable things happening in her country post-invasion. Victoria therefore returned to Ukraine from abroad two days after the onset of the great war and started helping others at home. She worked in a humanitarian warehouse in Lviv, interpreted for Ukrainian and foreign volunteers, sourced medicines, raised money to buy vehicles and drones for the troops, helped evacuate people and pets from all corners of Ukraine, and took many of them in to her apartment in Lviv.

Still, her faith in the power of the written word had not abandoned her, and so she began her quest for the genre that would be the most accurate and most truthful in the time of war. At this point her documentary poetry emerged[14]. It recorded the reality of war and how it shattered your language "as if hit by a shell."[15] In addition, Victoria wrote essays in English for numerous international media outlets, in which she explained the historic reasons behind Russia's colonial war against Ukraine.

But this was not enough for her. She wondered: Could the written word be used not only to document the war, but to accelerate

---

[14] After Victoria's death, her poems were published in the collection *Svidchennya* (*Testimonies*) (2024). The English translation of the collection is forthcoming.

[15] Quote from Victoria Amelina's poem "Ne poeziya" ("Not Poetry").

the advent of justice? As she phrased it in the book you have just read:

> *Law is ultimately about human beings, or at least it should have people at the center; this makes law similar to literature. Maybe I can do something other than sorting medicine, moving boxes, and collecting money?*

On April 3, 2022, immediately following the liberation of the Kyiv region, Victoria went to Kyiv to meet the writers Larysa Denysenko, Olena Stiazhkina, and Svitlana Povalyaeva, who had not left the city at the beginning of the invasion. On April 8, the Russians hit the railway station in Kramatorsk with a missile strike. Sixty-one people died and 121 were injured. Her meetings in Kyiv and the tragedy in Kramatorsk made Victoria realize that, besides her volunteer work, she could help people by documenting the war. At the end of May, Victoria was trained to document war crimes by the organization Truth Hounds. At the beginning of June, she joined PEN Ukraine's first volunteer trip to Kharkiv, a city near the front lines.

During this time, Victoria grew more and more aware of the importance of her transition from fiction to nonfiction literature. She wanted to help preserve the stories and voices of people living through war. As Victoria shared with a friend on June 15, 2022:

> I want to write, and I'm thinking whether I can, a book of reportage on those who are documenting the war. I'm still trying to understand if something will come of it. There are people who write about the war with various goals in mind. I am especially interested in those who document war crimes with the goal of holding the perpetrators accountable.

By the end of June, she had already embarked on an advocacy trip to Brussels and London accompanying the human rights activist Oleksandra Matviichuk, and in August she went on her first field mission to the Kherson region, in southern Ukraine.

Thus arose the concept of her book: a collection of reported stories about Ukrainian women documenting war crimes. While conceptualizing it, she shared her developing ideas and drafts with her husband and friends. Individual stories about her would-be women protagonists laid the foundation of the work, with the working title *Write Your Own War* or *Looking at Women, Looking at War*.

In the same way Victoria had searched for her new role in the first months of the full-scale invasion, in writing this book, she searched for her new voice and her new genre as a writer. Her archive demonstrates how the structure of this book changed many times before she eventually arrived at a form of documentary prose that combined diary entries, story excerpts taken from her subjects' investigations, accounts using the voices of witnesses to the crimes, investigations and reports taken during her field missions, as well as interviews, essays, historical excursions, and poetry. The one thing that remained unchanged was the decision to write the book in English. This was in order to reveal to the world Russia's centuries-long genocides and unpunished crimes against Ukrainians. As she stated in this book:

> The quest for justice has turned me from a novelist and mother into a war crimes researcher. Over the last year, I have photographed shell holes in library walls and the ruins of schools and cultural centers; I have recorded the testimonies of survivors and eyewitnesses of atrocities. I've done this to uncover the truth, ensure the survival of memory, and give justice and lasting peace a chance.

From June 2022 to June 2023, Victoria dedicated her life to this book: she joined field missions with Truth Hounds and volunteer trips with PEN Ukraine to areas near the front lines and liberated territories; she sought out witnesses and collected testimonies from people who had experienced Russian occupation. Endowed with extraordinary empathy that reminded us of the hero of her first novel, *Fall Syndrome*, Victoria was able to listen and provide support, and often became friends with those who shared with her their accounts of the war. She would often visit her book's protagonists or accompany them in their work, such as joining Vira Kuryko in Chernihiv, Tetyana Pylypchuk and Evhenia Zakrevska in Kharkiv, Iryna Novitska in Kryvyi Rih, and Oleksandra Matviichuk on her trip to Brussels, Paris, and London. This year of Victoria's life consisted of endless journeys, though she interrupted them regularly to make at least short stops in Kraków to see her son.

In September 2022, a few days after the Kharkiv region was liberated from the Russians, Victoria joined another mission by Truth Hounds and convinced her colleagues to stop by the small village of Kapytolivka, near Izyum, where in March 2022 the Russians had kidnapped the writer Volodymyr Vakulenko. No one knew his fate. A few months later, it was revealed that the occupiers had killed Volodymyr with two shots from a Makarov pistol and had buried him in a mass grave in the forest on the outskirts of Izyum. Victoria recorded the witness statements of Volodymyr's parents and neighbors and became the initiator of Truth Hounds' investigation into her fellow writer's kidnapping. During her first visit to Kapytolivka, Victoria helped Volodymyr's father search the garden for the diary which the writer had kept during the occupation. Vakulenko had buried it in his garden under a cherry tree just one day before his abduction by Russian soldiers. It was Victoria who found it and dug it up. In June 2023, Victoria, along with Volodymyr's loved ones and colleagues, presented the publication of this diary at the Book Arsenal literary festival in Kyiv. A month later Victoria initiated the publication of the diary, and in June 2023, along with Volodymyr's loved ones and colleagues, she took part in the presentation of the book at the Book Arsenal literary festival in Kyiv.

Soon after the festival, Victoria planned to leave Ukraine for a longer period; she had a residency with Columbia University in Paris. She intended to use the time to concentrate on this book and finally devote more time to her son. As she put it in her afterword, written before the book's completion,

> Since February 24, 2022, I have turned from a writer into a war crimes researcher and then learned to be both to tell you, the world, the story of Ukrainian civil society's quest for justice. Now there should also be a story of me learning to be a mother to my eleven-year-old son.

A few days before the Book Arsenal literary festival, Victoria decided to go to Kherson one more time to record the story of the wife of the conductor Yuriy Kerpatenko, who had been killed by the Russians. On her way south, on June 23, she sent a friend a file with the unfinished manuscript, accompanied by the words "It's uncertain which missile might hit me in Kherson, so this document can stay with you just in case."

But that was not to be. Instead, on June 27, Victoria joined a delegation of Colombian authors to the Donetsk region. At the end of a long day, they were relaxing in a pizzeria in Kramatorsk. It was hit by a Russian missile, injuring sixty-four people and taking the lives of thirteen others. One of the severely injured was Victoria. She died a few days later, in Mechnykov Hospital in Dnipro, from the injuries she had sustained. The date of her death is July 1, Volodymyr Vakulenko's birthday.

We opened the file of the last working version of the manuscript back in July 2023, not long after saying farewell to Victoria in Kyiv and in Lviv. Reading and editing this text in the following months became a continuation of our pain; it became a great responsibility, but a great source of support as well. Life under the conditions of war, with its daily losses, has taught us that there is only one way to deal with the pain: to continue the work of the people we love.

Victoria had managed to write nearly 60 percent of what she had planned, but even so, is it possible to estimate an author's progress in a creative process where the text is born, changed, and polished while being written? Furthermore, if we evaluate Victoria's desire to bring justice to her country, how much closer did she manage to bring it before her life was taken by Russia?

The file we started working on contained the structure laid down by Victoria and the chapters she had written and edited several times. The document had a beginning and a finale, yet some chapters in the middle were left completely blank, while others contained only sketchy notes: theses of transcribed conversations, or thoughts that were to become polished writing later. In several places, Victoria had inserted quotes from books or journalistic materials in order to rework them in her text. The manuscript also included reports from Truth Hounds field missions, as well as an interview with the British lawyer and human rights defender Philippe Sands. Although these text extracts differed from the style of the rest of the manuscript, we know for sure from conversations with Victoria that for her it was crucial to include them in the book. They were meant to enrich the reader's understanding of how war crimes researchers—and later international courts—work with testimonies. Further to this, these parts of the book demonstrate the path that Victoria took in turning from novelist to war crimes researcher. She wrote some parts of the reports included in the manuscript, and in them, her literary skill is evident.

In addition to the last working copy, dated June 23, 2023, Victoria's family worked on arranging her archive. In it we found various versions of individual chapters, photographs, and videos from her trips to territories near the front line and those that had been recently liberated, and hundreds of hours of recordings of conversations with her book's protagonists and war crimes witnesses. At times it also seemed that Victoria had left us hints and instructions in our online chat histories.

As we worked with the text, we aimed for minimal intrusion into Victoria's concept and style while at the same time, when necessary, easing the reading process. With that in mind, our editorial group accompanies the reader through the text warning them about which chapters remained unfinished or what the author intended to include in a certain section, according to the drafts. We also prepared more than one hundred editorial footnotes in order to explain important historical or personal contexts. If, in the draft versions, we found more detailed accounts of events or notes for chapters that were left blank in the last working copy of the manuscript, we transferred them into the book and identified our intervention to the reader.

Each of our editorial group's decisions was born in discussions during which we felt that Victoria was with us, that she was helping us do exactly what she would have wanted and what would be best for her text. These months of editing the book became a continuation of our communication with Victoria. We would argue, sometimes having to read older drafts and listen to archival audio files; sometimes we would laugh and crack jokes—exactly like it had always been in our conversations with

Victoria. Each one of our edits is the result of earlier, detailed discussions with her, as well as our great love for her.

It was painful to realize that Victoria had not finished writing those chapters for which she had gathered the most material, and had not developed those topics she talked about most in her advocacy trips and in opinion pieces. The reader will find only outlines of chapters about the writer Volodymyr Vakulenko; only fragments of impressions about trips she had taken with the human rights activist Oleksandra Matviichuk. The portraits of some of her other heroines—such as Larysa Denysenko, Olena Stiazhkina, and Kateryna Rashevska—remain just sketches. Victoria never managed to add even drafts of stories about the journalist and military servicewoman Lesia Hanzha or about Maryna Atsekhovska, wife of murdered conductor Yuriy Kerpatenko. Victoria met each of them, but her archives contain only audio recordings of their conversations. Another important encounter foregrounding significant links between past and present was with Solomiia Stasiv, a representative of the Clooney Foundation in Ukraine, whom Victoria met while investigating the case of Volodymyr Vakulenko. It was only later that she discovered that Solomiia was a close relative of the Soviet dissident Levko Lukyanenko, author of the Act of Independence of Ukraine and protagonist of a book written by another of Victoria's chosen subjects, Vira Kuryko. This is merely one of the stories the author wished to preserve in the pages of this book but which, due to her death, remained empty.

We are cognizant that in certain places it was difficult for the reader to read the unfinished text in the form of notes or fieldwork reports. Therefore, we wish to thank you for your patience and attention to this book. The book would never have existed had Russia not unleashed its full-scale war against Ukraine. It would have emerged very differently if Russia had never taken away Victoria's life. We hope that as you hold this document in your hands, you now understand the meaning of the empty pages in it. This book is not only a work of literature, but a testimony to the awful crimes that Russia has been committing against Ukrainian culture and people for centuries. This book also bears witness to that emptiness that we have been feeling ever since Victoria has been gone, and which can never be filled.

In one of the draft versions of the book found in Victoria's archive, she uses a different structure for the text, dividing it into chapters with the subheadings Lesson One, Lesson Two, Lesson Three, and so on. They were included because, on the one hand, Victoria had explored in her earlier literary works the history of her family and how Russia's colonial politics had caused them to forget about certain pages of their own history and the crimes committed against them. Thus, these lessons, for her, were also personal ones. On the other hand, as a researcher of Russia's anti-Ukrainian crimes, she wanted to share important lessons in testifying to these crimes, with each lesson concluding with the start of court proceedings that would serve justice. At the same time, thinking about a non-Ukrainian audience, it was critically important for Victoria to show that Russian aggression against Ukrainian culture and identity did not start in 2022 and that, without understanding the historical contexts and parallels, it would be impossible to grasp the true nature of this genocidal war. Victoria frequently drew parallels between the present and the history of the Executed Renaissance, when the Soviet authorities tortured, repressed, and murdered thousands of Ukrainian artists and intellectuals, and destroyed or banned their creative heritage. For the same reason, Victoria mentions the Holodomor and the millions of Ukrainians killed during the artificial famine of 1932–1933. This is why Victoria informs the reader about the dissidents of the 1960s, who, like her, were the first in Ukrainian history forced to combine the role of artists and war crimes researchers. As Victoria wrote about her predecessor, Alla Horska, an artist and an investigator into the violations committed by the Soviet Union, "I have yet to become a part of this sad tradition of Ukrainian creatives having to find out what happened to their dead colleagues."

Victoria saw the purpose of her book thus: "To uncover the truth, ensure the survival of memory, and give justice and lasting peace a chance". She believed that truthful testimony could bring justice closer and finally break the circle of Russian impunity, crimes, and genocides committed against Ukraine, unnamed and unrecognized by the world. Having taken Victoria away from us, from her family and friends, and from Ukrainian and world culture, Russia was not able to take away the power of her word. As she put it, "Because whenever a writer is still being read, it means that they are still alive."[16]

TETYANA TEREN
YARYNA GRUSHA
SASHA DOVZHYK
ALEX AMELIN

[16] This quote is from Victoria Amelina's foreword for the posthumous edition of Volodymyr Vakulenko's diary, *'Ya peretvoriuius . . .' Shchodennyk okupatsii* (*I Am Transforming . . . The Diary of the Occupation: Selected Poems*) (Vivat, 2023).

APPENDIX I

Fragments

Fragment A

Kateryna Rashevska is; somewhere here, in 1399, Western civilization, represented by the Lithuanian prince Vytautas, lost a battle to the Eastern civilization, represented by the Tatar horde.

In the last days before the full-scale invasion, Kateryna, a young lawyer from a small village in Sumy Oblast, watches yet another documentary about the Nazi policies toward Jews. She is very interested in the history of the Holocaust and also in the Article 6 of the Rome Statute. And the Article 6 is, of course, Genocide.

Maria Lvova-Belova has blonde hair, wears lovely long dresses, and helps Putin transfer Ukrainian children to Russia. He appointed Lvova-Belova as Russia's so-called Presidential Commissioner for Children's Rights four months before the invasion to become a partner in one of his crimes. The crime is defined in Article 6 in the Rome Statue under point (e) "forcibly transferring children of the group to another group."

Kateryna Rashevska is a young lawyer from a small village in Poltava oblast; somewhere here, in 1399, the Western civilization, represented by Lithuanian prince Vytautas, lost a battle to the Eastern civilization, represented by the Tatar horde.

In the last days before the full-scale invasion, Kateryna watches another documentary about the Nazi policies toward Jews. She is very interested in Article 6 of the Rome Statute, Genocide.

Maria Lvova-Belova was born in the Russian city of Penza. As a child, she sang in a church choir and dreamed of marrying a priest and having many children. Her dreams have largely come true. She is married to a Russian Orthodox priest. She has five biological, eighteen adopted, and one stolen child, a teenager named Philippe from Mariupol, whose bravery I admire. According to Lvova-Belova, Philippe hasn't been a very obedient "son," to put it mildly.

Kateryna Rashevska also dreams of having children, yet she has been too busy in the past eight years of the Russian-Ukrainian war, so she has none. She works for the Regional Center for Human Rights or RCHR, an NGO founded by the internally displaced Ukrainians from the temporarily occupied Crimea. In fact, before 2022, she was the only one in the office whose life was not affected by the Russian aggression. The RCHR first encountered cases of Ukrainian children's transferring to Russia in 2014: the children from the occupied Crimea were adopted by Russian families. Gathering information about these cases was the first task given to Kateryna at RCHR.

Kateryna Rashevska has blonde hair, wears suits, and defends people from grave human rights violations. Children transferring to Russia is just one of them. Yet Kateryna is especially passionate about it. Firstly, because she loves children. Secondly because as a lawyer she is interested in the crime of genocide.

Maria Lvova-Belova has blonde hair, wears lovely long dresses, and helps Putin transfer Ukrainian children to Russia. Putin appointed her as Russia's so-called Presidential Commissioner for Children's Rights four months before the invasion to become a partner in one of his crimes. The crime is defined in Article 6 in the Rome Statute under point (e) "forcibly transferring children of the group to another group." Kateryna and Maria are very different women. It's the Article 6 of the Rome Statute that connects them.

Maria does not know the connection. Kateryna has been thinking about Maria since March 2022. In April 2022, she learned that first children taken from Ukraine were transferred into Russian families. Among those, she saw two boys who had a grandmother. Kateryna wrote about children transferring and adoptions on social media, but her messages did not attract much attention. In March and April there were more hot themes.

What Kateryna finds and saves since March 2022, literally following Maria Lvova-Belova everywhere from social media to the Russian state-sponsored television channels, will feed into the submission RCHR will make to the International Criminal Court on October 25, 2022.

Fragment B

To go on this mission, I canceled my trip to Sweden to the Gothenburg Book Fair. I was supposed to talk about war crimes there. But Izyum was liberated, there was still no news about Volodymyr Vakulenko, and instead the mass grave in Izyum forest was all over the internet. I apologized and chose Izyum, not Gothenburg.

We have a pl[1]

We are traveling there through Merefa and Pervomaysk. For the first time since March 2022, Casanova is going the same roads she traveled to evacuate people in the Kharkiv region. We spent too much time at the meeting with prosecutors in Kharkiv, perhaps. Now we are late. It is dark as it can only be dark at war, with no lights along the road and no lights in the houses, ruined or intact. Casanova is driving, I sit next to her at the front passenger seat in our minivan nicknamed Cucumber. Fisher is driving the second car, his own, nevertheless nicknamed Long-nosed by the Truth Hounds team.

We had several options for accommodation. One of them came from my contacts in Izyum: a young woman offered us her apartment for free in exchange for bringing some help to her grandmother. The apartment has no electricity, running water, or heating, like all other apartments in Izyum. It is missing some windows, like most of them. Yet staying there would allow us to complete more work as we would not have to spend time traveling each day.

He did not expect any guests. The luxury resort was a place of survival for the past half year. They can only offer us Greek salad, four portions, and a bottle of good red wine. The owner asks if he could join us at the dinner; he appears to be a prominent architect and restaurateur. He says their specialty is fish; if they knew we would come, they would catch the best carps for the six of us. In March, after all the bridges in the area were blown up, they thought fishing would be their only source of survival. It was a significant part of their survival strategy indeed. Yet we do not talk about survival and war much but switch to discussing food and the best restaurants in Kyiv and Kharkiv. The Russian invasion does not dominate even at the table; we talk about far more important things like the best feta cheese from Greece, last pieces of which the local chef has put into our salads.

In the morning I would see the dead frog in the pool outside my window, dust and flies in the glasses in the cupboard in the fashionable restaurant room: war is here. But at night everything looks perfectly untouched by it.

---

[1] This sentence was left unfinished.

Fragment C: Original Testimony

My brigade and I used to gather every day at twelve o'clock at Shakespeare Cemetery, where the deceased were buried. Then these meetings took place at nine in the morning near the administration building.

The company Ritual Services organizes all burials on Shakespeare Street. There are also other cemeteries: Nekrasova (where many were buried during the occupation), Pivnichne, Arkhangelske (Russian military were stationed in the nearby forest, so there were no graves), and Kapitana Orlova.

In addition to our brigade, there was another volunteer brigade in Izyum called the 200s,[2] organized by the city administration, consisting of only six to eight people. They collected the bodies of the deceased. Often people buried their deceased and fallen in their yards, and these volunteers reburied the bodies. They traveled in one bus. One of these volunteers is named Serhiy. I don't have any other information about him. You can ask my colleague Vitaliy << who leads our organization's burial brigade and is in charge of the Shakespeare Cemetery >> about him. Both the 200s and our brigade were the only ones allowed on the left bank of the Donets River when the traffic was restored. Prior to that, the bodies were transported by hand across a pedestrian bridge. And no one except us and the 200s were allowed into the Shakespeare Cemetery. Both brigades brought bodies for burial with notes about the deceased or the missing person. There were bodies that couldn't be identified. We buried everyone under numbers and recorded them in the burial journal of our company. Currently, the SBU investigators have confiscated this journal and the computer for investigative actions.

---

[2] Cargo 200 (in Ukrainian, dvokhsoti, or two hundreds) is a Soviet code word used for the transportation of military casualties. In post-Soviet states, 200s has become a euphemism for killed in action.

APPENDIX II

Conversation with Philippe Sands, Lviv Bookforum 2022

RAPHAEL LEMKIN CITY, SUNDAY, OCTOBER 9

The international human rights lawyer and author of *East West Street*, *The Ratline*, and *The Last Colony* talks about his work and ideas about justice and criminality that have their origins in the city of Lviv with the novelist Victoria Amelina.

Victoria Amelina: Hi everyone. We are at the Lviv International Book Forum, which is happening in a digital partnership with Hay Festival. This event is taking place in Lviv, Ukraine, thanks to the Ukrainian Armed Forces that protect us and thanks to the support of our allies, including the UK, France, and everyone sending weapons to Ukraine for us to defend ourselves. We thank everyone who made this event happen.

This is a talk between me, Victoria Amelina, and Philippe Sands, who is a professor of law at University College London, a brilliant writer, and author of *East West Street: On the Origins of Genocide and Crimes Against Humanity*, a book which is very popular in Lviv and Ukraine in general. It was translated into Ukrainian by Pavlo Myhal, a translator who is now a soldier of the Armed Forces of Ukraine fighting at the front line.

Why am I talking to Philippe? We have a lot in common, I think. Both of our grandfathers used to live in the city of Lviv (or Lwów, Lemberg), and Philippe Sands has made this city popular among the international audience. His grandfather Leon used to live at 12 Sheptytskykh Street. My grandfather, Oleksiy, used to live on a neighboring street, now Andreya Sheptytskoho Street, about a hundred meters from that apartment. Of course, at the time distance was much greater. My grandfather Oleksiy was born near Vinnytsia. Perhaps you know this city now since it was attacked by Russian missiles and civilians, including children, were killed. My grandfather was born there. He fought Nazis in the Soviet Army and then became an accountant in the state bank in the Soviet Union and received a small room in that apartment. In that sense, we could have been neighbors.

But the history is much more complex than that. Of course, it never happened.

Philippe Sands traveled to Lviv, Ukraine, first in 2010 to give a lecture and has been returning since. First, I would like to talk about how your relationship with this city evolved. How does it feel to be in the city when it is under attack? Of course, it looks very peaceful now, but we all know what might happen at any moment. What is your relationship with Lviv and how does it feel now?

Philippe Sands: Thank you so very much for this lovely introduction. How fantastic to imagine that we are neighbors! Not just now, but in this historical and familial sense. I think we are going to have a wonderful conversation.

Can I just begin by saying how incredibly moving it is to be here? I have spent three days now in Lviv. It's a city I've come to know very well. It's a city, undoubtedly, where a part of my heart is. It feels like coming home. There is, as you know, not just for me but in my community, in both of my countries a very strong sense of solidarity with Ukraine. It probably doesn't need to be said, but I want to say it. You in Ukraine are not alone. There is an incredible amount of support, and it is widespread and very strongly felt. I've come, in a sense, for a reason that is the answer to your question. I wanted to be here as an expression of solidarity. Perhaps, for my mother, the idea of coming to what she thought, and many will think of as a war zone, seemed a risky thing to do. In fact, I send her regular WhatsApp messages to inform her that I am fine, that everything is fine, that the people are well, and there is food. But there is also an atmosphere, and it is different. It feels different. And the conversations are different from when I first came here in 2010.

I was not aware of this place called Lviv in April 2010, when I received an invitation to give a lecture on the cases that I do on crimes against humanity and genocide at the law faculty. I did not know, I am very sorry to say, where Lviv was. I googled it and I saw that it used to be called Lwów and Lemberg. The moment I saw this, I knew I was going to come here.

My grandfather used to mention that he'd been born in a place called Lemberg during the Austro-Hungarian Empire in 1904. He'd never wanted to talk about anything that happened before 1945. So I came to Lviv to find out who my grandfather was, and it was the way of finding out who I was—because his identity is, in part, my identity.

I came, to be very honest, not to give a lecture but to find a house in which he was born. My mother found his birth certificate, and we knew that the place was called 12 Sheptytskykh Street. But we didn't know, being these English people who turned up in the strange place, that there are two Sheptytsky streets. There's the big one, the avenue, which I think is the one that your grandfather lived on. And, very excitedly, we went to number twelve.

Victoria Amelina: That must be the Mytropolyta Andreya Street, for those who know the Ukrainian names of the streets.

Philippe Sands: So we went there, and we found the house. We were very excited because it seemed like a very fancy building, and we were surprised because my grandfather was very poor. We went inside and, I remember, we went up to the first floor. We knocked. Eventually, we heard someone coming, and a man opened the door, wearing nothing but his underpants—very tight underpants. And I was with my mother, who is already in her late seventies. She was a bit surprised. Having had a conversation with him, we realized that we were on the wrong Sheptytsky Street. The next day, we went through exactly the same procedure. And it was wonderful. I fell in love with Lviv the first moment I set foot here. I felt completely at home, instantly.

Victoria Amelina: Thank you so much for sharing this story. I would like to bring the discussion more to current events, to the Russian-Ukrainian war. I also have to inform you that I am writing a book which is called *Looking at Women Looking at War: A War and Justice Diary*. This conversation fits into the diary part, the justice part. Perhaps, it will be a part of my book. So if you come up with questions, you too can be included.

For any Ukrainian now, discussion on the International Tribunal for Crime of Aggression is very important. My book starts with my personal story, of course. In February, I denied all the warnings, I didn't want to believe that this full-scale Russian aggression would eventually happen. When it did, I was on vacation and I only managed to come back to Ukraine on February 26, because Ukraine became a no-fly zone. Not, unfortunately, in the sense of protected sky; planes couldn't land in Ukrainian airports anymore. Coming back to my hometown Lviv took me two days. I think at that time, Philippe

Sands was already thinking about his column for the Financial Times about how it is necessary to create an International Tribunal for the Crime of Aggression, which would allow us to get to the top table. I would like to quote your column here.

On February 28, the column was published. Philippe writes: "President Vladimir Putin's decision to launch attacks on Ukraine poses the gravest challenge to the post-1945 international order, one premised on the idea of a rule of law and principles of self-determination for all peoples and the prohibition of the use of force. It is not the first time that Russia has taken a military interest in the territories it now seeks to occupy: in September 1914, Russia occupied the city of Lviv, causing tens of thousands to flee westward, including my ten-year-old grandfather. The Soviet Union returned in September 1939 for a second bite, and then again in the summer of 1944, remaining in control until Ukraine achieved independence in 1991 . . . Putin has gambled, hoping that the west will blink. Following its own failures, including an illegal, failed war in Iraq, and the recent collapse of political will in Afghanistan, along with the embrace of oligarchical money and dependence on Russian gas, he hopes that the west doesn't have the stomach to stand up to his actions. He may be right, but his bet poses a grave challenge, and one that sanctions and financial measures alone cannot address."

And then Philippe suggests the idea to create an International Tribunal for the Crime of Aggression, which would allow us to have a trial on Putin and all his accomplices. I would like to talk about that. How did this idea come to you? Did you expect this war to happen? What was your February like and what was the reaction to this article?

Philippe Sands: I am very pleased to be a part of your diary. I have to say I've heard wonderful things about your two novels. I've not read them because they do not exist yet in English or French, but I know that they will, and you can count on my support to try to make that happen.

In 2016, I published the book *East West Street: On the Origins of Genocide and Crimes Against Humanity*, in which one of the major characters is the city of Lviv. Frankly, it permeates everything. Because, remarkably, the origins of the two concepts of crimes against humanity and genocide can be traced to the city of Lviv and to the two men who were students at what then was the Jan Kazimierz Law School, today the Ivan Franko Law School in the University of Lviv.

These two men were Hersch Lauterpacht and Raphael Lemkin. In Lauterpacht's case, all of his family lived in Lviv or in Zhovkva (Żółkiew) nearby, which is where my family also has its origins. Lemkin's family was a little further out, but in the course of the period between 1939 to 1945, both men, like my grandfather, lost every single member of their family who came from over here. What I found so remarkable about these two men was that instead of lying down in a corner and weeping about what had happened, they took their ideas, wrote them up and persuaded countries around the world to support these concepts of crimes against humanity and genocide. I'd found that incredibly inspiring.

I, of course, did not live during WWII, but I've spoken to many people who have and was very struck by those who were strong, as well as those who were weak. My own family history has been very influenced by that period. So, my reaction, like yours, Victoria, was that I couldn't believe it. In January and February, as these reports were coming, I was wondering whether this was disinformation from the intelligence services of the United States and the United Kingdom, whether they were, for some reason, trying to rally us against the dreaded Russian monster. I don't think any of us really believed that this was going to happen. And then it happened, and it was shocking. It was even more shocking than it would otherwise have been because I've been to Ukraine so many times in the last twelve years. I had been in Kyiv in October just before the war, and in Lviv too. I have many friends here, and it felt very local, very at home, and very much more personal than it would otherwise have felt. So my reaction was much like yours in that sense.

Because of *East West Street*, and because I live in a world of international law, the two issues of Ukraine and international law all of a sudden would thrust to the first pages of the newspapers. A lot of newspapers got in touch and asked me to write something about what has been going on. I accepted the *Financial Times*'s offer because it's one of those newspapers that gets read by the people who matter, people who actually make decisions. That's what I wanted to do. I wanted to reach people who mattered.

The *Financial Times* got in touch with me on the twenty-sixth of February, and I spent a day working out what I could say that would be helpful or useful. By then, I had already formed the view that, of course, a military response was needed, and I supported it from the first day. In fact, I go much further than what NATO has done and what Britain and the US have done. I supported a no-fly zone right from the very beginning. For me, it was an absolutely existential threat to Ukraine, but also an existential threat to a series of values that I really care about.

I was very familiar with the issue of Russian expansionism and essentially colonial and imperial designs. In 2008, I was hired as the lawyer for Georgia against Russia in a case of the International Court of Justice, which concerned the occupation of South Ossetia and Abkhazia. The only way we could get to the International Court was on an obscure International Convention on the Elimination of All Forms of Racial discrimination. The Russian occupier was essentially imposing linguistic and educational obligations to extinguish the Georgian language in those territories. So we went to court. And I am very sorry that the ICJ eventually, having ordered provisional measures, ruled that the court didn't have jurisdiction. It was a terrible decision. It was a formality, a technical, narrow-minded, little, frankly pathetic decision that somehow Georgia hadn't given enough notification to Russia. It was an appalling decision, and it was a mistake.

At the time I believed, and I very shortly after wrote, that this was a very dangerous decision because it signaled to Russia that it can take these kinds of actions and the international institutions won't do anything. Then, of course, the same thing happened in terms of turning a blind eye to Chechnya, and then Syria, Crimea and parts of Eastern Ukraine.

Again, I just want to put in a note of reality check here. What I'm about to say is not going to be popular in Ukraine. But throughout this period successive British governments not only did nothing but, in my view, actively supported the Russian sense that they could get away with this kind of stuff. And Boris Johnson, the very man who is considered a hero in this country (something that very frankly makes me feel sick to my stomach, although I agree with the positions he has taken, I do not believe that they are genuinely motivated), put into the House of Lords a Russian called Lebedev, whose father was a KGB agent.[1] This was opposed by the British establishment and Johnson overrode it because he was essentially in the pocket of a lot of Russian money and a lot of Russian influence. It was a late sudden

[1] Evgeny Lebedev is a current member of the House of Lords and Russian businessman who owns the *Evening Standard* and is a shareholder of the *Independent*, among other media companies. He was nominated for life peerage by Boris Johnson in 2020.

conversion to the Ukrainian cause, having done nothing as foreign minister, and then nothing as prime minister to address. London is disgustingly awash with Russian oligarchs' money. You cannot even begin to imagine how London opened its doors to filthy, dirty Russian money. It was unbelievable.

Against that background, I and many people felt deep-seated anger that Ukraine had been let down by the West, which had if not encouraged these actions, essentially turned a blind eye to things that had happened before, not just the United Kingdom, but other countries also.

So when the *Financial Times* asked me to write something, I thought: what can I do that's helpful? I'm not a military person, I'm not a money person. My world is the world of international law and justice. I decided to focus on that. Usually when you get an illegal war or wait when you get an illegal war, crimes follow. War crimes, crimes against humanity; we can talk, if you want, genocide. But that was covered by the justice system, either by the Ukrainian courts, other national courts or the ICC (International Criminal Court).

But there was one important gap, and that was the crime of aggression. In Nuremberg, it was invented and then applied retroactively. It was called crimes against peace in that period. There was a gap because the international criminal court doesn't exercise jurisdiction over the crime of aggression in relation to the territory of Ukraine for various technical reasons. Of course, it was possible that the crime of aggression could be addressed in the Ukrainian courts, but because it's a leadership crime, the only people who can be held to account for the crime of aggression are the people who decided to go to war and who continue to maintain the decision to go to war. So, basically, you're talking about Putin, Lavrov, and a very small group of people right at the top. And no Ukrainian court could easily exercise jurisdiction over such people with legitimacy in the eyes of public opinion.

I thought I'd focus on that and the need to fill this gap to avoid a terrible situation in the future, in three or five years, when this horror story is over. There will be crimes. There will be trials for crimes committed by low-grade military types in the Hague, Kyiv, and other places. The little people will be put on trial for terrible war crimes in Bucha, Mariupol, and other places, all crimes against humanity. But people at the top table will be off the hook. That, for me, is totally unacceptable and a travesty of justice. I thought that's what I will write about. I wrote my seven hundred words in an hour and a half. Sometimes you write and it just writes itself. I sent it off. You know this experience when you write something, and the next day seven people and one dog write to you and say that your article was fantastic or terrible, and then you move on with your life?

Did not happen. The column came out on the twenty-eighth. On the twenty-ninth, I got up in the morning and I went and checked my email. My wife always tells me off that the first thing I do in the morning is check my email—I should sit with her, talk, have coffee and do the email later. But I opened it. Four hundred emails about the crime of aggression from all over the world! Among all of the emails that came in the coming days was one from a former British prime minister, Gordon Brown, whom I didn't know personally. Of course, I knew who he was, we had a little bit of contact. And he said, "I write on behalf of a number of former British prime ministers. We're very interested in your idea. Could we have a conversation about it?" One thing led to another, I've been in pretty close WhatsApp contact with Dmytro Kuleba on this issue, and soon it became Ukrainian government policy and now it is supported by several governments.

Writing the article, I thought there is zero chance of this ever happening. Today, the situation is very different. It's curious how sometimes ideas hit the moment and they don't go away, taking on a life of their own, and then there is no putting them down.

To conclude, I would say, my inspiration for writing that article was the city of Lviv, Lauterpacht, and Lemkin. I went back to that moment in 1945, and I imagined Lauterpacht and Lemkin, who were both prosecutors in the Nuremberg Trial. You couldn't invent it. They prosecuted the man who killed their entire families without knowing that he had done that. I was inspired by them and by this city that I've come to love. It's as simple as that.

Victoria Amelina: Thank you so much for sharing this story. You are the president of the English PEN. I am a member of PEN Ukraine. We support a lot of justice initiatives. I was going to ask what we, as a civil society, could do more to advocate for the International Tribunal for the Crime of Aggression? What can I do?

Philippe Sands: Well, you are doing a lot already by being a member of PEN.

For those of you in the audience and those of you watching, the views of civil society matter hugely. Very early on in the process, the group called Avaaz started a petition campaign in support of the special criminal tribunal for the crime of aggression to investigate the leadership that had supported it. Unbelievably, within a month or so, it has achieved more than two million signatories from around the world, including, curiously, quite a few in Russia. But the country number one in this whole story is Ukraine.

So, go on Avaaz's website, and sign the petition. There is another one being prepared right now which will be made live quite soon. We feel that the moment is coming when another push will be significant. Ukraine is already supported by six or seven countries. But for this to happen, our feeling is, we need one of the big countries to provide support—the UK, the US, France, or Germany. The country we think is most likely to do it is the United Kingdom. The US is unlikely to do that for obvious reasons—Iraq hangs in the background. It too, in my view, was an illegal war and a crime of aggression in the view of many people. The Germans could be up for it but they are in a delicate situation. The French—and I am a dual national, British and French—are totally opposed to it. We're not really sure why, beyond the fact that they often oppose everything. But it's probably because they worry that if a special criminal tribunal is created today for one permanent member of the Security Council, why could it not be created tomorrow for another permanent member? I suspect that is the anxiety and the concern, but I'm quite optimistic that we're getting close.

I urge you to write to the French ambassador in Kyiv, thanking them for the support, sort of a bit limited I've got to say, that they've given so far. And then attack them for the total failure to support putting the accent on the leadership crime of aggression. And copy the letter to the French Minister of Foreign Affairs, who happens to be a close friend of mine, and explain why you are so upset with France's position. Public opinion really matters. Deluge them, bombard them with letters. I think we might even have a journalist from *Le Monde* here in this audience right now. Maybe *Le Monde* could interview a couple of you here, and you could give them quotes about how outraged and upset you are to see Macron sitting at long tables with Putin instead of saying that we don't negotiate with the criminals.

Victoria Amelina: Thank you so much for these pieces of advice. I'm sure Ukrainians have heard you, so now it will surely happen. Once again, Ukraine has a chance to change the world by changing international law. That's wonderful.

I would like to quote Hersch Lauterpacht, the man whom we both admire, who coined the term crimes against humanity. He said that the well-being of an individual is the ultimate object of all law. I think both of us agree with this saying.

I am not only a novelist, an essayist, and a poet, I document war crimes now. I became a war crimes researcher for a couple of NGOs, one of them recently was awarded the Nobel Peace Prize, the Center for Civil Liberties, and the other one is Truth Hounds. I'm going to the recently liberated areas or the areas very close to the front line and recording testimonies of people who suffered a lot from war crimes and crimes against humanity, and potentially genocidal crimes. Often I am the first person who comes to talk to those people and collect their testimonies. Why? Because there are so many crimes committed by the Russian army that the Ukrainian law enforcement system is unable to cope with this number of crimes, not because it is somehow incapable. They do their best. I didn't think I would say it, but right now Ukrainian civil society and the state work great together and we see them doing the best they can. But there are more than thirty thousand war crimes registered by the general prosecutors. I can tell you my personal example. In September, I went to the recently liberated Izyum in the Kharkiv region. Our team of six people stayed in Izyum for just a week. We have uncovered three new places where people were tortured. And we've identified more than seventy people who were abducted, tortured, and some of them killed. This is just one team's work during one week. You can imagine the scale.

Oleksandra Matviichuk and the NGO Center for Civil Liberties she is heading, advocate for another kind of international tribunal. They say that while the International Tribunal for the Crimes of Aggression is crucial, how do we address justice for all people who suffered in this war? I understand that justice is very expensive. But it is also precious.

So my question is: what do you think about the idea of the international hybrid tribunal, an additional one, that would also cover war crimes, crimes against humanity, and potential genocide? I know about the International Criminal Court, but it usually selects only several cases. What do I say to those people whose testimonies I record?

We do not have enough prosecutors to build the case and prosecute. And I want to stress one particular example. A Ukrainian writer Volodymyr Vakulenko, an author of many books for children, was abducted on March 24 in Kapytolivka near Izyum, and never returned home. We do not know what happened to him but we understand that he, perhaps, has been tortured. I recorded the testimony of his parents. I know one call sign of a man who is guilty, who led the abduction of Volodymyr Vakulenko. But what are the chances of bringing this man, a low-grade military type as you say, to court?

Philippe Sands: A lot higher now that you have told us the story. You must write this up. I admire what you're doing. We, who are far away, not emotionally or spiritually, but physically from the scene of what's going on, cannot easily do what you have done. You've chosen to do it, and that is an extraordinary thing.

You're a wonderfully gifted writer. I would invite you to follow the path that I have taken in following the paths the others have taken. I don't claim any originality for my approach, it is tried and tested. Write a short book about this story and I promise you it will gather attention, and it will be translated. I'm sure you can find a way to move the slow wheels of justice along. But you've raised a much bigger question. You've raised the question of what can be done in circumstances in which the number of crimes is so great that it overwhelms the institutional structures of any reasonable state.

Hersch Lauterpacht's quotation you mentioned is so revolutionary. A lot of people in the room won't realize the significance of what it means to say that the function of law in all circumstances is to protect the individual. In an international law context, that's a revolutionary statement because, until that moment in 1945 when Lauterpacht, Lemkin, and many others came along with their ideas, the function of the law was to protect the state, the emperor, the king, the queen, the monarch, or whoever it might be who's in charge and embodies the state. This is a revolutionary change of idea and it puts the individual at the beating heart of the legal order.

No legal system can deal with the sheer number of crimes that appear to have been committed, but there are many examples in which these issues have been addressed by a range of different means. One, for example, that comes immediately to mind, also on a horrendous scale, is what happened in Rwanda with the genocide back in the 1990s. The legal system too was overwhelmed. Instead, they created a system in which a small number of emblematic cases (and maybe your writer from Izyum will be one of those emblematic cases, we can talk about with the call signs and everything—it is possible to start tracking things down, and I'd really like to help you do that) go through the justice system.

Rwandans couldn't put everyone through a criminal trial, so they created a system of local justice called the gacaca courts, in which stories are told, and justice is delivered at a local level, in part by the telling of the story. In South Africa, we had truth and reconciliation. In Chile, we had truth and reconciliation. And one of the things that I've come to believe after more than thirty years of working in the field of international justice is that you don't need only the system of courts to deliver a sense of justice. What actually matters for many people is the sense that the facts have been established authoritatively and independently, and the stories are recorded in some form and made publicly accessible.

I am writing the third book, after *East West Street: On the Origins of Genocide and Crimes Against Humanity* and *The Ratline: Love, Lies and Justice on the Trail of a Nazi Fugitive* (also very much set in Lviv because it deals with the story of Otto Wächter, the Nazi governor of the District of Galicia between 1942 and 1944). The third book is about Chile. One of Wächter's friends escaped, got off justice, made his way to South America in 1950 and ended up in Chile, allegedly working with August Pinochet. And my next book tells that story.

Thousands of people were disappeared in Chile. Over the years, it set up a system of consecutive truth reconciliation processes. I've met quite a lot of people whose loved ones were disappeared. For example, a wonderful woman called Erika Hennings, who runs the museum called Londres 38, which was the address of the former headquarters of the Socialist Party in Chile where [President Salvador] Allende used to work. When Pinochet came to power, they took over the building and turned it into a torture center. Many people were disappeared. One of them is Erika's husband, who was disappeared in July 1974. He was taken into Londres 38, detained, interrogated, tortured, and disappeared. An absolute parallel story. Erika Hennings managed to bring the proceedings to France, but she also explained to me that for her and other people it was important for the stories to be told. Either in a nonfiction book, a novel, or an official government report.

We know that the government of Ukraine is right now dealing with these stories as best it can under very difficult circumstances. My own instinct—and I hope I do not disappoint you, is that we do not need another international criminal tribunal to deal with war crimes and crimes against humanity. It can be dealt with by the Ukrainian courts, by other national courts, those of Poland, Germany, the United Kingdom, maybe France, and also the ICC. But what we do need is a full accounting of what has happened and the stories to be told.

Stories really matter. In *East West Street*, I told the story of what happened to my grandfather, which I didn't know. I uncovered it seventy-fie years after it had happened. It mattered a lot to our family to know what had happened to his mother, to his siblings, to his nephews and nieces. This stayed with the family. In one part of the book, I talked about what happened in Zhovkva. On a single day, on March 25, 1943, three and a half thousand inhabitants of the small town of Zhovkva, half of the population, were executed. That was recorded by a sole survivor of the active execution. Someone who was shot in the head, but somehow survived, got out of the mass grave, went, recorded, and told the story of what had happened. But it was never formally recorded. And seventy-five years later, that leaves a big hurt. I've spoken to the current mayor of Zhovkva and suggested placing a little private memorial with the names of all the people there as an act of saying that individual stories really matter. They matter to everybody, whoever they are, whatever nationality, denomination, and religion.

So I think the key in answering your question is that the facts emerge, the stories come out, and the names are known. Those people who are on the receiving end, the victims, are recognized as human beings who are subjected to totally inappropriate treatment, but with exact names and with exact witness evidence. I'm pretty shocked when you tell me that no one has interviewed these people and found out what happened. We hear all these stories about how much money is going into war crimes investigations. But, obviously, the numbers are so enormous that it's simply not possible to deal with everyone. So, just gather information, record it, take photographs, get names down, get addresses down. This is absolutely invaluable information. We don't know what it'll be used for but gather, gather, gather.

Victoria Amelina: I think the ICC was going to send about forty-two prosecutors to Ukraine. This is of course too few. I've never met them on the ground. No one I know did.

Philippe Sands: Do they speak Ukrainian?

Victoria Amelina: I have no idea, we've never seen them.

Philippe Sands: We get told that millions are being put into war crimes investigation. But we have no idea what they're really doing. I have to believe that if a government did send those people there, they're doing something.

Victoria Amelina: I have no idea, and I am writing a book about that.

Philippe Sands: You've never met a non-Ukrainian war crimes investigator. How hard did you look?

Victoria Amelina: Well, it's not my goal of course. I am looking for war crimes, not the investigators. Actually, I was going to ask you about the ICC. What are your expectations? How many cases could they possibly take? I need a number.

Philippe Sands: I am really going to upset you with what I'm about to say. I'm afraid I have very low expectations.

Victoria Amelina: Me too, I just want to hear yours.

Philippe Sands: The ICC has a problem, and it's related to the current conflict in ways that I would like, with your permission, to briefly explain. The ICC has only investigated or prosecuted people who are black, from Africa. And people who are black and from Africa do not have a monopoly on international crime. And this has caused tremendous resentment around the world.

We're in Europe right here: pause, suspend your mental state, and imagine you're following this story from some other part of the world, South America, Africa, or Asia. Seeing stories that are being told about the support that has been given for investigations of crimes, let's be frank about it, committed against white people. Where are similar investigations in relation to the crimes committed by the Russian government in Syria? What's happened? What's the difference between the victims? We know what it is: it is the color of their skin and their religion, let's be frank about it. In order to restore its legitimacy around the whole world, the ICC needs to find some nice white people to investigate and prosecute. And it is being deluged with funds in order to be able to do that. I think it's entirely possible that the ICC ends up prosecuting nobody. Why?

Victoria Amelina: This was not something that I was expecting.

Philippe Sands: Because under the rules of the ICC statute there is something called a principle of complementarity. It is, first and foremost, for the courts of the country in which the crimes were committed or the crime of the nation of the perpetrator or victim to exercise jurisdiction.

The ICC only gets involved when, in this country's case, Ukraine is unable or unwilling to investigate and prosecute. Ukraine is not unwilling, it wants to. There is a bit of debate as to whether it can do all of these things when it comes to the kind of perpetrator who is not some, I have to say, a rather sad 18-year-old kid who has done something nasty and horrible, and been caught and put on trial in Kyiv. If an individual has violated the law, that individual must face punishment. That's absolutely right, there should be a trial. But in that one trial that we've all followed, frankly, that young man is not the problem. He has done something terrible, and the full force of the law should be applied. But that is not the kind of person you want. You want to go higher up the food chain.

Why is Ukraine going to hand over to the ICC someone higher up the food chain when they can do it themselves, in Kyiv? Will the people of Ukraine tolerate justice being done in some faraway place when it can be done locally? This is a big issue in the functioning of international courts. So I wonder, and I just raise this as a question, whether Ukraine will actually hand anyone over to the ICC? It may be the ICC can find perpetrators in other jurisdictions and get people that way, but it's far from assured. And the second concern I have is whether the ICC will get some of the top people. We can't exclude that possibility, but I don't think you should proceed on the assumption that there's going to be a massive trial at the ICC at some point in the future. It may happen, but just as equally it may not. So I would not hold your breath.

Victoria Amelina: Well, this is why we will keep insisting that after we have this incredibly important International Tribunal for the Crime of Aggression, we'll need to establish another international tribunal. Maybe in Kyiv, maybe in several cities, and one could be in Lviv. That would be quite symbolic taking into account that Hersch Lauterpacht and Raphael Lemkin, renowned international lawyers, come from here. And we also think about one in Mariupol somewhere.

You see, I think everyone in this wonderful Sheptytsky Center, is sure that the victory for Ukraine is not just defeating the aggressor and restoring territorial integrity, but also completing the reforms and becoming a full-functional liberal democracy, where rule of law is unquestioned, an example for everyone else. For that, we do need to believe in the rule of law. And it is very hard to do when so many crimes have just been committed by foreigners, by Russian invaders. But still, crimes were committed and we need people to believe that they can receive justice.

I was interviewing a man in Balakliya. He didn't suffer anything extraordinary—unless you agree with me that even surviving occupation by a foreign country is actually extraordinary. He is an old man, he hasn't been beaten or tortured. But he told me: "I felt like the smallest of insects during that time. They could do anything to me. There was no police department, no prosecutor's office, no place I could go and address my complaints." And I was standing there and thinking, how this ordinary man who used to work at a factory and survived Russian occupation now understands what democracy is made for, and what the rule of law means. It is so important to keep this faith so that he and other people like him can see justice. So perhaps an international hybrid tribunal for other international crimes would be needed as well. This is something I encourage you to think about because your voice in the international community of lawyers and as a writer is very important.

Philippe Sands: What you've just said resonates completely. Justice and the belief that you may obtain a sense of justice is part of the process of well-being. I wrote a small piece about this a few years ago in relation to a remarkable German, Turkish, and Kurdish psychologist called Jan Ilhan Kizilhan. Some of you will remember the story of the Yazidis, a very small community of about a million people in Northern Iraq and Syria, who were attacked by ISIS. It is not a Muslim community, it's a separate, distinct religious community targeted by ISIS for being "heathens" and "unbelievers." The ISIS people made a policy of abducting all the young women in order to subjugate them and rape them on an industrial scale, because having raped them, these women would then be unclean, they wouldn't be able to have children, and the community would extinguish itself. This is an example of the act of rape as an instrument of genocidal policy. Absolutely appalling story. Jan Kizilhan set up a program with the government of Baden-Württemberg in southern Germany to bring 1,100 of these young women there for post-trauma psychological treatment. He reached out to me asking to come and talk about the criminal justice system. I got to know Jan very well, and he explained to me as a psychologist that part of the process of restoration of well-being to the extent that was possible for some of the young women who'd been through . . . I am a parent, I have three kids, and two daughters of roughly that age when this happened. I literally couldn't believe what I was being told by them. At that moment I learned that the possibility of justice informally at the national level or international level alone was a significant part of the process of repair. I think you are absolutely right to focus on that, and I do hear your call to keep an open mind as to how it is done. And maybe you are right. Maybe we need more institutions or more mechanisms to ensure that, as part of that process of repair, the flame of justice can be kept alive.

Victoria Amelina: Thank you so much. I was also going to talk about my other grandfather. He comes from a place called Slobozhanschyna, a region close to Kharkiv, Sumy, and part of the so-called Donbas. He also, just like your grandfather Leon, lost a lot of members of his family. It happened in 1932 to 1933 during the Holodomor, the genocidal famine organized by the Soviets and described as a genocide by the inventor of the term Raphael Lemkin. Lemkin gave a speech in 1953 in New York in front of Ukrainians who gathered there to commemorate the victims of the Holodomor genocide.

I was able to find the people with the same last name as my grandfather in the books of memory we have in the Holodomor museum in Kyiv. There was not enough evidence. Holodomor wasn't as documented, and it would not be possible to find the perpetrators now, so we only have memory. This is all I have, and perhaps all I ever will have for justice. I can also write about this in my book, but that is, perhaps, all.

My question goes to the big G-word, as Peter Pomerantsev refers to it. I understand that the word genocide is not defined by the legal system as it was coined by Lemkin. At the same time, the world has come to see genocide as a crime of crimes. There is so much obsession with this word. Although both you and I agree that crimes against humanity are in no way less horrible. How do we overcome this obsession?

I was born in the Soviet Union. I know the harm of doublethink. Everyone in this room and people watching us from the so-called Global South or wherever else in the world would agree that humanity has committed many genocides, ethnocides, etc. This is not a unique crime. You've already mentioned Rwanda, we can go on and about Rohingya Muslims in Myanmar, and the Armenian genocide. We all agree that humanity, unfortunately, keeps having genocides all the time. At the same time, it is so hard to prove it in the legal system. And this is doublethink. This is an Orwellian thing. What can we do? Should we stress more crimes against humanity and create a convention on the prevention of those crimes? Or do we change the legislation for genocide and stop the doublethink? And if we are actually sure that a genocide has been committed, for example, against the indigenous people in the US, why don't we call it that? How do we end this doublethink? And then the obsession with the G-word?

Philippe Sands: My role is to say things as they are when it comes to legal issues.

Just before getting to your question, can we just mention, since you talked about the origins in this city. You mentioned the conversation that Lemkin had with his teacher, and I just wanted to namecheck the teacher. He was rather a remarkable person. Juliusz Makarewicz, Polish professor of criminal law who's buried in the wonderful cemetery here in Lviv, but whose house has recently been sold. I'm currently involved in discussions with the mayor of Lviv and Sofia Diak at the Center for Urban History to try to preserve the house and think about turning it into an International Center for Justice (ICJ). I just wanted to mention that because there might be more and more talk about that possibility.

Why has genocide come to be seen not by me but by so many people as the crime of crimes? I don't think genocide is worse than crimes against humanity. If you kill 100,000 people as a crime against humanity it's just as terrible as killing 100,000 people as genocide. For me, the principal difference for each of those 100,000 people is that what has happened to them is the most appalling thing. And yet you're right, in the court of public opinion, the word "genocide" attracts attention like no other.

If an American president, as President Biden did, in relation to Ukraine says genocide has happened or maybe a genocide has happened, it will be on the front page of every newspaper in the world, as it was when Biden, in my view mistakenly, said what he said about the possible genocide. In fact, as you probably know, he made two statements. He made his first statement off the cuff, without having really thought about it, and a second statement a few hours later when his lawyer advised him to be more careful about what he says. In fact, the *NYT* then asked me to write an opinion piece, which I did, on genocide and what was happening in Ukraine, and how one can characterize it. I didn't want to criticize President Biden because I think he was trying to be very supportive of Ukraine. So I said that he was probably using the term in its political sense rather than its pure legal sense.

The doublethink may even be a quadruplethink. Ordinary regular intelligent people think that genocide means doing really nasty things to large numbers of people. And then there is a legal definition, where you've got to prove that the person who is acting was motivated by an intention to destroy a group in whole or in part. The difficulty we have in relation to Ukraine at this point, and we've touched on some of the reasons why, we don't know enough about what was motivating some of the acts to know what the intention was.

The systematic targeting of civilian buildings could, under certain circumstances, be a genocidal act. But what we need to know and investigators have to establish is what was the motivation behind targeting those buildings. When you go into a small town and kill a certain number of people that could be a genocidal act. It has been suggested in Bucha. But we don't know enough about the motivations of individuals who perpetrated those horrendous acts, and that's where your work and the work of so many people become so important. What were they saying as they were abusing people? Why did they round up particular people? You can't tell, as Jonathan Littel said yesterday in the conversation we had in the afternoon, just from the photographs of a dozen dead people, some of them with their hands tied, killed in apparently horrible circumstances, that it was a genocidal act. To prove genocide, you had to get into the mind of the perpetrator.

The difference between crimes against humanity and genocide, between war crimes and genocide, is that you have to get into the head of the perpetrator and discover what the intention of that person was. This is a really difficult thing to do in law. The drafters of the convention did that on purpose to set the bar very high, to avoid some of the things that are given the label "genocide" in public discourse and the label "genocide" in legal discourse.

What is to be done about it? Well, one option is for judges to take the definition of genocide in the convention and reinterpret it. That's what courts do. I tried that in the case of Vukovar at the ICJ.[2] I made the argument explicitly: you, the judges, have set the bar too high and you should reinterpret the 1948 Convention and reduce the burden so that a greater number of acts are characterized as genocidal. That would be a socially useful thing to do. They refused to do it. All international courts and tribunals have refused to do it.

The second alternative is to amend the 1948 Convention. It is not going to happen. We are stuck right now in the UN on the possible Convention on Crimes Against Humanity. There is no political will to engage in that kind of act.

Another option is to engage in some sort of generalised form of re-education of the entire world that both crimes against humanity and the war crimes are pretty bad. One of the things I've been trying to do with *East West Street* is to try and tell a story of why our obsession with genocide is a bad thing. And one of the things I've been pleased about with *East West Street* being translated into many languages and this debate you are raising is that now there is a broader sense.

The word genocide was invented as a term, and it's a magical term, that's why it has a such powerful effect. This term actually has unintended negative consequences and here I would go even further, saying that the concept of genocide may have given rise to the very act it was intended to prevent. By focusing on the psychological element, the intention to destroy a group in whole or in part, you actually reinforce the sentiment of the group identity and you reinforce,

[2] When the Yugoslav People's Army and Serbian paramilitaries took control of the Croatian town of Vukovar after three months of siege on November 18, 1991, more than 200 Croat and other nationals were removed from the Vukovar city hospital where they were sheltering. According to the International Criminal Tribunal for the Former Yugoslavia, 194 people from the hospital were killed on November 20, 1991, near Ovčara farm. It is considered the largest massacre of the Yugoslav Wars.

including in the victim community, a sense of hatred of the perpetrator communities.

The bottom line is: Lemkin invented a word that has a huge power on the imagination. You are the writer of novels and literature, you know the power of words. If you put genocide on the screen and you put crimes against humanity on the screen, people will react to the word genocide because the word evokes, in a non-technical manner, absolute horror in a way that crimes against humanity do not—because it's legalistic, it's technical, it doesn't open up the imagination. I think Lemkin's brilliance was in part that he was a wordsmith. As you know from the book, there is a piece of paper I found in the archives of Columbia University where Lemkin writes out the word genocide 25 times, and then other possible variations. But he ended up with genocide and I think it was strategic. He knew he had to find a word that would open up the imagination, and he's done that, and of course, it's had some positive consequences, but I think it's also had some negative consequences. And we're stuck with it.

Victoria Amelina: Raphael Lemkin coined the term, and he considered Holodomor a genocide. Obviously, now he'd agree that another genocide is happening.

Philippe Sands: And he's banned in Russia because of it. Honestly, the senses in Moscow are pathetic. They ban Lemkin—you can't get his books or anything. But they don't ban Philippe Sands' Russian translation of *East West Street* which is all about Lemkin and his ideas. That sense of manifest incompetence maybe takes us to a Leonard Cohen song.

Victoria Amelina: I walked the streets of Lviv in March 2022. I kept my head down, I was very exhausted from the work at a humanitarian aid back then. And suddenly I saw the plaque on the building where Lemkin had lived, and I realized that I'm in Lviv, the city that gave so much to the world in terms of international law and I wondered whether I could write about that. I remembered your book, and that is how I started writing my *War and Justice Diary*. I do have a grandmother who's Russian, but Ukrainians are a political nation. If I want to be Ukrainian, it means that I am Ukrainian. We know that we are now targeted as a group. I have a sister. I won't name the place where she is because it's dangerous, but it is a territory temporarily occupied by Russia. There are plenty of books in her house, and all these books are in Ukrainian, including the Ukrainian literature school books. She is a teacher of Ukrainian literature. I know, and everyone knows here, that if her house gets searched she will be abducted, killed or maybe deported to Russia, like millions of Ukrainians.

Maybe they don't want to kill us all, but they would also be happy if we just agreed with them that we are not Ukrainians. This is what they say in their media. It might be difficult to prove in court. You have thirty-five years of experience. But in a political sense, we know that we are targeted as a group. So Raphael Lemkin, also my neighbor in Lviv in a sense, did a great job coining this term because as a writer I know that words matter, and now we have the language to talk not only about the Holocaust, some events of which also took place in Lviv, where more than 100,000 Jews were killed, but also Holodomor and all other genocides that happened and continue happening still.

We know that justice matters. We know that we are here in Ukraine, at the center of the events, and, perhaps, future changes to international law as well.

We have about ten minutes left. Does anyone have questions?

Question from the audience: At the beginning of the war, I was recording interviews with internally displaced persons with disabilities. Back then, not many of them were talking about art. In stressful situations, art usually is not the priority. People are worried about the most basic things. That's the reality. Now, when our brain has accumulated so many cruel things and has gotten accustomed, we are ready to reflect on them and put these reflections in different art forms. The art we're creating now has a kind of therapeutic function for us, and it is also a great language for us to communicate with each other. Now in Lviv there are many exhibitions of sculptors and painters who have already reflected on things happening in Ukraine now. What do you think about foreign audiences? Should there be a different form of art or conversation about what's happening in Ukraine? When we see our art here in Lviv, we understand it and can relate to it. When we talk to a foreign audience, should we use different words for them to understand us? People have different stories and traumas behind them, and not everyone would understand direct speech.

Philippe Sands: It is a very interesting question. Before I answer it, I would like to publicly thank my wonderful translator of *East West Street* who's also working on the translation of *The Ratline*, which I think will come out next year. Pavlo Myhal, who has volunteered and is now in military service. There was a moment when we thought he might be able to come back and I'd be able to spend a little time with him. And I just want to publicly express my solidarity and respect for him, because that too is a form of art, the art of translating.

There is so much that could be said about your question, and my answer might not go in the direction you expect or perhaps even encourage. I think it is very important that Ukraine feels a sense of solidarity. I think everyone in this room gets it. I myself and many people around me are in a complete sense of solidarity. There is communication. I happen to know many people in Lviv and in Ukraine, and I'm in contact with them the whole time, so there's that exchange. To be honest, I don't think the issue going forward is going to be the problem of exchanges with supporters.

I think that different forms of art are very useful in communicating messages. In fact, in ten days in London, I will be involved in an event interviewing Andriy Kurkov in relation to his new book *Diary of an Invasion*. And it's going to get a huge amount of attention. So I don't think you need to worry that what's happening here isn't going to result in people outside being interested in the art generated by Ukrainians.

What I want to put on the table is communications which are much more delicate and much more problematic, and that is communications with the other side. Which, as I know from my conversations over three days here, when you're in the midst of a war, is an enormously difficult conversation to have. But at some point, this will be over. The war will be over, and Ukraine and Ukrainians will have to grapple with some complex issues. There will be the issue of collaborators. How does a society or a community deal with that in its literature, in its art and other ways? We know, for example, that some of the greatest cinema out of World War Two came out of France and collaboration.

Then there is an even bigger issue of communication between Ukrainians and Russians. Russia is not going to go away, and Russians won't go away. What happens there? And here, with the most respectful of spirits, may I mention the experience of my Russian translator? She is a remarkable human being, a poet, totally opposed to this criminal war and crime of aggression as she calls it, who has herself been arrested, convicted and fined, I'm told on more than one occasion, including for reading out poems written by distinguished Russian poets.

I grew up in a household where nothing German was allowed in the house. Slowly I came to understand that German literature, German art, and German films were actually pretty interesting. And I began to exercise my own judgment on who I could talk about.

I think you've underscored a hugely important point. We have to at all times strive to find means of communication with people who are part of a community that has imposed unbearable pain and grief, and it may be that art and literature become the means by which one can begin to explore that possibility. So I thank you warmly for your question.

Victoria Amelina: In fact, I can't wait to be able to appreciate something Russian again, because this would only happen after Ukrainian territorial integrity is restored and after the Russian empire ceases to exist, and there are Russians, but no Russian empire. And so, after our Ukrainian victory and the victory of the free world, all of us can't wait to be able to just think about it again.

Thank you so much, Philippe, for talking to me here in Lviv at Lviv International BookForum, which happens in a digital partnership with the Hay Festival. I thank again the Ukrainian Armed Forces, including Pavlo Myhal, the translator of Philippe Sands' books into Ukrainian. Thank you so much.

About the Author

Victoria Amelina was killed by a Russian missile in July 2023. She was an award-winning Ukrainian novelist, essayist, poet, and human rights activist whose prose and poems have been translated into many languages. In 2019 and 2020 she lived and traveled extensively in the United States. She wrote both in Ukrainian and English, and her essays have appeared in *Irish Times*, *Dublin Review of Books*, and *Eurozine*.